RETHINKING EQUALITY PROJECTS IN LAW

The concept of equality has been a key animating principle of modern feminism, and has been highly productive for feminist legal thought and feminist politics concerning law. Today however, given the failure to achieve material and psychic equality for women, feminists have come to challenge the usefulness of equality as a concept, a particular definition, or a basis for strategising. The papers in this collection reflect these concerns, primarily in the context of English-speaking, common law cultures. Collectively, the papers analyse a range of equality projects across a number of areas of public and private law, considering both competing conceptions of equality and alternatives to it. In taking stock across a century and a half and around the globe, the book illustrates the range of ways in which equality projects in law have been challenged by, and remain a challenge for, feminism.

Oñati International Series in Law and Society

A SERIES PUBLISHED FOR THE OÑATI INSTITUTE
FOR THE SOCIOLOGY OF LAW

General Editors
Johannes Feest   Judy Fudge

Founding Editors
William L F Felstiner   Johannes Feest

Board of General Editors
Rosemary Hunter, University of Kent, United Kingdom
Carlos Lugo, Hostos Law School, Puerto Rico
David Nelken, Macerata University, Italy
Jacek Kurczewski, Warsaw University, Poland
Marie Claire Foblets, Leuven University, Belgium
Roderick Macdonald, McGill University, Canada

Titles in this Series

Rethinking Equality Projects in Law

Feminist Challenges

WITHDRAWN

Edited by

Rosemary Hunter

Oñati International Series in Law and Society

A SERIES PUBLISHED FOR THE OÑATI INSTITUTE
FOR THE SOCIOLOGY OF LAW

·HART·
PUBLISHING

OXFORD AND PORTLAND, OREGON
2008

Published in North America (US and Canada)
by Hart Publishing
c/o International Specialized Book Services
920 NE 58th Avenue, Suite 300
Portland, OR 97213–3786
USA
Tel: +1 503 287 3093 or toll-free: (1) 800 944 6190
Fax: +1 503 280 8832
E-mail: orders@isbs.com
Website: www.isbs.com

Hart Publishing, 16c Worcester Place, Oxford, OX1 2JW
Telephone: +44 (0)1865 517530 Fax: +44 (0)1865 510710
E-mail: mail@hartpub.co.uk
Website: http://www.hartpub.co.uk

British Library Cataloguing in Publication Data

Data Available

ISBN: 978-1-84113-840-4 (hardback)
ISBN: 978-1-84113-839-8 (paperback)

Typeset by Columns Design Ltd, Reading RG4 7DH
Printed and bound in Great Britain by
CPI Antony Rowe, Chippenham

Contents

Notes on Contributors

Rosemary Auchmuty is a Professor in the School of Law, University of Reading, UK, and a former Deputy Director of the AHRC Research Centre for Law, Gender and Sexuality at the University of Westminster.

Susan B Boyd holds the Chair in Feminist Legal Studies and is Director of the Centre for Feminist Legal Studies in the Faculty of Law, University of British Columbia, Canada.

Heather Douglas is a Senior Lecturer in the TC Beirne School of Law, University of Queensland, Australia.

Reg Graycar is a Barrister and Professor of Law at the University of Sydney, Australia, and a former Commissioner of both the Australian and New South Wales Law Reform Commissions.

Rosemary Hunter is a Professor in the Kent Law School, University of Kent, UK, and Chair of the RCSL Working Group on Gender and Law.

Jenny Morgan is a Professor of Law at The University of Melbourne, Australia, with a particular interest in issues of gendered violence.

Mary Jane Mossman is a Professor and Director of the Institute for Feminist Legal Studies at Osgoode Hall Law School, York University, Canada.

Hilary Sommerlad is Professor of Law and Society and Director of the Centre for Research into Diversity in the Professions at Leeds Metropolitan University, UK.

Karin van Marle is a Professor in the Faculty of Law, University of Pretoria, South Africa.

Introduction: Feminism and Equality

ROSEMARY HUNTER

TRADITIONALLY ASSOCIATED WITH the rise of the philosophy of liberal individualism, the concept of equality has been a key animating principle of modern feminism. In particular, the concept has been highly productive for feminist legal thought and feminist politics concerning law. Indeed, it has often been contended that it was advocacy of the idea that all human beings are by nature free, equal, and endowed with the same inalienable rights, that first led eighteenth and nineteenth century women to challenge their inferior legal status.[1]

Today, however, unequivocal celebrations of the principle of equality are much less common and feminists have come to challenge its usefulness on a number of fronts. For a start, reasoning in terms of equality begs the question 'equal to whom?', invariably pointing to a claim for equality with men, which tends to presume that men and women are, can or should be similarly situated in society.[2] Such claims are often charged with further consolidating existing power relationships and effectively constituting yet another male precept ensnared by the very gender system feminists oppose.[3] At the same time, formal equality with its rhetoric of likeness stands accused of accrediting a much greater degree of similarity than actually exists, not only between the sexes but also amongst women themselves, thereby construing 'Woman' in terms of a uniformity which negates the specificities of women's lives and experiences.[4] This in turn has precipitated a conflict between measures to protect sexual equality and

---

[1] Eg Wolstonecraft, M, *A Vindication of the Rights of Woman* (Harmondsworth, Penguin, 1975, 1st pub 1792).

[2] Cornell, D, *At the Heart of Freedom: Feminism, Sex, and Equality* (Princeton, NJ, Princeton University Press, 1998) 3, 6.

[3] Brown, W, 'Tolerance and/or Equality: The "Jewish Question" and the "Woman Question"' (2004) 15(2) *differences: A Journal of Feminist Cultural Studies* 1; MacKinnon, C, *Feminism Unmodified: Discourses on Life and Law* (Cambridge, Mass, Harvard University Press, 1987).

[4] Eg Behrendt, L, 'Aboriginal Women and the White Lies of the Feminist Movement: Implications for Aboriginal Women in Rights Discourses' (1993) 1 *Australian Feminist Law Journal* 27; Cain, PA, 'Feminist Jurisprudence: Grounding the Theories' (1989–90) 4 *Berkeley Women's Law Journal* 191; Harris, A, 'Race and Essentialism in Feminist Legal Theory'

those aimed at promoting cultural autonomy, for example in relation to female genital mutilation, native American citizenship rights, sexual abuse in Indigenous communities, Clarence Thomas's nomination to the US Supreme Court, the 'cultural defence' in criminal law, and so on.[5] Although there have been many attempts to resolve such dilemmas,[6] the debate over equality versus difference has consequently had a chilling, if not paralysing, effect on feminist theorising about equality.

If this were not enough to contend with, arguments about equality are also bedevilled by varying – and competing – conceptions of what is actually included in the term 'equality', with feminist and liberal theorists having advanced a panoply of arguments as to the most useful, desirable or defensible content of the concept. These have included the notions of formal and substantive equality (discussed further below), parité,[7] equality of opportunity,[8] equality of results or outcome,[9] equality of condition,[10] equality of power,[11] recognition of differences,[12] social equivalence,[13]

(1990) 42 *Stanford Law Review* 581; Spelman, EV, *Inessential Woman: Problems of Exclusion in Feminist Thought* (Boston, Beacon Press, 1988).

   [5] See, eg Eisenberg, A, 'Diversity and Equality: Three Approaches to Cultural and Sexual Difference' (2003) 11(1) *The Journal of Political Philosophy* 41; Huggins, J, et al, 'Letter to the Editor' (1991) 14 *Women's Studies International Forum* 506; MacKinnon, above n 3, at 63–9; Morrison, T (ed), *Race-ing Justice, En-gendering Power: Essays on Anita Hill, Clarence Thomas, and the Construction of Social Reality* (London, Chatto & Windus, 1993); Parashar, A, 'Reconceptualisations of Civil Society: Third World and Ethnic Women' in M Thornton (ed), *Public and Private: Feminist Legal Debates* (Melbourne, Oxford University Press, 1995) 221; Volpp, L, 'Feminism Versus Multiculturalism' (2001) 101 *Columbia Law Review* 1181.

   [6] Eg Eisenberg, *ibid*; Hunter, R, 'Deconstructing the Subjects of Feminism: The Essentialism Debate in Feminist Theory and Praxis' (1996) 6 *Australian Feminist Law Journal* 135; Phillips, A, *Which Equalities Matter?* (Cambridge, Polity Press, 1999); Scott, JW, 'Deconstructing Equality-Versus-Difference: Or the Uses of Poststructuralist Theory for Feminism' (1988) 14 *Feminist Studies* 33; Williams, JC, 'Dissolving the Sameness/Difference Debate: A Post-Modern Path Beyond Essentialism in Feminist and Critical Race Theory' [1991] *Duke Law Journal* 296.

   [7] See Scott, JW, 'French Universalism in the Nineties' (2004) 15(2) *differences: A Journal of Feminist Cultural Studies* 32.

   [8] See O'Donovan, K and Szyszczak, E, *Equality and Sex Discrimination Law* (Oxford, Basil Blackwell, 1988) 3–6; Thornton, M, *The Liberal Promise: Anti-Discrimination Law in Australia* (Melbourne, Oxford University Press, 1990) 17–20.

   [9] See O'Donovan and Szyszczak, *ibid*, at 4, 6; Thornton, *ibid*, at 16–17.

   [10] Baker, J, Lynch, K, Cantillon, S and Walsh, J, *Equality: From Theory to Action* (Basingstoke, Palgrave Macmillan, 2004).

   [11] Cooper, D, '"And You Can't Find Me Nowhere": Relocating Identity and Structure Within Equality Jurisprudence' (2000) 27 *Journal of Law and Society* 249.

   [12] Eg West, R, 'The Difference in Women's Hedonic Lives: A Phenomenological Critique of Feminist Legal Theory' [1987] *Wisconsin Women's Law Journal* 3, 81; and see Graycar, R, and Morgan, J, *The Hidden Gender of Law*, 2nd edn (Sydney, Federation Press, 2002) 29.

   [13] See Porter, E, 'Equality in the Law and Irigaray's Different Universals' in J Richardson and R Sandland (eds), *Feminist Perspectives on Law and Theory* (London, Cavendish Press, 2000) 149–51.

anti-subordination,[14] an equal minimum threshold enjoyment of capabilities,[15] equal concern,[16] complex equality,[17] and 'equal protection of the imaginary domain'.[18] In addition to the debate over the concept of equality there has been considerable discussion about the appropriate domain in which the achievement of equality for women is most important – whether this should be the public sphere – and within it, the economic[19] or political fields,[20] or both[21] – or the private sphere – and therein, the family[22] or sexual self-representation.[23]

The many different approaches to the principle of equality have not, however, resolved the real inequalities facing women. The failure to achieve material and psychic equality for women not only brings into question the effectiveness of the principle of equality but also casts serious doubts upon its ability to deliver the promise it once held for women; so much so that some theorists advocate a shift in focus away from equality. For example, the so-called humanitarian approach seeks to attack problems of hunger and poverty directly, independently of questions of in/equality, and argues for the development of absolute standards of justice.[24] Irigaray urges us to attend to sexual difference rather than equality, and, at least in her earlier work, advocates the development of a radical principle of sexual difference that would enable the representation of 'otherness' not to be premised on the masculine same.[25] Still others maintain that rather than cataloguing women's inequalities and consequent disadvantages, feminists should instead document and attack the current system of masculine advantage/privilege.[26]

Given these developments, it is hardly surprising that feminist legal discourse has been and still remains embroiled in intense debates regarding the jurisprudence of equality. The Workshop on 'Revisiting Equality',

---

[14]   MacKinnon, above n 3, at 32–45.
[15]   Nussbaum, M, *Women and Human Development: The Capabilities Approach* (Cambridge, Cambridge University Press, 2000).
[16]   Dworkin, R, *Sovereign Virtue: The Theory and Practice of Equality* (Cambridge, Mass, Harvard University Press, 2000).
[17]   Walzer, M, *Spheres of Justice* (New York, Basic Books, 1983).
[18]   Cornell, above n 2, at 23.
[19]   Dworkin, above n 16.
[20]   See Scott, above n 7.
[21]   Phillips, above n 6.
[22]   Okin, SM, *Justice, Gender and the Family* (New York, Basic Books, 1991).
[23]   Cornell, above n 2.
[24]   Eg Frankfurt, H, 'Equality as a Moral Ideal' (1987) 109 *Ethics* 287; Raz, J, *The Morality of Freedom* (New York, Clarendon Press, 1986); though cf Christensen, B, 'Equality and Justice: Remarks on a Necessary Relationship' (2005) 20(2) *Hypatia* 155.
[25]   Porter, above n 13, at 141.
[26]   Eg Eveline, J, 'The Politics of Advantage' (1994) 19 *Australian Feminist Studies* 129; Flood, M and Pease, B, 'Undoing Men's Privilege and Advancing Gender Equality in Public Institutions' (workshop on Reinventing Gender Equality and the Political, Academy of Social Sciences in Australia, The University of Sydney, 29–30 September 2005).

organised by the RCSL Working Group on Gender and Law and held at the Onati International Institute for the Sociology of Law in July 2006, sought to provide a discursive space in which to pause and reflect on this jurisprudence, to understand and learn from what has happened so far, and to generate new critical reflections upon the feminist jurisprudence of equality. Key questions addressed in the papers presented at the Workshop included: what is the history of the feminist use of 'equality' and what lessons are there for the future? What are the effects of the feminist pursuit of equality? What are the advantages and disadvantages of strategising in terms of equality? And, what potential is there to re-conceptualise equality, to mould it in a different form?

The papers included in this collection were originally presented at the Workshop and benefited from the discussions occurring there. The majority of the papers at the Workshop took a critical stance towards the concept of equality and to the deployment of that concept in various feminist legal projects. Disenchantment with both the liberal notion of formal equality, and its main rival in feminist legal scholarship, substantive equality, and the need for a fresh approach, were constant themes. Formal equality expresses the Aristotelian principle that likes should be treated alike, and requires that everyone in the same circumstances be treated according to their individual merits, without regard to sex or other 'irrelevant' characteristics. This version of equality has proved to be of limited value for feminism, however, given the manifold circumstances (such as sexuality, reproduction, family roles, economic situation, political and social histories) in which women are not *like* men, and therefore either cannot claim 'equal treatment', or find themselves disadvantaged by attributions of equality and consequent failures to recognise and respond to difference. The concept of substantive equality has appeared more promising, as it involves taking into account gender-related differences in order to produce substantively fair results. This model is designed to deal with the phenomenon of structural discrimination rather than simply focusing on individual treatment. It acknowledges that treating people as if they were the same as a norm from which they actually differ in significant ways is just as discriminatory as penalising them directly for their difference, and it suggests that dominant norms themselves need to be changed. Yet the (potential) application of this version of equality remains contested and it, too, has produced limited results. Assertions of women's difference have proved problematic due to their essentialising and decontextualised character, their limited political purchase, and the apparent imperviousness of law and the legal profession to the recognition and accommodation of difference.

The papers collected here reflect these concerns, primarily in the context of English-speaking, common law cultures. The contributors to the collection write from the UK, Australia, Canada and South Africa, while discussions at the Workshop also incorporated perspectives from the US and the European Union. Collectively, the papers analyse a range of equality projects in law, from the mid-nineteenth to the early twenty-first centuries, and across a number of areas of both public and private law.

Rosemary Auchmuty and Mary Jane Mossman in their chapters offer new appraisals of historical equality projects for women – the reform of married women's property laws in Britain in the second half of the nineteenth century, and the admission of women to the legal profession in the common law world and in Western Europe in the late nineteenth and early twentieth centuries, respectively – and demonstrate that concepts of equality provided uncertain, unstable foundations for these projects, or were even disavowed by their proponents. Rosemary Auchmuty argues that, despite modern assumptions about the liberalism of first wave feminists, the movement for married women's property reform in Britain was not an 'equal rights' campaign. The campaigners did not understand women to be equal to men, nor was the achievement of women's equality with men their aspiration. Rather, they adopted something more like what we would now recognise as a radical feminist analysis, concerned with men's power, domination and oppression of women, and the need to end that state of affairs.

The first women lawyers discussed by Mary Jane Mossman, by contrast, were far from being radical feminists, or indeed, in many cases, any kind of feminists. Although they often deployed equality rhetoric in order to argue that women should be 'let in' to the legal profession,[27] they tended to distance themselves from their gender once admitted, in favour of an embrace of the (masculine) professional norms of objectivity and rationality. They did not use the rhetoric of gender equality to question or disturb the norms of the profession, expressed ambivalence towards the women's movement, and failed to support campaigns for women's suffrage. At the same time, however, they were treated unequally by their male professional colleagues and were not accorded equal opportunities to obtain work. While they attempted to become lawyers on the same terms as men, they were not permitted to be lawyers on those same terms. The aspirations and experiences of these first women lawyers demonstrated an adherence to the concept of women's equality that was more strategic than committed, and also demonstrated the equivocal results of women's professional equality projects – a feature that was not confined to the late nineteenth and early twentieth centuries, but persists today.

The remaining chapters address contemporary equality projects, but among the authors, only Reg Graycar and Jenny Morgan express an

---

[27] The phrase 'let in' is Margaret Thornton's: *Dissonance and Distrust: Women in the Legal Profession* (Melbourne, Oxford University Press, 1996) 1.

unequivocal commitment to the concept of substantive equality. In their chapter, Graycar and Morgan consider the potential advantages and disadvantages of the fact that Australia lacks a constitutional equality guarantee. On the one hand, the lack of such a guarantee may have resulted in the persistence of a jurisprudence of formal equality in Australian courts, compared to the situation in countries such as Canada and South Africa, where courts have embraced substantive equality in the interpretation of their constitutional equality provisions. On the other hand, Graycar and Morgan argue, the lack of such a guarantee in Australia may have resulted in possibilities for more flexible and creative approaches to equality claims than has been possible in other countries. Through case studies of relationship recognition and abortion law reform, undertaken via political processes rather than litigation, they show that discussions of equality in these instances have reflected substantive understandings of equality, and in particular have not been constrained by the need for equality-seeking groups to advance their claims by asking to be treated in the same way as an advantaged comparator group (heterosexual married couples in the case of relationship recognition, or men in the case of abortion). In bringing the two parts of their argument together, Graycar and Morgan proceed to consider what a specific definition of substantive equality in a constitutional context might look like.

The chapters by Heather Douglas, Susan Boyd, Rosemary Hunter and Karin Van Marle, on the other hand, all provide critiques of substantive equality, from a variety of perspectives. Heather Douglas deals with the deployment of equality arguments in feminist efforts to reform the criminal law defence of provocation. Provocation has historically applied unequally to men and women, because men have been able to rely on the defence quite readily in situations where they have killed intimate partners in response to their infidelity or decision to end the relationship, but women have found it very difficult to invoke the defence in situations where, after suffering prolonged violence and abuse at the hands of their partners, they have killed their abusers. Feminists have thus attempted to reform the criminal law to make it as responsive to women's experiences and values as it has been to men's experiences and values – a project centred on substantive equality. In practice, however, formal equality has tended to prevail, so that increased availability of the defence for women has resulted in its increased availability for men as well. And to the extent that women's 'difference' has been recognised, this has tended to be in the form of expert evidence about 'battered woman syndrome', which has proved to be disempowering, essentialising and stigmatising for women who kill violent partners. Neither has the abolition of the provocation defence in some common law jurisdictions resolved these dilemmas. Ultimately, Douglas argues, however much feminist reformers may attempt to deconstruct equality-versus-difference and focus on multifaceted differences rather than simple gender categories,[28] law appears inherently unresponsive to these efforts and continues either to insist upon sameness, or to reinscribe gender difference, in both cases to women's disadvantage.

Susan Boyd argues that the area of child custody law 'might be said to provide an example of a rather spectacular failure of feminist substantive equality arguments', partly because of the complexity of those arguments, and partly because of the success of formal equality arguments made by fathers' rights advocates, who have demanded equal parental rights for fathers and mothers following separation. Boyd's main concern, however, is with the way in which equality-based arguments advanced by both feminists and fathers' rights groups in child custody reform debates have tended to focus on the cultural rather than the economic sphere, and have failed to place 'the family' within its broader economic context. She argues that it is essential for feminists to make this conceptual shift in order to question and challenge 'the material underpinnings of gendered roles in heterosexual families' and the role of the state in ordering family relationships, but in this process, she doubts the capacity of the concept of equality to 'encompass the complex socio-economic relations that frame and limit parenting patterns'. She calls, instead, for feminists to focus on the material and cultural conditions that would be necessary to promote women's autonomy, both within intact families and after separation.

Karin van Marle examines the concept of substantive equality as it has developed in South African constitutional jurisprudence and in academic commentaries on that jurisprudence. She shows how substantive equality is aligned with a version of the wider project of transformative constitutionalism, which seeks the creation of an egalitarian society. Within this version of transformative constitutionalism, material change is placed at the heart of constitutional equality jurisprudence. Yet Van Marle is cautious about the potential of substantive equality to make a radical difference to women's lives. She contrasts this version of transformative constitutionalism with a more tentative, critical version which would be open to change and contestation. This latter version would require a more complex understanding of equality that would take multiple values into account, and recognise that women's inequality is not only economic but multidimensional. This 'complex' or 'ethical' understanding of equality would also recognise that it is impossible for law and equality to serve justice fully, but rather, justice is something to strive towards, relying not only on constitutional litigation and judicial decisions, but also on a vibrant democratic politics. Van Marle delivers two warnings about the possible limits of this project, however. First, like Douglas, she questions

---

[28] This is the approach advocated by Scott, above n 6.

whether law can ever achieve anything more than formal equality. Secondly, she notes the tendency for all attempts at openness and inclusion to fall back into closure and exclusivity in the context of particular cases. This slippage means that 'every act of equality will [inevitably] be haunted by its own exclusions'.

Rosemary Hunter's response to the dilemmas and impossibilities of equality projects is to argue for less reliance on the concept of equality as the basis of feminist reform campaigns and advocacy. While feminist appeals to equality have been rhetorically useful, she maintains, they have proved problematic in practice, and produced either limited or counterproductive results for women. She contends that rather than appropriating liberal concepts for feminist causes, feminists need to develop their own, new concepts to describe the disadvantages women experience and create imperatives for change. Concepts such as 'sexual harassment' and 'date rape' have performed this function successfully, but more are needed. Through case studies of pay inequity and women's inequitable access to legal aid funding, Hunter proposes the concepts of 'undervaluation' and 'policy neglect' as alternatives to (in)equality, which may have greater rhetorical and practical value for feminist strategising in these areas, particularly in the current, neo-liberal economic and political climate.

Hunter also notes that alternative concepts to equality need to emphasise women's structural disadvantage and be attentive to the positions of differently situated women. These two points are finally taken up by Hilary Sommerlad in her chapter on the contemporary professional projects of 'outsider' entrants to the legal profession. As she notes, 'outsiders' to the profession are no longer only white, middle-class women. While equality arguments were previously deployed to advocate for the admission of women as a group into the legal profession, the advent of a wider range of non-traditional would-be entrants has coincided with broader cultural shifts producing a greater focus on individual identity and the formation of individualised mobility projects. Yet at the same time, older forms of categorical exclusion and social closure persist within the legal profession. Despite its rhetorical commitments to rationality, equality and diversity, its transformation in practice has been limited, so that masculinity, whiteness and class remain central to professional hierarchies. Sommerlad reports on the results of a research project involving students undertaking the Legal Practice Course, amongst whom black and minority ethnic, working class, and mature age students were disproportionately represented. Most of these students evinced individual rather than social justice motives for entering the legal profession, and although they perceived barriers to personal success based on their gender, class and ethnicity, they also believed that they could overcome these barriers by adopting new identities and bodily projections of professionalism and authority. Sommerlad concludes by observing that if individual equality projects on the part of minority entrants are seen as a means of overcoming collective subordination, paradoxically, 'in order to achieve equality, the cultural and linguistic attributes of collective identities must be abandoned'. Thus, once again, equality projects in the legal profession prove to be uncertain and equivocal for their subjects.

The book is organised into three parts, focusing on the different legal contexts of the equality projects discussed. Part I, 'Equality Projects in Law Reform', contains the chapters by Auchmuty, Douglas, Boyd and Hunter, which address appeals to the concept of equality and alternative feminist strategies in law reform processes taking place in courts, tribunals, law reform bodies, legislatures and policy arenas. Part II, 'Constitutional Equality Projects', contains the chapters by Graycar and Morgan and Van Marle, which discuss the value for feminist legal scholars of constitutional equality guarantees, both present and absent. Part III, 'Personal Equality Projects in the Legal Profession', contains the chapters by Mossman and Sommerlad, which analyse, at opposite ends of the twentieth century, the efforts of women and other 'outsiders' to gain equal access to, and to be accorded equal respect within, the legal profession. In all of these contexts, equality – as a concept, as a particular definition, or as a basis for strategising – is found wanting, giving rise to proposals for alternative understandings of equality, or alternative approaches to equality altogether. Yet as the chapters also demonstrate, none of the competing conceptions of equality, or alternatives to it, have achieved or are likely to achieve general adherence or success, although particular alternative approaches may be fruitful in specific contexts. These are not questions that feminists can turn away from, however, so long as inequalities, disadvantages and injustices for some women persist. In taking stock across a century and a half and around the globe, the book illustrates the range of ways in which equality projects in law have been challenged by, and remain a challenge for, feminism.

* * *

A number of participants in the Onati Workshop did not ultimately contribute to this collection. Nevertheless, I would like to acknowledge the important role played by all the participants who presented papers and discussed ideas at the Workshop, and thus helped to focus and sharpen the thinking of the authors represented here. Thanks, too, to the staff of the Onati Institute for the support they provided to the Workshop, and to the anonymous referees who offered constructive criticisms on the draft manuscript. Finally, I would like to express my gratitude to Sally Sheldon and Maria Drakopoulou. Both were instrumental in the conceptualisation of the Workshop, and Sally played a major part in its initial organisation, while Maria undertook a significant portion of the chapter editing before other commitments intervened. The RCSL Working Group on Gender and Law continues to provide a congenial and stimulating forum for the discussion of contemporary issues in feminist legal scholarship.

Part I

Equality Projects in Law Reform

1

The Married Women's Property Acts: Equality Was Not the Issue

ROSEMARY AUCHMUTY

N INETEENTH CENTURY BRITISH feminist[1] legal activism is often categorised as liberal, concerned with the pursuit of formal equality for women with men. For example, Hilary Sommerlad notes that:

> during both first wave and "second wave" feminism of the 1970s, the women's movement was primarily concerned with equal opportunities.[2]

While true in one sense, this is not the whole story. 'Equal opportunities' was the starting-point, certainly, but (in contrast to today) not necessarily on grounds of equal entitlement. Few feminists claimed that women were equal to men, still less that they wanted the right to *be* like men. What they were concerned with was removal of the restrictions and penalties – far more overt and direct than those existing today – that weighed so heavily upon women that their lives were constrained at every turn. Yet it is not uncommon for later generations of feminist legal writers, anxious to point out the limitations of a formal equality approach, to assume or imply that all Victorian feminists embraced liberal theories and argued for modern

---

[1] The Victorians did not use the word 'feminist', but there was certainly general agreement amongst those involved in the 'Woman Movement' about goals which were feminist in the modern sense. See Levine, P, *Victorian Feminism 1850–1900* (London, Hutchinson, 1987) 14; Bland, L, 'The Married Woman, the "New Woman" and Feminism: Sexual Politics of the 1890s' in J Rendall (ed), *Equal or Different? Women's Politics 1800–1914* (Oxford, Basil Blackwell, 1987) 142.

[2] Sommerlad, H, 'Can Women Lawyer Differently? A Perspective from the UK' in U Schultz and G Shaw (eds), *Women in the World's Legal Professions* (Oxford, Hart Publishing, 2003) 192. I am not even sure Sommerlad is right about the second wave – for example, the later demands around violence.

notions of equality, as if these were the only analyses open to them, and as if they themselves were unaware of the drawbacks of such an approach.[3]

Over the past 30 years, feminist historians have shown that nineteenth century feminist theorising and activism were much more varied and sophisticated than mere liberalism. In education, for instance, there were well-publicised debates over the meaning of equality – should girls and women receive 'equal' *and the same* education as males or should it be an equal *but different* education that took account of their different pasts and futures?[4] In matters of sexuality, writers and campaigners like Josephine Butler were less interested in conceptions of equality than in *justice*; and they had a very clear analysis of the workings of male power.[5] Many Victorian feminists were, as Jane Rendall explains:

> profoundly committed to the ideal of equality; but almost all in some way used the language of difference, of separate spheres arising from their own experience.[6]

Most of this knowledge seems, however, to have passed legal writers by, with the sad result that nineteenth century feminist legal strategies are often misrepresented (or, more commonly, ignored) in later legal writing.

This chapter will consider feminist attitudes to and uses of the concept of equality primarily in the context of the married women's property reforms but also with reference to other nineteenth century campaigns. This is because most of the movers in married women's property rights were also involved in other movements, Frances Power Cobbe being a prime example. I will argue that the Married Women's Property Acts were not 'equal rights' measures in the modern sense,[7] however they might appear to later commentators, and were not sought as such. Instead, feminists who campaigned for the Married Women's Property Acts were motivated by an

---

[3] For instance, Hilaire Barnett discusses the nineteenth-century feminist campaigns under the label of 'Early Struggles for Equality' and later comments on the limitations of the liberal analysis: *Introduction to Feminist Jurisprudence* (London, Cavendish Publishing, 1998) 38, 74–5.

[4] Girton and Newnham Colleges were founded at Cambridge in 1869 embodying those opposing philosophies. See McWillams-Tullberg, R, *Women at Cambridge: A Men's University – Though of a Mixed Type* (London, Gollancz, 1975); Spender, D (ed), *The Education Papers: Women's Quest for Equality in Britain, 1850–1912* (London, Routledge and Kegan Paul, 1987); Burstyn, J, *Victorian Education and the Ideal of Womanhood* (London, Croom Helm, 1980).

[5] See Butler's articles on prostitution and against the Contagious Diseases Acts in S Jeffreys (ed), *The Sexuality Debates* (London, Routledge and Kegan Paul, 1987) 111–90; Caine, B, *English Feminism 1780–1980* (Oxford, Oxford University Press, 1997) 108–10; Jordan, J, *Josephine Butler* (London, John Murray, 2001).

[6] Rendall, J (ed), *Equal or Different? Women's Politics 1800–1914* (Oxford, Basil Blackwell, 1987) 27.

[7] Nor in the technical legal sense, since they did not give married women the same rights as everyone else.

analysis that looks more like an early form of *radical feminism* than liberalism, and which neither understood women to be 'equal' to men nor wished them to become so.

Radical feminism is a political analysis usually dated from the late 1960s and the rise of the Women's Liberation Movement or the 'second wave' of feminism in western societies. Like all political theories, it encompasses a range of positions on certain aspects (for example, whether gender differences are biological or purely social in origin), linked by a common conception of male power: radical feminists regard gender as the primary organising principle of society and view men and women as separate classes which are not simply different from each other but in a relationship of dominance and oppression. While not excluding the economic or material analysis of Marxist feminists, they emphasise the significance of sexuality and sexual expression as a means of male domination over women. Male power is conceptualised as both systemic, the concept of patriarchy being employed to describe its operation, and personal – for example, through individual acts of rape or domestic violence. Classic radical feminists hold (in the words of Carol Ann Douglas) that:

> men and women are more similar than they are different, and that men use the differences that exist in reproduction to oppress women and define them as inferior. Love and sexuality have been defined by men to suit their interests. ... Women must confront men by direct action and fight for an end to male supremacy.[8]

The goal of radical feminists is the abolition of gender as a socially significant category.

A later development of radical feminism, sometimes called cultural feminism, rejects the focus on men as the 'enemy' and offers instead, as the way forward, a re-claiming and re-valuing of women's characteristics and experiences.

> Women's reproductive capacity is not a burden in itself ... Women's experience as mothers has not been entirely negative because women have developed a culture that is separate from male culture and more nurturing. Women can gain more from being with each other than with men. ... Perhaps there are some differences that should be preserved.[9]

While it would be anachronistic to impose a twentieth century politics upon nineteenth century ideas, there are sufficient similarities in Victorian feminism to radical feminism to indicate that liberalism was not the only important and unproblematised analysis of the movement. Josephine Butler in her crusade against the Contagious Diseases Acts pinpointed

---

[8] Douglas, CA, *Love and Politics: Radical Feminist and Lesbian Theories* (San Francisco, Ism Press, 1990) 11.

[9] *Ibid*, at 12.

sexuality as an instrument of male oppression of women. Frances Power Cobbe held views about women's moral superiority that resonate with later cultural feminism. For her, women were not 'equal but different' but 'different and *better*'. Her relationship with ideas of equality was equivocal at best, as we shall see.

THE MARRIED WOMEN'S PROPERTY ACTS – A LIBERAL REFORM?

This chapter owes its genesis to work I have been doing on the history of women and the family home in the twentieth century. Whilst researching the movement for community of property in Britain in the 1950s and 1960s, when joint ownership of the matrimonial home came surprisingly close to being implemented here,[10] I noticed how advocates of community of property repeatedly referred to the 'accident' of history by which English law had adopted separation of marital property, whereas many continental jurisdictions had community of property. For example:

> In the process of giving to women the legal status which reflected their status in society, English law adopted, almost by accident, a regime of 'separation of goods'.[11]

This 'accident' was attributed to the Married Women's Property Acts of the nineteenth century,[12] the first of which,[13] by an interesting coincidence, had been enacted precisely one hundred years before the Matrimonial Proceedings and Property Act 1970 emerged as the watered-down consequence of the community of property discussions.[14] This coincidence is of

---

[10] It was recommended in three Law Commission Reports and a Bill twice passed its second reading in the House of Lords.

[11] Kahn-Freund, O, 'Injustices and Inconsistencies in the Law of Husband and Wife' (1952) 15 *Modern Law Review* 135.

[12] Under the common law doctrine of coverture, a woman's property passed to her husband on marriage and all property subsequently acquired (including earnings) belonged to him, not to her. This meant that she lacked legal personality to sue or be sued on contracts and torts. In return for her property, husbands had a common law duty to maintain their wives, which was not, however, enforced.

[13] There were a number of Married Women's Property Acts. The first, in 1870, gave married women the right to keep their own earnings. The most important, that of 1882, repealed most of the 1870 Act and gave married women the right to keep *all* their property.

[14] Section 4 of the MPPA 1970 introduced the provisions now embodied in ss 24–25 of the Matrimonial Causes Act 1973 governing property division on divorce, which recognised (for the first time) a spouse's contribution to the welfare of the family; s 37 gave married people who had no formal interest in the matrimonial home the possibility of claiming a share on the basis of work they had undertaken to increase the value of the property. The Act fell far short of community of property, but was fairer to women at that period than the implied trust rules based on financial contributions alone.

course just that – happenstance – but the hundred-year gap between the two reforms offers evidence (if evidence be needed) of women's ongoing struggle for property rights.

The reason I found it curious that the separation of property brought about by the Acts was described as 'accidental' was that, from my reading of the sources of this period, I had always understood that separation of property had been the *goal* of the feminists who had pressed for the reform. Alert to the injustice of the common law rule that all women's property passed to their husbands on marriage, they wanted married women to be able to hold their property separately, just as men and single women could. So what could be accidental about it? Even liberal commentators viewed the legislative change as a good and necessary one which reflected the modernisation of Victorian society.

Pondering further, I found a second paradox. The Married Women's Property Acts are represented in these retrospective descriptions as *equality measures*, granted in recognition of women's enhanced status in society (as the quote above indicates), on the ground that equality of the sexes demanded equality of treatment in law. But my reading of Victorian feminist writing on the Acts indicates that *their promoters* never viewed them as equality measures. It is true they wanted equal treatment for married women, in the sense that they wanted them to receive *the same* treatment as men and single women, but not because they considered the sexes to be 'equal' in the modern sense. Few believed, and no one seriously argued, that women were or could be the equals of men in intellectual capacity, artistic creativity or physical strength. On the contrary, it was precisely *because* they were already unequal that the additional legal and educational restrictions imposed on them were so unfair. Those who supported the Married Women's Property Acts sought to release married women from a particular legal and economic disability, one which existed ostensibly to protect married women but in fact exposed them to the possibility of even greater exploitation.

This understanding led me in turn to consider why so many twentieth-century legal commentators have misread (or more probably not read) the arguments of the nineteenth century feminists who fought for the Married Women's Property Acts. I found myself tracing the genesis of the idea that the reform was an equality measure pure and simple back through its many repetitions in Law Commission reports and the writings of community of property advocates to the earliest (male) legal historians who, even as the Acts were themselves unfolding, were also engaged in rewriting history to remove feminist agency[15] and re-categorising the reforms as having nothing to do with men's abuse of power and everything to do with 'modern' notions of women's status. But even some feminist chroniclers of first-wave feminism perpetuated the equality myth, perhaps as a deliberate 'persuader' ploy of telling a tale of progress that must continue inexorably and inevitably.[16]

The problem with this approach is that subsequent developments make this apparent faith in inevitable progress seem naïve. Twentieth century feminists and the advocates of community of property were both very aware of the shortcomings of legislation which guaranteed women a right to their own property but did nothing to facilitate their access to any. They had become much more conscious of the distinction between equal treatment and equal outcomes, and between formal and substantive equality, than first-wave feminists had been a century earlier. This recognition became the focus for new strategies in the twentieth century, of which community of property was one and the Equal Pay Act another, and we have yet to find an adequate solution.

But it is wrong to criticise the first-wave feminists for not realising that the Married Women's Property Acts would not give women equal access to property. The truth is that they never expected them to. They did not campaign for formally equal property rights in order to gain substantively equal property rights, but to get rid of an egregious injustice which gave husbands indefensible power over their wives. They certainly never assumed that equal property rights would solve married women's economic problems. For the minority who suffered their husbands' abuse of power, the Acts provided much-needed practical relief. For the majority, feminists recognised that the greatest significance of the Acts was symbolic,

---

[15] This technique of denying feminist agency is perhaps the most striking characteristic of mainstream accounts of legal history, even today. Of course, it only strikes those who are looking for it; those who know nothing of feminist history will notice no omission, and will take a very different lesson from their reading from those who see the gap. The reason why feminist campaigners cannot be mentioned in mainstream accounts is that their authors do not wish to acknowledge that women might actually prompt a legal change *by their own efforts*. It suits the self-referential nature of legal reasoning to attribute change to a developing legal consciousness, but never to human agency. There is one exception to this silence: you may find women campaigners mentioned in accounts written at times of ongoing feminist agitation – that is, in the later decades of first-wave feminism or during the second wave. Where women are mentioned in this context, the author will always expressly deny their role in achieving reform. For example: 'It is very questionable whether woman has ever gained any great concessions by direct agitation. If we look back, and note the numerous changes in the laws concerning women, how many of these changes are attributable to women themselves?': Cleveland, AR, *Women Under the English Law* (London, Hurst and Blackett, 1896) 298. The change will be ascribed to some abstract evolution of progressive ideas, or to generous male law-makers. An explicit put-down of this sort is necessary to deter feminist sympathisers among the readers of these accounts.

[16] Most notably, Strachey, R, *The Cause: A Short History of the Women's Movement in Great Britain* (London, Virago, 1978, 1st pub 1928).

offering married women a psychological freedom from male power which was the starting-point, not the end-point, of their financial independence. Much more needed to be done before women could be truly 'equal', but one could not even begin to talk about equality without getting rid of coverture first. Hence the subsequent criticisms of the Acts for not bringing about *substantive* equality for women are largely misplaced, an example of the rather patronising assumption that more recent generations always see things more clearly than their forebears.

The final paradox lies in the fact that the author of the statement quoted above, about separation of property being an accidental outcome of giving women 'the legal status which reflected their status in society', himself understood that the Married Women's Property Acts were not equality measures. Otto Kahn-Freund, distinguished professor of law at the London School of Economics from 1951 to 1964 and later at Oxford, was probably the most influential advocate of community of property. In 1955 he wrote:

> What is of special importance for an understanding of the present law is that the principles of equality of status and of separation of property appeared on the scene together, and, moreover, that they appeared, as it were, through the backdoor of a statutory extension of a technical conveyancing device invented by equity.[17] ... [A]s a result of...the connection at common law between inequality of status and the combination of both spouses' property in the hands of the husband, the idea of separation of property became in the minds of people, lawyers and laymen, interwoven with that of equality with which it has little intrinsically to do.[18]

[17] The 'technical conveyancing device invented by equity' refers to the *form* that the Acts took, but the suggestion that the achievement of the reform was due to a development of equity is again misleading. This is an idea of mainstream legal history promulgated by AV Dicey, who claimed that the Married Women's Property Acts were an example of 'The Effect of Judge-Made Law on Parliamentary Legislation': *Lectures on the Relation Between Law and Public Opinion in England During the Nineteenth Century* (London, Macmillan, 1962) 371–98. But the very title of the Acts makes it unlikely they could have slipped 'through the backdoor'. What happened was that, following the failure of successive Bills in the 1870s, Lord Chancellor Selborne realised that the reform could be re-cast as a perfect illustration of the new fusion of law and equity introduced by the Judicature Acts 1873–75, for which he had been largely responsible. The government therefore adopted the Bill and entirely re-wrote it in terms of 'separate property' under a statutory settlement. 'In effect', writes Lee Holcombe, the historian of the Married Women's Property Acts, 'the act of 1882 bestowed an equal marriage settlement upon every married woman who did not have one': Holcombe, L, *Wives and Property: Reform of the Married Women's Property Law in Nineteenth-Century England* (Toronto, University of Toronto Press, 1983) 202. This was not at all what the feminists had wanted; *their* proposed Bill, drafted by Richard Pankhurst, would have given married women the right to hold their property (of any kind, acquired both before and after marriage) in exactly the same way as unmarried women and men did – that is, not 'separate' under a statutory trust, nor hedged about with restrictions and contradictions as to their own and their husbands' contractual and tortious liabilities.

[18] Kahn-Freund, O, 'Matrimonial Property Law in England' in W Friedmann (ed), *Matrimonial Property Law* (Toronto, Carswell, 1955) 277–8.

It is clear from this passage that Kahn-Freund realised that most lawyers and lay people were wrong to think that the Married Women's Property Acts were simply about equality. He knew that equality had not been a goal, and had therefore not been a result. Kahn-Freund's aim was to achieve a measure of *justice* for women in relation to the home (I suspect not actual gender *equality* more generally), and he was engaged in trying to persuade his readers that community of property was the solution for this particular problem. And he was quite right in observing that separation of marital property did not work well for the housewives of the 1950s and 1960s, denied much opportunity to make financial contributions to the home, who would have been better served by community of property or joint ownership of the family home.

On the other hand, if mid-twentieth century women had had the access to sufficient independent means that some first-wave feminists envisaged – and that many had worked towards in their parallel campaigns to improve women's education, work opportunities and pay – then community of property or joint ownership might not have been necessary; might, indeed, have been detrimental to successful women, as some opponents of community of property were to argue in the 1970s,[19] and as some might argue today.

FRANCES POWER COBBE ON MARRIED WOMEN'S PROPERTY

For a proper understanding of Victorian feminist perspectives on the Married Women's Property Acts, we must turn to nineteenth-century writings on the subject. The campaign to reform the married women's property laws began in the 1850s with the formation of a women's committee – 'the first organized group of women in England to discuss and promote women's rights', according to Lee Holcombe[20] – by Barbara Leigh Smith and some of her friends, many of them (including Smith) later to be associated with a range of feminist causes. Though not, of course, legally trained or indeed university educated – women were still barred from the universities at that date – Smith had already demonstrated that the arcane rules of common law and equity held no terrors for her in writing a book, published in 1854, called *A Brief Summary, in Plain Language, of the Most Important Laws Concerning Women, Together With a Few Observations.*[21]

---

[19] Deech, R, 'A Tide in the Affairs of Women' (1972) 122 *New Law Journal* 742–3.
[20] Holcombe, above n 17, at 58.
[21] In Lacey, CA (ed), *Barbara Leigh Smith Bodichon and the Langham Place Group* (London, Routledge and Kegan Paul, 1987) 23–35.

A petition for reform of the married women's property law was presented to Parliament in 1856, explaining why the legislation was needed:

> The newspapers constantly detail instances of marital oppression, 'wife-beating' being a new compound noun lately introduced into the English language, and a crime against which English gentlemen have lately enacted stringent regulations.

> But that for the robbery by a man of his wife's hard [won] earnings there is no redress, – against the selfishness of a drunken father, who wrings from a mother her children's daily bread, there is no appeal. She may work from morning till night, to see the produce of her labour wrested from her.[22]

What was needed from the legislature was protection, not for a small number of unfortunate wives, but for many who were vulnerable to this husbandly abuse. As the petition noted, 'such cases are within the knowledge of every one'.[23]

Despite the support of the Law Amendment Society and the introduction of two Married Women's Property Bills into Parliament in 1857, Smith's campaign ground to a halt with the passing of the Divorce Act in that year.[24] Critics argued that happily married women did not need a law protecting their property from their husbands, while unhappily married women could obtain a divorce or a judicial separation, and so achieve separation of property. Underlying these excuses was doubtless a masculine conviction that *one* reform of the marriage laws was quite enough for a decade.[25]

The campaign was revived in the 1860s. One of the most effective contributions to the debate was the essay entitled 'Criminals, Idiots, Women, and Minors', published in *Fraser's Magazine* in 1868.[26] It was the work of Frances Power Cobbe who was 'unquestionably the ablest and most prolific amongst the mid-Victorian feminists' in Barbara Caine's view.[27]

---

[22] Petition reproduced in Holcombe, above n 17, at 238.

[23] *Ibid.*

[24] In another not coincidental parallel, the feminists' plans for joint ownership of the matrimonial home in the 1960s also foundered on the enactment of a Divorce Reform Act, that of 1969.

[25] Anderson, O, 'Hansard's Hazards: An Illustration from Recent Interpretations of Married Women's Property Law and the 1857 Divorce Act' (1997) *English Historical Review* (November) 1202–15.

[26] Cobbe, FP, 'Criminals, Idiots, Women, and Minors' in S Hamilton (ed), *Criminals, Idiots, Women, and Minors: Victorian Writing by Women on Women* (Peterborough, Broadview Press, 1995) 108–31.

[27] Caine, B, *Victorian Feminists* (Oxford, Oxford University Press, 1993) 104.

Cobbe's essay carefully avoids claiming that women are, or should be, equal to men. Instead, Cobbe asks for the 'just and expedient treatment of women'[28]:

Of course it is not pleasant to women to be told they are 'physically, morally, and intellectually inferior' to their companions

she admits, and adds:

The humblest individual is neither more contented, nor (we believe) much the better for being reminded of congenital defects which he can never hope to overcome; and for a proud and gifted woman to be told that she is in every possible respect inferior to the footman who stands behind her chair, can hardly be thought pleasing intelligence.[29]

Sympathetic as she is, Cobbe thinks it is a waste of time getting upset about such insults. The commoner experience of a man's pretending to admire, while secretly despising, a woman is actually much worse, she says. This looks suspiciously as if she is sidestepping the issue, and her very next sentence shows that this is indeed so. 'In any case all such discussion is beside our present aim.'[30]

Her aim, it emerges, is to counter the three main arguments put forward in defence of the common law rule that a married woman's property should be given to her husband. The 'justice' argument contends that, as men are breadwinners and support their wives, it is right and proper for them to control all the family property. The 'expediency' argument points to the undesirability – indeed, impossibility – of having two independent wills in one household: *someone* must take the lead, and that someone ought to be the husband since women have no head for money management. The 'sentiment' argument is, however, in Cobbe's view the most important. The substance of this argument is that men have an idealised view of marriage and design their laws to promote this.

Cobbe then proceeds to refute each point one by one. Justice first: how *just* is a legal system that allows a man to take everything his wife owns and earns but does not enforce his obligation to maintain her? Here follow one or two tragic stories drawn from the newspapers in which unfortunate women, whose husbands have taken their every penny, are refused Poor Law assistance on the ground that their husband has a duty to support them, and are at the same time unable to obtain an order in a magistrate's court to sue him because 'husband and wife are one' so cannot sue each other. Some of these women had subsequently starved to death.

---

[28] Cobbe, above n 26, at 109.
[29] *Ibid*, at 109–10.
[30] *Ibid*, at 110.

How *expedient*, then, was a legal arrangement that assumed a man would be a better financial manager than a woman when, in fact, he might be a gambler or a drunkard? Cobbe also wrote extensively on domestic violence and knew a great deal about men's abuse of their wives.[31] On the disjunction between the ideal and the reality she is particularly bitter, pointing the finger at a legal system which condoned men's exploitation of women by recourse to the familiar argument that:

> laws cannot take note of exceptional cases; they must be laid down to suit the majority, and the minority must do as best they can. But is there any other department of public justice in which the same principle is applied? What else is law *for*, but to be 'a terror to evil doers'? – always, as we trust, in a minority in the community. The greater number of people are honest, and neither steal their neighbours' goods nor break into their houses. Yet the law takes pretty sharp account of thieves and burglars.[32]

Set against this reminder of the potential for male abuse is the image of married women's vulnerability under the current law. In the essay's most famous metaphor, Cobbe portrays the English wife as a bird in the zoo, whose keeper explains to visitors:

> This, ladies and gentlemen, is an inoffensive bird, the *Mulier Anglicana*. The beak is feeble, and the claws unsuited for grubbing for worms. It seems to be only intelligent in building its nest, or taking care of its young, to whom it is peculiarly devoted, as well as to its mate. Otherwise it is a very simple sort of bird, picking up any crumbs which are thrown to it. ... Therefore you see, ladies and gentlemen, as it is so helpless, we put that strong chain round its leg, and fasten it to its nest, and make the bars of its cage exceptionally strong. As to its rudimentary wings we always break them early, for greater security; though I have heard Professor Huxley say that he is convinced it could never fly far with them, under any circumstances.[33]

Abandoning this very graphic image to leave its mark on her readers' imaginations, Cobbe moves on to a more practical point. '[T]he great and overwhelming argument against the Expediency of the Common Law', Cobbe explains, is that no Victorian parent with the means to do so would ever surrender his daughter into marriage without a marriage settlement to provide her with an independent income which her husband could not touch.[34]

---

[31]   See Cobbe, FP, 'Wife Torture in England' in Hamilton (ed), above n 26, at 132–70. She was later instrumental in bringing about the Matrimonial Causes Act 1878 which enabled the wives of violent men to separate from their husbands and obtain maintenance from them.

[32]   Cobbe, above n 26, at 117. The idea that law cannot deal with 'exceptional' cases is commonly found in case law concerning women up to the present day.

[33]   *Ibid*, at 118–19.

[34]   *Ibid*, at 119.

Cobbe saves her most withering scorn for the Sentiment argument. It is sentiment, she believes, that lies at the heart of men's objection to their wives' having independent means. Reason plays little role in this:

> Legislators talk in Parliament with a certain conviction that the principles of fairness and policy are the only ones to be referred to *there*. But whenever the subject is freely discussed, in private or in a newspaper, there is sure to burst out sooner or later the real feeling at bottom.[35]

'Sentiment', however, turns out to mean something very different from the poetic vision of marital unity lovingly described by opponents of reform: for example, the description of coverture in *The Times* as a system in which:

> men undertake to provide for women a safe and sheltered sphere within which they may develop all the gentle powers of their nature.[36]

Instead, Cobbe asks:

> Is it not this – that a woman's whole life and being, her soul, body, time, property, thought, and care ought to be given to her husband; that nothing short of such absorption in him and his interests makes her a true wife?[37]

Unfortunately, she recognises, most women accept this role, leaving men to assume 'so far as legislation can create such an ideal', that it will do so.[38]

At the end of the essay, Cobbe considers the more general question of how English law should deal with women. Rather as Mary Wollstonecraft had done three-quarters of a century before,[39] she admits that many women are 'unequal' to men in character, though, like Wollstonecraft, she ascribes this to lack of educational opportunity, something from which she had herself suffered sorely.[40] This allows her to draw attention to the forthcoming opening of the first university college for women, the future Girton.[41] But once again she shies away from further engagement with the idea of equality:

---

[35] *Ibid*, at 121. Albie Sachs sees this 'sentiment' as an excuse for male self-interest: see Sachs, A and Wilson, JH, *Sexism and the Law: A Study of Male Beliefs and Judicial Bias* (Oxford, Martin Robertson, 1978).

[36] Quoted in Mitchell, S, *Frances Power Cobbe: Victorian Feminist, Journalist, Reformer* (Charlottesville, University of Virginia Press, 2004) 209. This led Cobbe to remind the editor that no week passed 'without the police reports recording some pitiful story of a wife beaten to death by her husband': Mitchell, *ibid*.

[37] Cobbe, above n 26, at 121.

[38] *Ibid*.

[39] Wollstonecraft, M, *A Vindication of the Rights of Woman* (London, Joseph Johnson, 1792).

[40] Cobbe, FP, *Life of Frances Power Cobbe by Herself,* 3rd edn (London, Bentley, 1894) vol 1, 58–68.

[41] Cobbe, above n 26, at 126. Barbara Leigh Smith (now Madame Bodichon) was one of the founders of Girton College, Emily Davies the other.

Much time and more temper have been lost in debating the sterile proposition of the 'equality' of men and women, without either party seeming to perceive that the solution either way has no bearing on the practical matters at issue, since civil rights have never yet been reserved for 'physical, moral, and intellectual' equals.[42]

In other words, the rights of citizenship – 'the right to hold property, to make contracts, to sue and be sued' (the very rights claimed for married women) – should be available to all competent adults, regardless of capability. Thus can Cobbe draw a distinction between 'equality' in terms of innate capabilities and 'equality' in terms of equal treatment. She refuses to claim the former, and indeed declares it irrelevant; but the latter can be justified by recourse to a liberal notion of 'civil rights' familiar to the Victorian intellectuals who were her readers.

She concludes:

But whatever a woman may think on these subjects, she has no need to argue, much less to grow shrill and angry about it. 'Granted,' she answers to all rebuffs; 'let me be physically, intellectually, and morally your inferior. So long as you allow I possess moral responsibility and sufficient intelligence to know right from wrong (a point I conclude you will concede, else why hang me for murder?) I am quite content. It is *only* as a Moral and Intelligent Being I claim my civil rights.'[43]

THE FEMINIST REJECTION OF EQUALITY

Given that the campaigners for married women's property rights were effectively asking for *equal treatment* for women, we have to ask ourselves why Cobbe (and others) avoided using equality arguments so assiduously. The first reason was undoubtedly the widespread perception in Victorian society that women *were* unequal, and that this inequality was *natural* and demonstrable by women's own presentation, behaviour and achievements (or lack of them). This made the climate of nineteenth century opinion very different from that of today when women's equal abilities are generally conceded, though there might still be arguments over differences of 'nature' and behaviours. Many Victorian women as well as men accepted the idea of women's natural inequality: Sarah Ellis, for example, advised women that they must:

be content to be inferior to men, inferior in mental power in the same proportion that you are inferior in bodily strength.[44]

---

[42] *Ibid*, at 128
[43] *Ibid*.
[44] Quoted in Murray, JH, *Strong-Minded Women and Other Lost Voices from Nineteenth-Century England* (Harmondsworth, Penguin, 1984) 211.

More startling, perhaps, is the number of Victorian feminists who made a point of repudiating any claim to equality with men. In this, Frances Power Cobbe was in distinguished company. Here is Caroline Norton, for instance:

> The natural position of woman is inferiority to man. Amen! That is a thing of God's appointing, not of man's devising. I believe it sincerely, as a part of my religion: and I accept it as a matter proved to my reason. I never pretended to the wild and ridiculous doctrine of equality.[45]

It is hard to credit that these words were written by a woman whose husband had bullied and beaten her, taken her children from her, and lived off her earnings – a woman, moreover, of great literary talent and political acumen, not to speak of courage, resilience and dedication. But they were, and we have to ask, *did she mean it?*

Listen, too, to Emily Davies who, though firm in demanding that her women students at Cambridge should study the same subjects as the men and take the same examinations, yet declared that:

> my feeling against raising barriers between men and women has nothing to do with the assertion of equality or identity, in neither of which I believe.[46]

Cobbe echoed her when herself advocating university study for women:

> A man and a woman are *parallel* to each other, but never *similar*. ... They are *equivalents* to each other, but never *equals*. ... All these differences are innate, unchangeable, ineradicable.[47]

Why did Victorian feminists reject the idea of equality – shun the very word – so thoroughly? Four explanations occur to me. First, the rejection of equality could have been strategic, so that the feminist demands might appear moderate and unthreatening to men. Second, it could have been the result of decades of disappointment and disillusionment with the political reality of liberalism, which had proved so unhelpful to women. Third, the insistence on *in*equality might have been ironic, allowing women's real feelings to be concealed from all except those who were in the know, while conservatives, not seeing the in-joke, could take the words at face value. Or, finally, we must allow for the possibility that it was sincere: these women might really not have believed in the equality of the sexes.

---

[45] Norton, C, 'A Letter to the Queen on Lord Chancellor Cranworth's Marriage and Divorce Bill' (1855) in P Hollis (ed), *Women in Public: The Women's Movement 1850–1900* (London, George Allen and Unwin, 1979) 183.

[46] Letter from Emily Davies to Mr Tomkinson, 16 Jan 1869, in Hollis, *ibid*, at 154.

[47] Cobbe, FP, 'The Education of Women, and How it Would be Affected by University Examinations' (1862) in D Spender (ed), *The Education Papers*, above n 4, at 42.

Strategy

As a second-wave feminist, I have always assumed that the denial of equality-seeking was in part tactical. Caroline Norton could *surely* never have thought that women were inferior to men, knowing what she did not only about her own husband's abominable behaviour but about the experiences of the hundreds of other women whose sufferings she publicised to help bring about changes in the laws of child custody, divorce, and married women's property.[48] But she must have needed powerful support for her proposed reforms, and the sentiments quoted were in an open letter to the Queen, well-known for her conventional views. Obviously, then, she would have tried to demonstrate appropriate 'womanliness' and asked, not for equal rights, not even for justice, but for 'protection'.

Emily Davies, too, was anxious not to appear to be encroaching on masculine privilege and knew, moreover, that the success of her college of higher education for women depended on her students' parents being reassured that their daughters would remain 'ladies', with their femininity unimpaired, in spite of their masculine studies. Any hint that they might come to resemble men (and perhaps become unmarriageable) would be disastrous. Strategy demanded, therefore, that she eschew equality claims, while actually arguing for an equal education. Barbara Caine suggests that maybe:

> it was only because of her conservative social and political framework that Davies was able to be as radical as she was on the education question.[49]

For Cobbe, too, tackling the notion of women's supposed inferiority was bound to seem tactically foolish when the matter could not be proved or disproved at that time. Physically constrained as they were, poorly educated and excluded from most employments, women had little chance of successfully disputing this truism. Certainly Cobbe was not in a position to do so. It was only at the end of the nineteenth century, when women began to obtain grades which equalled or exceeded those of men in university examinations, that they could begin to challenge men's intellectual superiority, and even then many areas of 'natural' inequality (physical, creative) remained sufficiently taken for granted to keep women in their place. This is clearly demonstrated by Mary Jane Mossman's account in Chapter 7 of this volume of women's struggles to enter the legal profession.

Cobbe's aim was to try to persuade, so, knowing that equality was not her strongest argument, she avoided it. Moreover, as a professional writer

---

[48] The Infant Custody Act 1839 and the Matrimonial Causes Act 1857. See Shanley, ML, *Feminism, Marriage, and the Law in Victorian Britain 1850–1895* (Princeton, NJ, Princeton University Press, 1989) 22–48; and Caine, above n 5, at 66–70.

[49] Caine, *ibid*, at 101.

she realised she could make much more effective use of alternative arguments such as the illogicality of the wedding service where the groom spoke of endowing his wife with all his worldly goods, when the opposite was the case,[50] and the injustice of the law's claiming to protect women when in fact it facilitated their oppression. These were points she could make most strikingly through the use of anecdote, metaphor and irony, techniques for which she was renowned, and which helped to make her essays so accessible and convincing.[51] Claiming a right on the basis of women's intrinsic equality, on the other hand, would have put most of her readers on the defensive from the start, producing quite the wrong effect if one sought reform. As Sally Mitchell notes, Frances Power Cobbe would sometimes make 'significant rhetorical concessions to conservative arguments about women's sphere' in order to place her articles advocating radical reform in socially conservative journals.[52]

That said, Cobbe did point out that until women were given exactly the same conditions and opportunities for self-development as men had, one could not say for certain what their capabilities might be. She could not resist showing how much women's 'natural' inequality was due to their circumstances. Her image of the chained, caged bird makes this point very clearly, and even calls into question the very notion of any inferiority that was *not* socially constructed. But she never tried to claim that women deserved equal treatment in property matters *for this reason*.

The Limits of Liberalism

A second explanation for the feminist avoidance of equality claims might have been a recognition that liberalism had done little to further women's rights. It is true that the campaign for married women's property rights was a *liberal* campaign in the sense of the goal being the removal of a legal barrier to the exercise of the individual's capabilities. Barbara Leigh Smith, daughter of a Liberal MP, expressed this view in her *Brief Summary of the Laws of England Concerning Women* when she wrote:

> Philosophical thinkers have generally come to the conclusion that the tendency of progress is gradually to dispense with the law – that is to say, as each individual man becomes unto himself a law, less external restraint is necessary.

---

[50] She illustrates this point with a story that opens the essay, where a visitor from outer space chances on a wedding and enquires about its significance.

[51] Her biographer, Sally Mitchell, comments that Cobbe was known for her 'memorable phrases as well as provocative ideas': above n 36, at 2.

[52] Mitchell, above n 36, at 169. Davies and Cobbe may not have found it so difficult to adopt this stance since they were both Tories in party politics.

And certainly the most urgently needed reforms are simple erasures from the statute book. Women, more than any other members of the community, suffer from over-legislation.[53]

It was also helpful in a self-consciously progressive era to associate feminist goals with liberalism as an inexorably progressive movement.

For Victorian feminists, however, this apparent inevitability of liberal reform was both boon and burden. Liberal ideas could be used (as they were by Barbara Leigh Smith) as a persuader technique: by linking improvements in women's condition to progressive ideas generally, feminists could head off potential opposition from people who considered themselves forward-thinking. But this strategic usefulness was more than offset by numerous disadvantages. First, reforms which appeared to be just around the corner could be put off again and again: this happened with the Married Women's Property Acts, but the parliamentary vote took far longer.[54] Secondly, liberalism tended to remove agency from the picture: if injustices existed in society, they were never the fault of any particular individual or group; and if reform was going to happen anyway, it could be represented as occurring of its own accord – not because feminists fought for it.

Victorian feminists were therefore cautious in their use of liberal arguments, knowing that these could work against them. Yet such arguments exercised a powerful appeal as the dominant ideology of the day. As Barbara Caine explains:

> feminism is necessarily bound by the preoccupations of the society in which it develops and by the terms in which the situation of women was currently being discussed.[55]

Frances Power Cobbe's call for 'civil rights' at the end of the essay discussed above is a good example of this. One is struck by the way that, after expounding a clear analysis of male power, she falls back on the language of natural rights that had sustained nineteenth century liberalism with all its equality claims. This is a very different discourse from one of male power and one which had never really been favourable to women who, alongside working-class men and non-white people generally, had not been seen as falling within its remit.[56] The answer is that it was both respectable and accepted, as well as tactically satisfactory in enabling her to sidestep the issue of women's inferiority.

---

[53] Smith in Lacey, above n 21, at 30–31.
[54] It was not granted (to women of 30 and over) until 1918, and not until 1928 on equal terms with men.
[55] Caine, above n 27, at 17.
[56] But many male historians mistakenly locate feminism within the spread of Enlightenment ideals. See, eg Cleveland, above n 15, at 295.

Irony

That the feminist rejection of women's equal worth might have been ironic occurred to me when I read the sentence that followed Caroline Norton's remarks on women's inequality. She wrote:

> I will even hold that (as one coming under the general rule that the wife must be inferior to the husband), I occupy that position, *Uxor fulget radiis Mariti*; I am Mr. Norton's inferior; I am the clouded moon of that sun.[57]

Everything about this sentence – the careful distinction Norton makes between herself personally and herself *as a wife*; the Latin aphorism, the use of which belies her intellectual 'inferiority' as surely as the wit of the final clause, whose effect is to render the whole notion absurd; that very descent into bathos – seems calculated to undo the seriousness of the earlier declaration. This humour (if such it was) passes in an instant, so quickly one begins to doubt it, and we are back to a passionate but logical appeal to civil rights: 'Put me then – (my ambition extends no further) – in the same position as all his other inferiors!'[58]

Irony is not a quality one associates with Emily Davies, but Frances Power Cobbe's work, as we have seen, is full of it: she is one of the wittiest feminist writers, with a skill honed in decades of work as a professional journalist charged with making social issues accessible to a wide audience. Here is Cobbe on the parlous position of the middle-class daughter at home:

> If she be a Roman Catholic, she may leave her home and go into a nunnery in all honour and credit; but the exchange is perhaps no great gain. If she be a Protestant, friends, parents, neighbours, and all her little world cry out lustily if she think of leaving her father's roof for any end, however good or noble, save only that one sacred vocation of matrimony, for which she may lawfully leave a blind father and dying mother, and go to India with Ensign Anybody.[59]

In that last clause, incidentally, is revealed Cobbe's contempt for the cult of marriage – and for men generally.

Sincerely Held Belief

Yet, while her argument that men and women were essentially different might well have been tactical, I do not think it was ironic – even given Cobbe's own masculine demeanour, lifestyle and profession. I think she really did believe that men and women were different and unequal, but the

---

[57] Norton in Hollis, above n 45, at 183.
[58] *Ibid.*
[59] Cobbe, above n 47, at 39.

issue was not women's inferiority: it was *men's*. On the matter of intellect, she might concede men's superiority, though with the admission of women to higher education she could see that the gap was closing. On moral issues, there was no contest. Women were less likely to be criminals, she observed; they were generally less selfish, and certainly more conscientious than most men. 'In short, *in the lump*, women are better than men,' she concluded.[60]

There is an apparent contradiction here between her inner conviction of women's moral superiority and her need, for strategic reasons, to allow that women might be inferior to men under existing social conditions, which she used as the *reason* for removing the restrictions on their ability to hold property. If women were already weak, she demonstrated in her writings on married women's property, their legal restrictions put them in an even weaker position by making them vulnerable to their husbands' abuse of power. This was rather like kicking someone who was already down. The best justification for property law reform was therefore the need for genuine and adequate *protection* for married women – not because of any abstract philosophical idea of their equality but because they were in fact *unequal*, and the law made it worse.

In later writing Cobbe was to abandon natural rights and any concessions to men's superiority in favour of a more robust assertion of women's abilities, but she could only do this once the assumed inferiority of the sex had been thoroughly challenged by their increasing participation in the public sphere, higher education and the professions. She then co-opted another conservative image of Victorian woman – that of the guardian of public morality – to argue that women's *special qualities*, particularly their special moral responsibilities, made a female contribution to political and social life both expedient and necessary.

IS THIS A RADICAL FEMINIST ANALYSIS?

The central goal of classic radical feminism is the abolition of gender. Whether radical feminists regard gender differences as socially constructed or innate, they do not seek for women to become more like men in their pursuit of equality but rather for the best values, which are often those associated with women, to become the dominant values of society irrespective of sex. In such a scenario, gender becomes irrelevant.

Victorian feminists never, to my knowledge, spoke of the abolition of gender; such an idea remains contentious today. But in their analysis of married women's property and some other issues of their time, they

---

[60] From an article on 'Woman Suffrage' published in the *Contemporary Review* in 1903: quoted in Mitchell, above n 36, at 365.

employed a number of arguments that resemble elements of the radical feminism of a century later. First, they saw women as a class. In a sense this was a different understanding of class from that of radical feminism which in the 1960s was reacting against the social-class basis of Marxist or socialist feminism (though this, too, of course, had its roots in the nineteenth century). But in another sense it is the same, for Victorian feminists were interrogating the assumption that married women's rights were necessarily encompassed in their husbands – the idea of coverture – just as twentieth-century radical feminists were critical of the way women's separate position was ignored and taken for granted within the working and middle classes of the socialist analysis.

One would have imagined that the idea of women as a class would have been readily accessible to a society which already assumed that men and women had separate spheres. But the Victorian feminist insistence that married women formed a class needing independent rights seems to have appalled and terrified the very men who would exclude women from political rights precisely *because* they were not within the 'class' of men. An article in *The Times* in the mid-1860s protested that women 'are not a class at all' and had 'no separate interests' or, if they had, that these were adequately catered to by their male relations.[61] MP John Bright declared in the debates on the 1867 Reform Act that 'it was a scandalous and odious libel to say that women are a class' or that they suffered from non-representation.[62]

It is not difficult to account for the vehemence of men's opposition to the idea of women as a separate class of persons. Many men were accustomed to thinking of their wives as their own property, to treat as they wished. Though legally inaccurate, this idea was common enough for Frances Power Cobbe to note in her article on domestic violence, 'Wife-Torture in England', that:

> It is even sometimes pleaded on behalf of poor men, that they possess *nothing else* but their wives, and that, consequently, it seems doubly hard to meddle with the exercise of their power in that narrow sphere.[63]

And even those men who would not dream of beating their wives were uneasy at the thought that their wife's financial independence might loosen their control over her. In this they were perfectly correct. Recognising women as a separate class with an independent existence went some way towards freeing wives from their husband's 'protective' rule and might even

---

[61]   Quoted in Mitchell, *ibid*, at 169.
[62]   *Ibid*, at 243.
[63]   Cobbe in Hamilton, above n 31, at 139.

allow them to put themselves first, for a change.[64] Woman, Cobbe wrote, is not an adjective, whose value lies in her relation to others, but a noun, who exists for herself.[65]

This in turn opened up the threatening possibility of *choice* for a woman. A wife with her own property, as MPs cautioned in the debates on the Married Women's Property Acts, might be able to *leave* her husband if she did not like him.[66] Of course, leaving one's husband would not have been easy for women with very little property of their own, but the men's anxiety showed that a larger principle was at stake: *their own behaviour*. Men might actually have to behave better if they wanted to keep their wives.

Feminists rarely drew explicit attention to this fear, but everyone recognised that it simmered just below the surface of the discussions. Their technique was rather to publicise the most egregious tales of cruelty and hardship that appeared in the press, *especially among the working class*, for:

> to convince members of Parliament to act, it was far easier to arouse benevolence towards poor victims than to demand an examination of their own behaviour.[67]

Cobbe referred to the idea that all women's needs were satisfactorily provided for by individual men as 'the great Masculine Myth'.[68] Indeed, Cobbe's response to John Bright's indignant denials noted above was to argue that women:

> form the class of all others which needs the protection of direct representation, seeing that their special interests concern not only money or land, but things tenfold dearer – personal rights, and rights over children.[69]

Men could not be trusted to prioritise the things that women valued – personal and family rights, which were, in Cobbe's eyes, much more important than money and property. But she recognised that these, too, mattered to women.

[64] Eg when the father of novelist Ann Bridge faced a financial crisis in the late nineteenth century he used all the family assets, 'including [his wife's] rather meagre marriage-portion...to meet this emergency; and as she had been married before the Married Women's Property Act was passed in 1874 it never occurred to my Father to replace it when he was in funds again, so that to the day of her death my Mother never had a penny to call her own': Bridge, A, *Portrait of My Mother* (London, Chatto & Windus, 1955) 103.

[65] Cobbe, FP, 'The Final Cause of Woman' in J Butler (ed), *Woman's Work and Woman's Culture* (London, Macmillan, 1869) 21.

[66] Holcombe, L, 'Victorian Wives and Property: Reform of the Married Women's Property Law, 1857–1882' in M Vicinus (ed), *A Widening Sphere: Changing Roles of Victorian Women* (Bloomington, Indiana, Indiana University Press, 1980) 15.

[67] Mitchell, above n 36, at 50.

[68] *Ibid*, at 332.

[69] *Ibid*, at 243.

Underlying all these arguments was an understanding that male power operated in the interests of men and was devoted to sustaining those institutions which benefited men. Victorian feminists did not speak of patriarchy, but they often described it. Coverture was seen as one aspect of a system that gave men an unfair advantage over women, which worked globally to keep men dominant and women subordinate, but also on an individual level in favour of particular men and against particular women.

The Problem of Men

Thus, as well as recognising men and women as separate classes, Victorian feminists clearly defined their relationship as one of exploitation. The Married Women's Property Acts were necessary because women needed protection against *men*: men who exploited their wives through their unrestricted access to all her worldly goods. The feminist analysis of coverture was one of male power and the solution sought was justified, not in terms of women's greater equality or independence, but in terms of limiting that power.

Smith's *Brief Summary* was the first important feminist statement on this subject. Its brilliance lay in the fact that, while purporting merely to set out the law in accessible language, Smith managed to convey through an apparently objective choice of phrasing the *loss of rights and control* that women experienced on marriage and the potential for abuse – though she never mentions the word – at the hands of a husband who, even if he had not explicitly married the woman for her money,[70] nevertheless got his hands on everything she possessed:

> A man and wife are one person in law; the wife loses all her rights as a single woman, and her existence is entirely absorbed in that of her husband. ... What was her personal property before marriage, such as money in hand, money in the bank, jewels, household goods, clothes, etc. becomes absolutely her husband's, and he may assign or dispose of them at his pleasure.[71]

Even her body 'now belongs to her husband; she is in his custody'.[72] By setting out the facts in this stark way, Smith provided some justification for

---

[70] Though it was well known that some men *did* marry women for their property – see Marshall, T, 'Love and Money' (1869), quoted in Levine, above n 1, at 138.
[71] Smith in Lacey, above n 21, at 25–6.
[72] *Ibid*, at 25.

the belief that married women, like slaves, were the property of their husbands – an analogy later used by a number of writers including John Stuart Mill.[73]

'The cumulative effect of this simple listing of married women's disabilities was devastating', comments Mary Lyndon Shanley of Smith's pamphlet.[74] To appreciate Smith's achievement one needs to contrast her account with the benign descriptions of coverture in the legal textbooks of the time:

> From the time of the intermarriage the law looks upon the husband and wife as but one person; and therefore allows of but one will between them, which is placed in the husband, as the fittest and ablest to provide for and govern the family; and, for this reason, the law gives the husband an absolute power of disposing of her personal property, no account of hers being of any force to effect or transfer that by which the intermarriage she has resigned to him.[75]

It is a tribute to the success of the Married Women's Property campaign in shifting the terms of the debate that, when Thomas Barrett-Lennard came to write his account of *The Position in Law of Women* in 1883, he had to explain the equitable intervention that protected middle- and upper-class women before the Acts as a response to:

> The hardship inflicted by the common law upon femes covert [married women] in not permitting them to enjoy their own property.[76]

Of course, in *his* account, the 'hardship' is taken for granted, the cause (men) omitted in favour of the genderless 'common law', and the reform rendered natural and inevitable.

In 'Criminals, Idiots, Women and Minors', Cobbe's observation that all middle- and upper-class fathers provided marriage settlements for their daughters was probably her clinching argument. If well-to-do women were protected, what could be the objection to offering the same protection to women further down the social order? Certainly Dicey chose to interpret the Married Women's Property Acts in this light, describing the reform in classic Whig terms as part of the general extension of rights from the well-to-do to the less well-off in the nineteenth century.[77] Cobbe's interpretation is a very different one. If most middle- and upper-class women were

---

[73] Mill, JS, *The Subjection of Women* (1869) in AS Rossi (ed), *Essays on Sex Equality: John Stuart Mill and Harriet Taylor Mill* (Chicago, University of Chicago Press, 1970) 123–242.

[74] Shanley, above n 48, at 32.

[75] Barrett-Lennard, T, *The Position in Law of Women* (London, Waterlow and Sons, 1883) 69.

[76] *Ibid*, at 82.

[77] Dicey, above n 17, at 393. The historian of the Acts, Lee Holcombe, seems to me rather too inclined to accept Dicey's reasoning: above n 17, at 230–31.

protected by equity from the powerlessness experienced by many working-class women, this showed that *even middle-class and upper-class men were not to be trusted*. Otherwise, why insist on a settlement? Thus, while Dicey might reframe the married women's property reforms as solely a class issue – the horror stories were generally of working-class women – it was in fact an issue of gender pure and simple.

As the essay proceeds, Cobbe shines the spotlight more and more closely on men as she develops her argument that reform is needed to protect women from men's abuses of power. She shows how men's wish to have wives who are completely absorbed in their interests is both complacent and egotistical and, moreover, that the law (man-made, as she points out)[78] promotes this unattractive masculine quality. By the end of the essay a further reason for Cobbe's avoidance of equality arguments becomes abundantly clear when the reader is left in no doubt that she does not consider the male model a suitable standard for women to aspire to. If men were inferior to women, there was really no reason for feminists to call for equality with them – that would, in truth, have been a retrograde step. Rather, men needed to be raised up to women's standard. But it is one thing to argue that women are morally superior, and quite another thing to impugn men's right to be morally *inferior*. Feminists like Frances Power Cobbe managed to turn something that had always worked to men's advantage on its head by systematically exposing and publicising the depths to which men sank, and the extent to which their behaviour was condoned in a society that professed to be just and Christian.

Like second-wave feminists, Cobbe linked her analysis to her politics, revealing by her choice of imagery that she saw feminism as a war between the sexes. 'Let us try to fathom this sentiment,' she wrote, 'for till we understand it we are but fighting our battles in the dark'.[79] We can therefore see a direct line of descent from the married women's property campaigns to the later critique of male sexual behaviour that was to have its most famous manifestation in Christabel Pankhurst's suffragette slogan, 'Votes for Women and Chastity for Men'. Sheila Jeffreys[80] and Lucy Bland[81] have detailed the feminist critique of men's uncontrolled right of sexual access to women in marriage – the tenacious last remaining feature of coverture – in the closing decades of the nineteenth century. Bland writes:

[78] Cobbe, above n 26, at 125.
[79] *Ibid.*
[80] Jeffreys, S, *The Spinster and Her Enemies: Feminism and Sexuality 1880–1930* (London, Pandora, 1985).
[81] Bland, L, *Banishing the Beast: English Feminism and Sexual Morality 1885–1914* (Harmondsworth, Penguin, 1995).

On the one hand, we find feminists working to change the law on marriage, and on the other, women writers using the vehicle of fiction to expose matrimonial horrors and to suggest alternative ways of living and relating.[82]

While male authors like Thomas Hardy[83] and Grant Allen[84] focused on the sexual 'freedom' of their 'New Woman' heroines, women novelists paid more attention to men:[85]

It was male sexual behaviour which was singled out as the key problem: demanding, selfish, frequently injurious to its female recipient.[86]

Philippa Levine suggests that many women 'cut their feminist teeth' on the married women's property campaigns and 'through addressing the problems of property within marriage came to a clearer understanding of other aspects of female subjugation'.[87] When Frances Power Cobbe wrote 'Criminals, Idiots, Women and Minors' in 1868, she had a better idea than most women of the role played by the absence of property rights in married women's subjection; but, as the decades passed, she developed her analysis into a comprehensive attack on the entire legal and moral framework of marriage.[88] The property campaigns can therefore be said to have paved the way for what Levine characterised as 'a fully-fledged moral critique of Victorian value systems'.[89]

CONCLUSION

To the extent to which all the variety of objectives subscribed to by nineteenth-century feminists can be described as tending to produce equality for men and women alike, then it can be said that the ideal of equality was generally shared, but it is difficult to go further than this.[90]

So wrote Rosalind Delmar in 1986. She went on to explain how, as the nineteenth century progressed, the feminist reliance on Enlightenment ideals of *human entitlement* gave way to a call for *equal treatment* for

---

[82] Bland, above n 1, at 148.
[83] Hardy, T, *Jude the Obscure* (London, Macmillan, 1895).
[84] Allen, G, *The Woman Who Did* (London, John Lane, 1895).
[85] Eg, George Egerton (penname of Mary Chavelita Dunne), *Keynotes* (London, Elkin Nathews and John Lane, 1893); Sarah Grand, *The Heavenly Twins* (London, Cassell, 1893); Emma Brooke, *A Superfluous Woman* (London, William Heinemann,1894); Mona Caird, *The Daughters of Danaus* (London, Bliss, Sands and Foster, 1894). See also Caird, M, *The Morality of Marriage* (London,George Redway, 1897); and Cunningham, G, *The New Woman and the Victorian Novel* (London, Macmillan, 1978).
[86] Bland, above n 1, at 151.
[87] Levine, above n 1, at 140.
[88] Caine, above n 27, at 135.
[89] Levine, above n 1, at 141.
[90] Delmar, R, 'What is Feminism?' in J Mitchell and A Oakley (eds), *What Is Feminism?* (Oxford, Basil Blackwell, 1986) 20.

women and men set alongside an acknowledgment of *gender difference*. Rights were claimed for women – or *some* women, at least – as representatives of a sex 'class' with its own interests, skills, and points of view. Feminists sought to rid themselves of legal and educational disabilities, but not necessarily in the hope of achieving equal status with men. They rejected the male standard of behaviour as the desirable norm and tried to inject a measure of superior feminine morality into public life.

The identification of women as a class was as fundamental to Victorian feminists' claims for women's rights as it was repugnant to those men who resisted granting them. But naming women as a category needing rights did not necessarily mean, as it would mean today under discrimination or human rights law, a call for *equal rights* for women. When Frances Power Cobbe expounds on gender differences, it becomes obvious that she stands in a tradition that not only goes back to traditional conservative Victorian ideas (hardly surprising, since that was the milieu she came from) but also forward to cultural feminist ideas and an essentialist interpretation of Carol Gilligan's ethic of care:

> Woman learns differently from man; and when she is able to teach, she teaches differently and with different lessons. If ever the day arrives when women shall be able to deal worthily with the subjects of our highest interests, we shall all be the better, I believe, for completing man's ideal of religion and morals by that of woman, and learning to add to his Law of Justice her Law of Love.[91]

Here she seems to me completely sincere, describing what she saw of men and women all around her, just as Gilligan described what she and her researchers found a hundred years later.[92]

Cobbe's refusal to entertain an equality analysis as long as men continued to exploit women also resonates with the radical feminist politics of Andrea Dworkin, who wrote (in an essay of 1974 entitled 'Renouncing Sexual "Equality"'): 'There is no *freedom* or *justice* in exchanging the female role for the male role.... There is only equality'.[93] Dworkin explained that, unlike the 'equality' feminists of her own generation, she could not view equality as:

> a proper, or sufficient, or moral, or honourable final goal. We believe that to be equal where there is not universal justice, or where there is not universal freedom is, quite simply, to be the same as the oppressor.[94]

---

[91] Cobbe, above n 47, at 42.

[92] Gilligan, C, *A Different Voice: Psychological Theory and Women's Development* (Cambridge, Mass, Harvard University Press, 1982).

[93] Dworkin, A, 'Renouncing Sexual "Equality"' in A Dworkin, *Our Blood: Prophecies and Discourses on Sexual Politics* (London, The Women's Press, 1982) 12.

[94] *Ibid*, at 11.

Cobbe would not, I think, have gone as far as Dworkin in wishing to see the abolition of gender itself, yet she certainly favoured the removal of artificial legal and social restraints on the ability of all citizens, male or female, to fulfil their potential. And she would probably have agreed with Dworkin that the ideal human behaviour of the future would not be based on *the male model*.[95] Barbara Caine agrees that Cobbe, whose comprehensive grasp of the 'woman question' – she contributed to almost every debate on women, enabling her to make connections across the whole range of issues – 'came closer to propounding a theory of patriarchy than did any other Victorian feminist'.[96]

Perhaps the most significant legacy from nineteenth century feminist thought has been, as Mary Maynard puts it:

> the clear understanding that men have historically created a system of patriarchal privilege, that they maintain such a system in their own interests, and, further, that they are not likely to deliver up their stake in such a system without a struggle.[97]

Yet these insights are the very ones that are lost in accounts of Victorian feminism which see only a focus on equality and/or the inexorable progress of liberal reform.

---

[95] *Ibid*, at 13.
[96] Caine, above n 27, at 104.
[97] Maynard, M, 'Privilege and Patriarchy: Feminist Thought in the Nineteenth Century' in S Mendus and J Rendall (eds), *Sexuality and Subordination: Interdisciplinary Studies in Gender in the Nineteenth Century* (London, Routledge, 1989) 242–3.

2

The Demise of the Provocation Defence and the Failure of Equality Concepts

HEATHER DOUGLAS*

INTRODUCTION

T HE LEGAL RESPONSE to intimate violence has been a central concern of feminist law reform projects for a long time.[1] Women are more likely to be killed by their current or previous intimate partner than by anyone else.[2] Further, women are more likely to kill their current or previous intimate partner after a history of violence than to kill in any other context.[3] There is some ambivalence about the role of the criminal law in responding to intimate violence,[4] nevertheless many feminists have continued to critique and attempt to improve the criminal law so that it operates more fairly for women.[5] Although there has been concern about the way in which men are prosecuted (or more often not prosecuted) for criminal offences when they harm their intimates,[6] more recently feminist critique has been preoccupied with the operation of the criminal law defences, both where battered women kill and are killed. In Australia and the United Kingdom, this preoccupation has been most

---

* The author wishes to thank Rosemary Hunter for her careful reading of drafts of this chapter and for her many constructive suggestions.

[1] See Nancy Lemon's overview in Lemon, N, *Domestic Violence Law* (Minneapolis, West Group, 2001) ch 1.

[2] New South Wales Law Reform Commission, *Provocation, Diminished Responsibility and Infanticide: Discussion Paper 32* (Sydney, NSWLRC, 1993) 14.

[3] See Easteal, P, *Less Than Equal* (Sydney, Butterworths, 2001) ch 6.

[4] See, eg Mills, L, 'Killing her Softly: Intimate Abuse and the Violence of State Intervention' (1999–2000) 113 *Harvard Law Review* 551, 554.

[5] Schneider, E, *Battered Women and Feminist Law-Making* (New Haven, Yale University Press, 2000).

[6] Douglas, H and Godden, L, 'The Decriminalisation of Domestic Violence: Examining the Interaction Between the Criminal Law and Domestic Violence' (2003) 27 *Criminal Law Journal* 32, 42.

pronounced in considerations of the operation of the provocation defence.[7] In cases involving domestic violence the provocation defence was unequally applied. The defence was overly restrictive to women defendants and too expansive for male defendants.[8] Consequently, debates around reforming provocation law have frequently relied on the concepts of formal and substantive equality.[9] This chapter shows how these concepts of equality have been used, in different ways, to modify the provocation defence. It concludes that the use of equality concepts in this context has had ambivalent results.

In order to reform the provocation defence, feminist critics have attempted first to expose the assumptions that underpin provocation law and then to critically scrutinise those assumptions.[10] Graycar suggests that part of the process of (criminal) law reform requires that law's stories about women are challenged and that the legal framework is dismantled and rearranged.[11] Other critics have recognised that in order to be usefully challenged and rearranged, the criminal law must be understood in relation to its historical, social and political contexts. For example, Horder tracked the historical development of the provocation defence and showed that its origins lay in recognising the human frailty of men who, in order to protect their honour, killed other men in the context of a duel. He described how the defence later expanded to recognise the human frailty of men who killed adulterous wives and their wives' lovers in order to protect their honour. His analysis showed that the provocation defence privileged male values and experiences.[12] Men have continued successfully to claim the provocation defence when they have killed their intimates in response to jealousy and separation or in response to an act that has appeared to them

---

[7] Arguably less so in Canada where counsel for battered women have more squarely focused on self-defence: see Baker, B, 'Provocation as a Defence for Abused Women who Kill' (1998) 11 *Canadian Journal of Law and Jurisprudence* 193; Sheehy, E, Stubbs, J and Tolmie, J, 'Defending Battered Women on Trial: The Battered Women Syndrome and its Limitations' (1992) 16 *Criminal Law Journal* 369, 377.

[8] Howe, A, 'Provoking Polemic – Provoked Killings and the Ethical Paradoxes of the Postmodern Feminist Condition' (2002) 10 *Feminist Legal Studies* 39, 41; Schneider, above n 5, at 114.

[9] See Schneider, above n 5, at 4, 112–14. See also Baker's discussion of the role of substantive equality in reforming provocation law, above n 7, at 193.

[10] See generally Lacey, N, Wells, C and Meure, DJ, *Reconstructing Criminal Law* (London, Weidenfeld and Nicholson, 1990) xi.

[11] Graycar, R, 'Telling Tales: Legal Stories About Violence Against Women' (1996) 7 *Australian Feminist Law Journal* 79, 80. See also Morgan, J, 'Provocation Law and Facts: Dead Men Tell No Tales, Tales Are Told About Them' (1997) 21 *Melbourne University Law Review* 237, 238 where she notes the importance of recognising the disconnection between legal stories and factual stories.

[12] Horder, J, *Provocation and Responsibility* (Oxford, Clarendon Press, 1992) 25, 74, 88. Note that his research also tracks the shift in the focus of provocation from honour to self-control.

to be sexually provocative.[13] Women kill their intimates far less frequently than men and usually they kill in response to years of domestic abuse.[14] However, when battered women have attempted to defend the killing of a violent spouse, they have struggled to fit their experiences within the requirements of the provocation defence.

Baker suggests that the underlying concern, when considering how to reform provocation law, is an equality concern because the aim is to make the criminal law as responsive to women's experiences and values as it is to men's experiences and values.[15] Her analysis implies a focus on substantive equality, as it recognises that women may not have the same experiences as men.[16] Thus, any change to provocation law should ensure that jealous and possessive men are held criminally responsible for the harm they cause their intimates, but at the same time should ensure that women have access to the provocation defence when they kill an intimate partner after experiencing long-term abuse.[17] These aims potentially conflict because there is a risk that any reforms made to expand the operation of the defence for battered women may also expand its operation for men who kill in response to infidelity and jealousy.[18]

Various reforms have been made to the provocation defence that have allowed some recognition and contextualisation of women's experiences. However, as Schneider points out, feminist law reform has not tended to achieve linear progress, and reforms to the provocation defence have been no exception.[19] Some have criticised reforms on the basis that they conflict with notions of formal equality.[20] Others have criticised them because they

---

[13] Howe, above n 8, at 41.

[14] According to research conducted in Australia between 1989 and 2002, only 20% of intimate partner killings involve women killing their intimate male partner, while 75% involve men killing their intimate female partner: see Mouzos, J and Rushforth, C, 'Family Homicide in Australia' (paper presented to the 8th Australian Institute of Family Studies Conference, 12–14 Feb 2003), 5.

[15] Baker, above n 7, at 193. Howe has also recognised this concern although she suggests that it is overtaken by other concerns: above n 8, at 43.

[16] Graycar, R and Morgan, J, 'Thinking about Equality' (2004) 27 *University of New South Wales Law Journal* 7, 8.

[17] See generally Stubbs, J and Tolmie, J, 'Feminisms, Self-Defence, and Battered Women: A Response to Hubble's "Straw Feminist"' (1998) 10 *Current Issues in Criminal Justice* 73, 74.

[18] Office of Women's Policy, *Report of the Taskforce on Women and the Criminal Code* (Brisbane, Queensland Government Office of Women's Policy, 2000) ch 6, pt 5, available at http://www.women.qld.gov.au/?id=75 (accessed 5 Feb 2007).

[19] Schneider, above n 5, at 5.

[20] Walker, G, *The Rule of Law* (Melbourne, Melbourne University Press, 1988) 217. See also Graycar and Morgan, who have pointed out the 'pull of a notion of formal equality': Graycar, R and Morgan, J, 'Examining Understandings of Equality: One Step Forward, Two Steps Back?' (2004) 2 *Australian Feminist Law Journal* 23, 31.

have had the practical effect of directing battered women to the provocation defence and away from the complete defence of self-defence.[21] Further, as predicted above, although reforms to provocation have expanded the range of circumstances where women can claim the defence, they have also tended to expand the availability of provocation to men. In relation to this latter point, it seems that despite attempts to contextualise the operation of the defence, notions of formal equality have tended to trump Baker's more substantive vision of equality.[22] The progress of provocation law reform reflects feminist debates about equality versus difference.[23] Minow points out that to ignore difference may leave in place a faulty neutrality, while focusing on difference may serve only to underscore deviance from a male norm.[24] Arguably, both faulty neutrality and the underscoring of deviance have resulted from various reforms to provocation.

This chapter provides an overview of the development of the provocation defence and shows how both formal and substantive concepts of equality have been applied in order to reform the operation and application of the provocation defence. Although the way that the defence operates has indeed changed over time, critics of the process of law reform more generally have demonstrated that one of law reform's limitations is that it tends to build on existing ideas. As a result, reforms may have the effect of reinforcing existing inequalities.[25] This chapter argues that concepts of equality have been, at best, of ambivalent value in assisting feminist reforms to the provocation defence. The legal changes made to provocation law have failed to significantly assist battered women. This has led many feminist critics to call for the abolition of the defence, and these calls have been successful in a number of common law jurisdictions. In conclusion the chapter questions whether abolition will transcend the equality versus difference conundrum evident in previous law reform efforts.[26] Before exploring the application of concepts of equality, I outline the current operation of the provocation defence.

---

[21] See, eg Tarrant, S, 'Something is Pushing Them to the Side of Their Own Lives: A Feminist Critique of Law and Laws' (1990) 20 *Western Australia Law Review* 573; Tolmie, J, ' Provocation or Self-Defence for Battered Women Who Kill' in S Yeo (ed), *Partial Excuses for Murder* (Sydney, Federation Press, 1991) 61.

[22] Morgan, J, *Who Kills Whom and Why: Looking Beyond Legal Categories* (Melbourne, Victorian Law Reform Commission, 2002) 39.

[23] See, eg Scott, J, 'Deconstructing Equality-Versus-Difference: Or the Uses of Poststructuralist Theory for Feminism' (1988) 14 *Feminist Studies* 32.

[24] See Minow, M, 'Learning to Live with the Dilemma of Difference: Bi-Lingual and Special Education' (1984) 48 *Law and Contemporary Problems* 157, 160, referred to in Scott, *ibid*, at 39.

[25] Mossman, MJ, 'Running Hard to Stand Still: The Paradox of Family Law Reform' (1994) 17 *Dalhousie Law Journal* 5, 10

[26] See Crimes (Homicide) Act 2005 (Vic), and the concerns raised by Howe, A, 'Reforming Provocation (More or Less)' (1999) 12 *Australian Feminist Law Journal* 127, at 135; Scott, above n 23.

THE PROVOCATION DEFENCE

In many common law jurisdictions, the provocation defence is available in situations where the accused is charged with murder. It is a partial defence that will reduce murder to manslaughter. In those jurisdictions where the penalty for murder is mandatory life imprisonment, the reduction of criminal responsibility is particularly important as the sentence can then be mitigated.[27] Broadly speaking there are three requirements to establish the defence of provocation. There must be a provocative incident, the accused must have lost self-control and killed under the influence of the provocation and the provocation must have been such that it would have caused an 'ordinary person' to act similarly.[28]

The provocation test set out by Australia's High Court contains both subjective and objective elements.[29] First, the test reflects the position generally followed in common law jurisdictions. It requires that the accused was acting under provocation when she or he killed. At this point, the content and extent of the provocative conduct is assessed from the point of view of the accused. The test also incorporates an objective element which requires that the provocation be of such a nature as could, or might have, motivated the ordinary person to respond as the accused did.[30] The objective part of the test is divided into two further stages.[31] The first stage allows that the:

personal characteristics or attributes of the particular accused may be taken into account for the purpose of understanding the implications and assessing the gravity of the wrongful act or insult.[32]

The second stage then requires assessment of:

the possible effect of the wrongful act or insult, so understood and assessed, upon the power of self-control of a truly hypothetical 'ordinary person'.[33]

The first stage of the objective test could include evidence about the history and impact of previous violence on the defendant or other characteristics if

[27] Eg United Kingdom, Canada and in Australia, Queensland, Western Australia, and Northern Territory.

[28] See The Law Commission, *Partial Defences to Murder (Consultation Paper)* (2003) part V, available at http://www.bailii.org/ew/other/EWLC/2003/173.html, for a discussion of the position in common law jurisdictions (although the defence has now been abolished in Victoria and Tasmania since the summary was prepared).

[29] *Stingel v R* (1990) 171 CLR 312.

[30] See Bronitt, S and McSherry, B, *Principles of Criminal Law* (Pyrmont, LBC, 2005) 273, citing *Masciantonio v The Queen* (1995) 183 CLR 58, 66 per Brennan, Deane, Dawson and Gaudron JJ.

[31] The United Kingdom test for provocation is now similar to Australia: see *Attorney General for Jersey v Holley* [2005] UKPC 23 (15 Jun 2005) para 25.

[32] *Stingel v R* (1990) 171 CLR 312, 327.

[33] *Ibid*.

they were deemed relevant.[34] The second stage is focused on the ordinary person and asks whether, considering the gravity of the provocation, the ordinary person would have lost self-control and formed the intention to kill.[35] Ultimately the behaviour of the accused must represent a normal response to an abnormal event in order to come within the requirements of the provocation defence.[36] Various incremental changes have been made to the defence in response to criticism about the narrow application of the defence to battered women compared with its broad application to men in a range of circumstances. The role of equality arguments in the development of the defence is discussed below.

EQUALITY AND CHANGES TO THE PROVOCATION DEFENCE

Concepts of equality have not proved to be especially useful tools in developing legal responses to assist battered women. MacKinnon has pointed out that attempts at law reform have tended to reflect the Aristotelian model of equality, that is, like is to be treated as like and vice versa.[37] In the Australian context, Graycar and Morgan have also noted the persistence in law and in law reform of strategies that foster formal equality.[38] 'Equality before the law' is a frequently cited expression in provocation case law and the phrase has usually reflected an idea of formal equality.[39] This approach has offered little assistance for battered women charged with murder who have sought to rely on provocation.[40] Their experiences and circumstances are usually very unlike the experiences and circumstances of men relying on the provocation defence.

The recognition of differences in circumstances and experiences has been used to justify expanding the definitions or elements within the provocation defence so that battered women's real life stories can be taken into account. This approach has reflected the concept of substantive equality. Such reforms have increased battered women's access to the defence. While in some individual cases this has been advantageous to women,[41] there have been many negative outcomes for women more generally. One negative outcome has been that changes to the defence in the name of equality have had the effect of expanding the range of circumstances in

---

[34]   *Ibid*, at 326.
[35]   See *Green v R* (1997) 191 CLR 334, 382.
[36]   Wilson, W, *Central Issues in Criminal Theory* (Oxford, Hart Publishing, 2002) 328.
[37]   MacKinnon, C, 'Reflections on Sex Inequality Under Law' (1991) 100 *Yale Law Journal* 1281, 1291.
[38]   Graycar and Morgan, above n 20, at 33. See further their chapter in this volume.
[39]   See, eg *Stingel v R* (1990) 171 CLR 312, 329.
[40]   Graycar and Morgan, above n 20, at 31.
[41]   See, eg *Chhay v R* (1994) 72 A Crim R 1.

which men can rely on it.[42] It is suggested that another negative outcome has been the development of a notion of a stereotypical battered woman.[43] This latter development may have meant that in some circumstances battered women who do not fit the established stereotype may not be able to claim provocation successfully.[44] Finally the focus on the expansion of provocation has also averted consideration away from the possibility of applying self-defence in circumstances where women kill their batterers.[45] Thus, reforms aimed to promote formally equal access for battered women to the provocation defence as well as reforms designed to promote substantively equal access to the defence have been problematic. These negative outcomes are discussed further below.

A Specific Triggering Incident

The first example of reform to the provocation defence that attempted to ensure substantive equality by recognising the different context of battered women's killing was reflected in the shift away from the strict requirement of a discrete act or specific trigger of provocation. The requirement of a specific trigger of provocation mirrored the historical development of the defence. For example, the discovery of the defendant's wife in the act of adultery provided a specific trigger.[46] However, the requirement for a specific trigger did not reflect many battered women's experiences. Often a specific trigger incident was difficult to identify. In the context of a long history of domestic violence, something had occurred which was, in effect, the last straw. For example, in the cases of *Chhay* and *R*, the defendant women were subjected to a lengthy period of abuse from their intimates before killing them.[47] The Crown case for each was that the women had killed their intimates while they were asleep. The courts in both matters found that the loss of self-control in relation to provocation could develop after lengthy abuse and without the need for a specific triggering incident.[48]

---

[42] Morgan, above n 11, at 253.
[43] Nicholson, D, 'Telling Tales: Gender Discrimination, Gender Construction and Battered Women Who Kill' (1995) 3 *Feminist Legal Studies* 185, 188–9.
[44] See, eg *Osland v R* (1998) 197 CLR 316.
[45] Tarrant, above n 21, at 596.
[46] *R v Morhall* [1995] 3 All ER 659.
[47] See *Chhay v R* (1994) 72 A Crim R 1, and also *R v R* (1981) 28 SASR 321.
[48] *Chhay v R*, *ibid*, at 14; *R v R*, *ibid*, at 323. In the UK see *R v Ahluwalia* (1993) 96 Cr App R 133.

Anger versus Fear

Another change to the operation of provocation related to the kind of emotion assumed to underlie the defence. Horder found that, historically, because the provocation defence was embedded in the need to protect a man's honour in the context of duels or in response to adultery, the underlying emotional feeling was a response embedded in anger.[49] In contrast, it was suggested that the underlying emotion experienced by battered women was different. Rather than anger, it was suggested that panic and fear usually triggered their response.[50] Clearly in individual cases this change was important and positive. However, it is self-defence that has historically been associated with fear, and self-defence is a complete defence that leads to an acquittal, while provocation is only a partial defence leading to a manslaughter conviction. The underlying emotions that lead a woman to kill are undoubtedly complex.[51] However, broadening the provocation defence to give equal recognition to the emotion of fear and panic on the assumption that this emotion underlies the experience of battered women who kill has had an ambivalent effect. It has made the partial defence of provocation more available to women who kill in response to fear, while, at the same time, shifting the emphasis away from the complete defence of self-defence. It also assists in the development of a story of battered women as fearful rather than angry, a story that may not fit all battered women's experiences.[52]

A Sudden and Temporary Loss of Self-Control

Another requirement traditionally associated with the provocation defence was that any response to the specific trigger or provocation should be 'sudden'. This was stated in the 1942 case of *Duffy* where the court held that the defence required a 'sudden and temporary loss of self-control'.[53] Duffy killed her husband after he had abused her for a number of years. In the trial she claimed provocation. However, there was a lapse of time between the alleged provocative conduct and Duffy's response. Because of the time lapse, her claim of provocation was not successful and she was convicted of murder. As the provocation doctrine has moved away from requiring a specific trigger incident, the requirement for a sudden response

---

[49]   Horder, above n 12, at 27–9.
[50]   *Chhay v R* (1994) 72 A Crim R 1, 14; see also *Van Den Hoek v R* (1986) 161 CLR 158, 169.
[51]   Baker, above n 7, at 196.
[52]   See, eg Heather Osland's story, which was arguably a provocation story based on anger: *Osland v R* (1999) 159 ALR 170.
[53]   *R v Duffy* [1949] 1 All ER 932 per Devlin J.

has become more relaxed. There would be a different result if *Duffy* were to be decided in Australia today.[54] Although this development was recognised earlier in the case of *Parker*, where Parker lost control and killed in response to his wife's affair,[55] the extended time has been particularly emphasised and supported in cases involving battered women. Some battered women have not acted immediately in response to a provocative act. In a number of cases battered women have waited until their batterer is asleep or until their back is turned.[56] For example, in *Hill's* case[57] there was evidence of a history of domestic abuse. It was alleged that the usual pattern of abuse was that Hill's husband would become drunk and then abuse her. On the day of his death, Hill's husband had left the house suggesting to Hill that he would kill her on his return if he was drunk. He later returned home drunk. Hill was prepared for him. She killed him with a rifle as he walked towards her. The prosecution argued that her response had not been sufficiently sudden; many hours had elapsed between his comments earlier in the day and her subsequent response. However, despite this argument, the court found that, against the background of prolonged abuse, a crisis was evident that brought Hill (slowly rather than suddenly) to 'breaking point'.[58]

The practical results of this shift are, ultimately, also ambivalent. Morgan's research suggests that the extended time available for response has simply been extended for men who kill as well.[59] Specifically, the time frame appears to have been extended in situations where men kill in response to jealousy and perceived infidelity.[60] A notion of formal equality has triumphed here and an extended timeframe has become available to all defendants claiming provocation, regardless of different circumstances.

---

[54] Yeo, S, 'The Role of Gender in the Law of Provocation' (1997) 26 *Anglo-American Law Review* 431, 436. In England *R v Duffy* [1949] 1 All ER 932 was followed in *R v Ahluwalia* (1993) 96 Cr App R 133, 138. Ahluwalia had endured years of violence from her husband before causing his death by setting him on fire while he was asleep. The court found her guilty of manslaughter on the basis of provocation. It extended provocation to the situation of a defendant experiencing a 'slow burn' reaction to cumulative provocation, but nevertheless still held that at the time of the killing, the defendant must have suffered a 'sudden and temporary loss of self-control'. See McColgan, A, 'General Defences' in L Bibbings and D Nicholson (eds), *Feminist Perspectives on Criminal Law* (Cavendish, London, 2000) 145.

[55] *Parker v R* (1963) 111 CLR 610.

[56] See, eg *R v R* (1981) 28 SASR 321. See also Beri, S, 'Justice for Women Who Kill: A New Way?' (1997) 8 *Australian Feminist Law Journal* 113, 117.

[57] *Hill v R* (1981) 3 A Crim R 397.

[58] *Ibid*, at 400 per Street CJ. See also *Parker v R* (1963) 111 CLR 610 which opened the door for this expansion.

[59] Morgan, above n 11, at 253.

[60] See, eg *R v Szabo* [2000] NSWCCA 226 (11 Jul 2000); *R v Georgatsoulis* (1994) 62 SASR 351; *Ahwan v R* [1989] NTSC 12 (22 Mar 1989); *R v Schubring; ex parte A-G (Qld)* [2004] QCA 418 (5 Nov 2004).

The Reactions of the 'Ordinary' Person

A key aspect of the provocation defence is its reliance on the concept of the 'ordinary person'. In Australia, the response of the defendant to the provocation is measured against the response that would be expected of the ordinary person and this concept has caused feminist scholars some concern. In *Stingel* the Australian High Court stated:

> The principle of equality before the law requires...that the differences between different classes or groups be reflected only within the limits within which a particular level of self-control can be characterised as ordinary.[61]

Some have argued that the ordinary person has actually been understood as male.[62] Boyle has also suggested that there is assumed to be a relationship between ordinary and reasonable. She suggests that foreign experiences (in the sense of being foreign to law) or unrecognisable stories often appear to be unreasonable.[63] In the context of this discussion, this means that a battered woman's response has tended to appear unreasonable and therefore not the response expected of an ordinary person. Arguably, the response of the ordinary person should be able to reflect a diverse range of experiences and outlooks in order to be relevant to the range of defendants appearing before the courts. Morgan has pointed out that there has been a great deal of argument about the cultural diversity of ordinary men,[64] but she suggests that this debate has masked the debate about the values of ordinary men as compared with the values of ordinary women.[65] If we return to Baker's view that the 'equality' aim is to make the criminal law as responsive to women's experiences and values as it is to men's experiences and values,[66] it follows that the context of the killing needs to be taken into account in order to interpret the concept of the ordinary person. The different circumstances in which women and men usually kill their intimates should inform the concept of 'ordinary'.[67] Relaxing or expanding the rules of evidence in relation to battered women's experiences of violence seemed to provide a way of fostering the

---

[61]   *Stingel v R* (1990) 171 CLR 312, 329.

[62]   Leader-Elliot, I, 'Passion and Insurrection in the Law of Sexual Provocation' in N Naffine and R Owens (eds), *Sexing the Subject of Law* (North Ryde, LBC, 1997) 161; Roberts, D, 'Foreword: The Meaning of Gender in Criminal Law' (1995) 85 *Criminal Law and Criminology* 1, 2.

[63]   Boyle, C, 'The Role of Equality in Criminal Law' (1994) 58 *Saskatchewan Law Review* 203, 213–14.

[64]   See, eg Yeo, S, 'Power of Self-Control in Provocation and Automatism' (1992) 14 *Sydney Law Review* 3; *R v Dincer* [1983] 1 VR 460; *Mungatopi v R* (1991) 2 NTLR 1.

[65]   Morgan, above n 11, at 264.

[66]   Baker, above n 7, at 193.

[67]   Morgan, above n 22, at 30.

equal recognition of women's experiences in the application of the provocation defence. However this move has also had ambivalent effects.

Through admitting evidence of 'battered woman syndrome' (BWS), it was aimed to show how different kinds of responses might be made in circumstances where women had experienced battering over a prolonged period. For example, it could help to explain why women often remain in a violent relationship rather than leave.[68] Evidence of BWS was initially admitted to ensure that battered women who behaved in a particular way could be recognised as having an 'ordinary' response, allowing them access to the provocation defence. Although this approach may have had the effect of ensuring the court heard battered women's stories, the approach also had the effect of promoting stereotypes of battered women.[69] Evidence of battering came to be understood as supporting a type of psychiatric 'syndrome' and women were frequently perceived to be sick and/or irrational when measured against an ordinary standard (which could be understood as a male standard).[70]

Stubbs and Tolmie have suggested that when Australian case law started to allow BWS evidence, courts came from the position 'that battered women have developed different perceptions from others' rather than that the law is gendered.[71] Stubbs and Tolmie argued that evidence of BWS should be reconfigured as 'social-framework evidence' along the lines originally envisaged by Wilson J in *Lavallee's* case.[72] Such an approach, they argued, could recognise the gendered nature of legal doctrine, and following from this establish objective standards that reflect women's experiences.[73] It is not an approach that Australian courts have generally accepted.[74] Morrissey suggests that the use of BWS to support the provocation defence continues to recuperate women to the status of victim, give them sympathy and then pathologise them as freaks.[75]

---

[68] See Walker, LE, *The Battered Woman Syndrome* (New York, Springer Publishing, 1984). See also Craven, Z, 'Topic Paper: Battered Woman Syndrome' (Sydney, Australian Domestic Violence Clearinghouse, 2003).

[69] Nicholson, above n 43, at 188–9.

[70] See also Freckleton, I, 'When Plight Makes Right: The Forensic Abuse Syndrome' (1994) 18 *Criminal Law Journal* 29 on the use of the terminology of syndrome. In *Luc Thiet Thuan* [1996] 2 All ER 1033, 1049, Lord Steyn suggested that BWS was a mental abnormality. See also *R v Ahluwalia* [1993] 96 Cr App R 133.

[71] Stubbs, J and Tolmie, J, 'Falling Short of the Challenge? A Comparative Assessment of the Australian Use of Expert Evidence on the Battered Woman Syndrome' (1999) 23 *Melbourne University Law Review* 27, 35.

[72] *R v Lavallee* (1990) 1 SCR 852.

[73] Stubbs and Tolmie, above n 71, at 35; see also Sheehy, Stubbs and Tolmie, above n 7, at 389–94 for a discussion of efforts to redirect the consideration of BWS.

[74] Although there have been some exceptions: see Tolmie, J, 'Battered Defendants and the Criminal Defences to Murder – Lessons from Overseas' (2002) 6 *Waikato Law Review* 10, 19.

[75] Morrissey, B, *When Women Kill* (London, Routledge, 2003) 101; see also Schneider, above n 5, at 6, 113; Roberts, above n 62, at 11.

Women can currently call BWS evidence in provocation cases, however they have needed medical experts, or other experts, to provide this type of evidence.[76] Experiences of battering appear to remain outside what the law can recognise as ordinary. These experiences must be translated into something that the law can digest[77] and the criminal law has relied on medical expertise for direction in this area.[78] In contrast to the situation for women who kill, men continue to successfully claim provocation when they kill in response to nagging and adultery without any expert evidence being required.[79] The requirement for expertise suggests that the ordinary person concept has not really been transformed at all. The necessity for BWS evidence perpetuates a special understanding of the experience of battered women. In contrast, men's experience continues to be perceived as the truly 'ordinary' benchmark and does not require expert evidence.

When battered women defendants come to court with stories that are not recognised as provocation stories, there has been a tendency on the one hand for courts to acknowledge women as different, but then on the other hand to try to fit their experiences within the existing legal frameworks. Such an approach reflects both substantive and formal equality aims. This approach has tended to essentialise battered women. The reforms discussed above suggest that battered women experience loss of self-control for much longer periods than their male counterparts, in response to much more uncertain triggers and that their loss of self-control is often based on fear. The allowance of evidence of BWS appears to create a legal space from which women can tell their stories and this approach has arguably allowed more equal access to the defence of provocation for battered women. However, unlike men's stories, battered women's stories need to be mediated by an expert. This expert is usually a health professional such as a psychologist or a psychiatrist. The approach has meant that battered women are further typecast. In Stubbs's view, BWS evidence has been used as prescriptive of the reasonable responses of battered women rather than descriptive of the experiences of some battered women.[80]

---

[76]   See, eg *R v Secretary* (NTSC, 11 May 1998, Gray AJ, unreported) trial transcript at paras 279–81. See also Sheehy, Stubbs and Tolmie, above n 7, at 385.

[77]   Smart, C, *Feminism and the Power of the Law* (London, Routledge, 1989) 11.

[78]   For a discussion of problems with medical evidence in this area see McMahon, M, 'Battered Women and Bad Science: The Limited Validity and Utility of Battered Woman Syndrome' (1999) 6 *Psychiatry, Psychology and Law* 23.

[79]   See, eg *R v Khalouf* [2003] NSWCCA 179 (8 July 2003).

[80]   Stubbs, J, 'The (Un)reasonable Battered Woman? A Response to Easteal.' (1992) 3 *Current Issues in Criminal Justice* 359, 360.

The Impact of Reforms

Although individual defendants and their lawyers have embraced many of these reforms for strategic reasons,[81] such changes do not necessarily reflect good law reform for battered women. The construction of battered women pursuant to these reforms corresponds with the negative characteristics ascribed to women within liberalism as 'emotional, irrational ...unstable, fickle...weak, neurotic'.[82] This can be contrasted with the male alternative version of the operation of the defence, where there is an underlying expectation that men are quick to regain their self-control, they respond to a clear instance of provocation (suggesting greater levels of rationality) and their responses are based on anger (which can be linked to assertiveness and aggression).[83] Unlike battered women who are dependent on experts to tell their stories, men can tell their provocation stories all by themselves.

In spite of the suggested problems with using concepts of equality to change underlying principles, occasionally decisions suggest shifts in approach. Men have continued to argue the defence of provocation in situations of alleged sexual infidelity, nagging and separation.[84] However some members of the judiciary may be growing increasingly reluctant to accept that adultery or verbal taunts about sexual ineptitude are provocation for the purpose of the defence.[85] For example in *Hart's* case, the defendant killed his estranged wife after he saw her kissing another man. The judge refused to recognise any issue of provocation.[86] The judge in this case discussed the idea of equality before the law and the relationship of that principle to the concept of the ordinary person. He concluded that allowing the defence of provocation in the case 'would set far too low a standard for the conduct which a civilised society is entitled to expect from an ordinary person'.[87] Further, there may be more acceptance by some jurors that an ordinary person may kill after years of battering.[88] However,

---

[81] Tolmie, above n 74, at 14; Carline, A, 'Women who Kill Their Abusive Partners: From Sameness to Gender Construction' (2005) 26 *Liverpool Law Review* 13, 35; Sheehy, Stubbs and Tolmie, above n 7, at 388; Stubbs, *ibid*, at 361.

[82] Nicholson, above n 43, at 188.

[83] See Carline, above n 81, at 22; Baker, above n 7, at 197.

[84] See, eg *R v Singh* (2003) CCASA (6 Oct 2002).

[85] *R v Margach* [2006] VSC 77 (8 Mar 2006); *R v Szabo* [2000] NSWCCA 226 (11 Jul 2000); cf *R v Khalouf* [2003] NSWCCA 179 (8 Jul 2003). This point is also noted by Stubbs and Tolmie, above n 71, at 27.

[86] *Hart v R* [2003] WASCA 213 (9 Sept 2003) para 109. See also *R v Margach, ibid*.

[87] *Hart v R, ibid*, at para 110.

[88] *R v MacDonald* (2006) VSC (3 Mar 2006).

these examples are merely discrete instances relying on the discretion of individual judges and juries. These developments do not necessarily follow any coherent principle.[89]

The approaches taken to reforming the provocation defence so that it can equally recognise men's and women's stories of provocation have been fraught. One of the central problems with respect to the application of the provocation defence to battered women who kill is that it has required that women be constructed in a particular way; as 'battered women' helplessly out of control. This approach has consistently denied battered women's killing as an act of resistance or as an act of taking control of their situation. Many have argued that a renewed focus on the defence of self-defence will deal with the problems so far experienced in attempting to reformulate provocation. The final section of the chapter examines the arguments for abolition of the provocation defence.

CONCLUSION: THE END OF PROVOCATION

In spite of the shifts in the application and interpretation of the provocation defence discussed above, many feminist scholars have argued that the developments to the provocation defence have failed to give women equal access to the defence or to equally recognise women's experiences and that therefore the defence is ultimately 'beyond redemption'.[90] A number of commentators have called for its abolition.[91] Recently the Victorian Law Reform Commission (VLRC) recommended abolition of the provocation defence. The Commission found that the provocation defence, even though it had been incrementally changed over time in an attempt to ensure it applied equally to men and women, had continued to reinforce gender inequality.[92] It argued that homicide defences should reflect the context in which homicides occur, rather than abstract philosophical principles (like equality), and that they should deal fairly with men and women who kill.[93] Provocation has now been abolished in some jurisdictions including Victoria.[94] Abolition without other legal reforms could be viewed as yet

---

[89]   Gleeson CJ noted similar concern in *Chhay v R* (1994) 72 A Crim R 1, 9–14.

[90]   Howe, above n 8, at 43.

[91]   Howe, above n 8. See also Beri, above n 56, at 123; Horder, above n 12, at 192; Coss, G, 'Editorial: Revisiting Lethal Violence by Men' (1998) 22 *Criminal Law Journal* 5, 9.

[92]   See Crimes (Homicide) Act 2005 (Vic); VLRC, *Defences to Homicide: Final Report* (VLRC, Melbourne, 2004) xxviii.

[93]   VLRC, *ibid*, at 15. See also Graycar, R and Morgan, J, 'Law Reform: What's in it For Women?' (2005) 23 *Windsor Yearbook of Access to Justice* 393, 402.

[94]   See Criminal Code Amendment (Abolition of Defence of Provocation) Act 2003 (Tas); Crimes (Homicide) Act 2005 (Vic). See also Model Criminal Code Officers Committee, *Report on Fatal Offences against the Person* (Canberra, Australian Government, 1998) 87–91. It is mainly in jurisdictions in which a mandatory sentence for murder of life

another application of the concept of formal equality to law reform. After all, once provocation is abolished everyone has equal lack of access to the defence. However, abolition was part of a package of reforms in the Victorian context.

The legal reforms generated by the VLRC in Victoria also clarify self-defence and establish a new offence of 'defensive homicide'. This approach attempts more equally to reflect the experiences of battered women. In most common law jurisdictions, self-defence is available where the accused believes on reasonable grounds that the responsive force used was necessary in self-defence.[95] Like provocation, self-defence has been argued to be unequally available to men and women. Self-defence regularly succeeds for men who kill in response to attacks in public places,[96] while the application of self-defence to women who kill in the context of extended intimate violence has encountered strong resistance.[97] Although commentators have suggested that battered women's stories are often more appropriately understood as stories of self-defence,[98] the requirement of necessity has been interpreted in a way that excludes women's experiences. For example, many of the killings by battered women have been considered to be pre-emptive strikes and thus not 'necessary' for self-defence.[99] Further, when women kill they are often armed while their victim is unarmed.[100] In such circumstances, the force used has been viewed as a disproportionate (and therefore unnecessary) response to the threat.[101] In an attempt to ensure that women's experiences of violence inform the analysis of the question of the necessity of the self-defence response, the Victorian reforms also specifically recognise the potentially cumulative effect of family violence on an individual and the particular dynamics of relationships. The new legislation draws on the critique of Stubbs and

imprisonment exists that there has been reluctance to call for the abolition of the defence. In those jurisdictions, feminists have feared that without the availability of the provocation defence, battered women are placed at too high a risk of being imprisoned for life for murder: see, eg Office of Women's Policy, above n 18, at 195.

[95] See *Zecevic v DPP* (1987) 162 CLR 645, 661 per Wilson, Dawson and Toohey JJ; *Palmer v R* [1971] AC 814, 831.

[96] VLRC, above n 92, at 61, 63.

[97] See *Secretary v R* (1996) 5 NTLR 96; *Osland v R* (1999) 159 ALR 170. See also newspaper coverage of *R v MacDonald* (2006) VSC (3 Mar 2006): one headline read 'Woman Killed Husband from Sniper's Nest': Gregory, P, *The Age* (21 Feb 2006).

[98] Howe, above n 26, at 43; Stubbs and Tolmie, above n 17, at 82; cf Brown, H, 'Provocation as a Defence to Murder: To Abolish or Reform?' (1999) 12 *Australian Feminist Law Journal* 137, 141; Schneider, above n 5, at 114. For a good example of the tensions involved, see *R v Secretary* (1996) 5 NTLR 96.

[99] This was essentially the initial stumbling block in *R v Secretary, ibid*. See also *R v R* (1981) 28 SASR 321; *Chhay v R* (1994) 72 A Crim R 1, 14.

[100] VLRC, above n 92, at 67. See, eg *Hill v R* (1981) 3 A Crim R 397.

[101] These concerns were illustrated in the *Secretary* trial: *R v Secretary* (1996) 5 NTLR 96. See Gray, S, 'Aboriginal Women and the Battered Woman Syndrome' (1998) 4 *Indigenous Law Bulletin* 57.

Tolmie[102] in relation to the application of BWS, and attempts to frame family violence evidence as social-framework or social-context evidence.[103] In addition the new offence of 'defensive homicide' provides a kind of 'halfway house' between complete acquittal and conviction for murder[104] in circumstances where the belief in the necessity of the response was not based on reasonable grounds. This offence is effectively a reintroduction of a form of 'excessive self-defence'.[105] The new social-context evidence provisions are also designed to inform the understanding of 'reasonable grounds' for this offence. In response to recognition of the failure of the provocation defence equally to recognise women's experiences, these changes aim to make the criminal law equally responsive to women's experience as it is to men's experiences in the self-defence context.

A more comprehensive critique of these developments is beyond the scope of this chapter. However, there appear to be two obvious risks in the approach of these reforms. The first is that the defensive homicide charge will be preferred for battered women who kill, perpetuating the view that battered women's perceptions are unreasonable. Further, despite these reforms, there remains a risk that provocation will continue to be relevant at the sentencing stage. More particularly, men may still be able to claim provocation as a result of, for example, sexual infidelity, in order to mitigate sentence.[106] Morgan has worried that reframing provocation as a sentencing issue is risky. She points out that sentencing decisions are often unreported, difficult to locate and therefore difficult to read and critique.[107] These potential approaches to the application of the law risk re-entrenching inequalities that existed prior to the reforms.

The use of an equality approach to law reform in this context shows that gains to women have been at best ambivalent. Can an approach to law reform based on concepts of equality, when women and men are so

---

[102]   Stubbs and Tolmie, above n 71.

[103]   Crimes (Homicide) Act 2005 (Vic), s 9AH.

[104]   *Ibid*, s 9AD.

[105]   Excessive self-defence was available as a defence in some Australian jurisdictions (see *R v Howe* (1958) 100 CLR 448) until it was abolished in 1987, because it was seen as overly complex and because it might lead to unfair convictions: see *Zecevic v DPP* (1987) 162 CLR 645, 664. Excessive self-defence has been reintroduced in a simpler form in NSW (see Crimes Act 1900 (NSW), s 421) and South Australia (see Criminal Law Consolidation Act 1935 (SA), s 15(2)). A defence of excessive self-defence has been rejected in England: see *R v Palmer* [1971] AC 814.

[106]   See Howe, above n 8, at 40.

[107]   Morgan, above n 11, at 275. These concerns are currently being examined by a Sentencing Advisory Council that has been established in Victoria: see Sentencing Advisory Council, *Annual Report 2005–2006* (Melbourne, Victorian Government, 2006) introductory notes.

differently situated, ever yield (unambiguously) positive results?[108] This question returns us to the equality versus difference debate. As Scott suggests:

> it is not sameness *or* identity between men and women that we want to claim but a more complicated historically variable diversity than is permitted by the opposition male/female.[109]

She argues that there must be criticism of the operations of categorical difference and the hierarchies and exclusions it constructs, and she recommends that we aim for a version of equality that rests on multiple differences, 'differences that confound, disrupt, and render ambiguous the meaning of any fixed binary position'.[110] Ultimately, however, it is difficult to be confident that Scott's suggested approach will assist law reformers. Some of the provocation reforms discussed above have attempted to look beyond binary male/female categories. Stubbs and Tolmie's attempts to reframe evidence about battered women as social framework evidence rather than using medical evidence to construct 'the' battered woman, and Morgan's attempts to reform the law by looking at the specific contexts of violence and beyond legal categories,[111] may be examples of such attempts. However, the pull back towards binary constructions, which focus on formal equality or deviant difference in the application and interpretation of the law, appears formidable.[112]

---

[108] Carline asks a similar question: above n 81, at 33.
[109] Scott, above n 23, at 46.
[110] *Ibid*, at 48.
[111] See Stubbs and Tolmie, above n 71; Morgan, above n 22.
[112] See Morgan, above n 11. The pull is also recognised by Scott, above n 23, at 47.

3

Is Equality Enough? Fathers' Rights and Women's Rights Advocacy*

SUSAN B BOYD

CHILD CUSTODY LAW reform appears on its face to address 'cultural' (gender) rather than economic matters. It thus provides an example of a political and legal struggle (often characterised as the 'gender wars') that severs cultural from economic equality, partly because parenting issues appear to be located in the 'private' sphere of family rather than the 'public' sphere of the economy. As a result, law reform debates tend to proceed in a manner that divorces them from their larger political/economic context including neo-liberalism, which asks families to assume economic and caregiving responsibilities beyond their means. The assignment of these responsibilities to 'the family' in turn generates gender difficulties, notably increased caregiving responsibilities for women that are masked by the gender neutrality inherent within neo-liberal policies. This chapter studies the arguments and strategies deployed by fathers' rights and women's advocates in the field of child custody and access law reform in order to raise questions about the capacity of the concept of equality to encompass the complex socio-economic relations that frame and limit parenting patterns.

By highlighting the political economy of child custody law, I heed calls by various feminists working from different theoretical spaces to remember that political equality and economic equality are inseparable issues.[1] So too

* This research was supported by the Social Sciences and Humanities Research Council of Canada and a Hampton Grant from the University of British Columbia. Thanks to Karey Brooks for research assistance, Emma Cunliffe for comments, and Cindy Baldassi for editorial assistance.

[1] Christensen, B, 'Equality and Justice: Remarks on a Necessary Relationships' (2005) 20 *Hypatia* 155; McCluskey, MT, 'How Equality Became Elitist: The Cultural Politics of Economics from the Court to the "Nanny Wars"' (2005) 35 *Seton Hall Law Review* 1291; Phillips, A, *Which Equalities Matter?* (Malden, Mass, Polity Press, 1999); Duggan, L, *The Twilight of Equality? Neoliberalism, Cultural Politics, and the Attack on Democracy* (Boston, Beacon Press, 2003). See also Fineman, MA and Dougherty, T (eds), *Feminism Confronts*

are the so-called culture wars and the economic order. On its surface, the term 'culture wars' appears to capture controversies over the 'social' or 'moral' order as distinct from the economic, and yet the two are interrelated. As Martha McCluskey shows, another way of thinking about this (false) distinction is the relationship between neo-conservatism, which seeks to restore traditional ideas of 'morality,' 'responsibility' and 'community,' and neo-liberalism, which focuses on restoring traditional laissez-faire policies of 'market efficiency' and 'competitiveness'.[2] I am hopeful that these approaches will assist in rethinking feminist equality strategies in relation to parenting. To that end, I will ask to what extent fathers' rightists and women's groups contextualise their arguments in relation to material as well as cultural questions.

The chapter first analyses discursive invocations of equality in relation to post-separation parenting law reform in Canada, before critically analysing these invocations and placing them in the context of the larger political economy. I try to take seriously the equality claims by a group that is arguably not historically disadvantaged – that is, fathers. Until fairly recently, fathers had more legal rights in relation to children of a marriage than mothers did.[3] Can fathers' rights advocates be regarded as part of a progressive social movement, arguing as they do that they are now subjected to discrimination, marginalisation and exclusion? How does this claim fit into the political economy of child custody law? How does the economic potential of individual fathers to pay financial support for children fit into the neo-liberal impetus towards privatisation of economic responsibilities?

In taking fathers' rights discourse seriously, I am guided in part by Davina Cooper's effort to consider whether all groups who can claim that they experience some unequal treatment or social asymmetry (eg smokers, divorced fathers) can be equated with groups who experience social inequality (eg persons of colour, lesbians).[4] Cooper does not analyse the case of divorced fathers, but it engages acutely her question of which

---

Homo Economicus (Ithaca, Cornell University Press, 2005); Boyd, SB, 'Family, Law, and Sexuality: Feminist Engagements' (1999) 8 *Social and Legal Studies* 369; Conaghan, J, 'Reassessing the Feminist Theoretical Project in Law' (2000) 27 *Journal of Law & Society* 351.

   [2] McCluskey, above n 1, at 1291. See also Cossman, B, 'Family Feuds: Neo-Liberal and Neo-Conservative Visions of the Reprivatization Project' in B Cossman and J Fudge (eds), *Privatization, Law, and the Challenge to Feminism* (Toronto, University of Toronto Press, 2002) 169.

   [3] Boyd, SB, *Child Custody, Law, and Women's Work* (Don Mills, Oxford University Press, 2003).

   [4] Cooper, D, *Challenging Diversity: Rethinking Equality and the Value of Difference* (Cambridge, Cambridge University Press, 2004) 60.

experiences of social asymmetry constitute organising principles of inequality – precisely because fathers typically invoke gender, a widely accepted organising principle of inequality.

Can fathers complain of discriminatory treatment in the same way that women or racialised persons might? Does their claim that they experience *gender* inequality set them apart from other lobby groups that have emerged to 'defend the rights of the unfashionable' such as gun users? Cooper suggests that it is a necessary – but not sufficient – element of an organising principle of social inequality to be able to show, as fathers' rightists' do, unequal treatment based on conduct, beliefs, or social location.⁵ But she rejects the notion of equality as sameness, or that it need be interpreted arithmetically, something that some fathers' rightists suggest.⁶ Cooper's two further necessary elements may resonate somewhat more with fathers' rightists' claims, albeit, I will suggest, in a complicated manner that weakens their claim. First, she asks whether the inequality has the capacity to shape other dimensions of the social or to become socially pervasive. Second, can the inequality significantly impact on social dynamics such as the intimate/impersonal or capitalism? Cooper finds that smoking fails these two tests. In order to answer whether fathers' rights claims fail, it is important to consider how they present their arguments, for instance in relation to feminism, and the way in which their arguments are taken up in public policy, and why. In other words, it is important to consider their arguments in the context of the political economy of custody disputes and the material position of mothers and fathers. This I attempt in the last part of the chapter.

The empirical base of my argument is oral submissions made at public consultations held by the Special Joint Committee on Child Custody and Access (SJC) in Canada in 1998, the most recent public consultation for which systematic data are available. I reviewed the transcripts of 42 oral submissions by advocates who either adopted a fathers' rights perspective or offered a position aligned with fathers' rights (some were technically 'women's groups' and many had female spokespersons), and 34 oral submissions by advocates speaking to women's interests. In reading the transcripts, I highlighted themes that related to invocations of equality or equality-seeking strategies.⁷ Most advocates addressed opposite sex rather

---

⁵ *Ibid*, at 195.

⁶ Linde, C, 'Unethical Lawyers Abuse Children', brief presented to the Special Joint Committee on Child Custody and Access, online: Divorce for Men Homepage <http://www.divorce-for-men.com/jointcom.pdf> (accessed 29 Oct 2006).

⁷ Other work has highlighted anti-mother and anti-feminist discourses: Boyd, SB, 'Demonizing Mothers: Fathers' Rights Discourses in Child Custody Law Reform Processes' (2004) 6 *Journal of the Association for Research on Mothering* 52; Boyd, SB, 'Backlash against Feminism: Custody and Access Reform Debates of the Late 20ᵗʰ Century' (2004) 16 *Canadian Journal of Women and the Law* 255.

than same sex parenting; both fathers' rightists and women's advocates tended to speak of parents as heterosexual. As a result, this chapter mainly addresses parenting in the heterosexual context, despite the clear reality of same sex parenting in Canadian society.[8]

INVOKING EQUALITY IN A COMPLEX FIELD: AN OVERVIEW

Early liberal feminists were optimistic about involving men as equal parents and removing residual gender-based assumptions about parenting in family law. Since the 1970s, however, many feminists have moved from a formal equality to a substantive equality approach in this field. In the face of significant social and economic impediments to the equal sharing of parental responsibilities, a substantive equality analysis emerged both to explain the apparent failure of formal equality and to argue for a more nuanced understanding of women's inequality in relation to family and child care.[9] During this period a strategy focused around a primary caregiver presumption emerged. This analysis illuminates the material underpinnings of women's relationship to family, but is more difficult to develop and understand than formal equality. Moreover, it is easily misunderstood as reinforcing the sexual division of labour because it consistently points to the social reality of women's more onerous responsibilities. As such, it can be portrayed as regressive in comparison to liberal feminist and fathers' rightists' claims. Feminists who take a substantive equality approach can also be charged with essentialism and failure to take account of differences related to race, sexuality, and class – overlooking differences between women as mothers, men as fathers, and men in relation to power.[10]

The comparative aspect that equality claims typically involve has never worked straightforwardly in this field either, not least because the focus is supposed to be children's interests, not parental rights. As well, while in many fields, women have sought equality with men – sometimes by seeking to be treated like men – in custody law, women were not seeking equal treatment with men. Rather, under the formal equality argument, women argued that gender-based assumptions related to parenthood should be

---

[8] Complex and important questions arise as a result of this reality: Boyd, SB, 'Gendering Legal Parenthood: Bio-Genetic Ties, Intentionality, and Responsibility' (2007) 25 *Windsor Yearbook of Access to Justice* 63.

[9] See, eg 'Women and Custody' Special Issue of the *Canadian Journal of Women and the Law* (1989) 3; Fineman, MA, *The Illusion of Equality* (Chicago, University of Chicago Press, 1991); Smart, C and Sevenhuijsen, S (eds), *Child Custody and the Politics of Gender* (London, Routledge, 1989).

[10] See Collier, R and Sheldon, S, 'Fathers' Rights, Fatherhood and Law Reform – International Perspectives' in R Collier and S Sheldon (eds), *Fathers Rights Activism and Law Reform in Comparative Perspective* (Oxford, Hart Publishing, 2006).

eliminated, and that *men* should behave more like women – by participating equally in child care in the 'private' sphere of the family. When that strategy failed, the substantive equality approach argued that the impact of men's failure to behave more like women on women's *in*equality in the family should be taken into account. That is, women's disproportionate responsibility for children should be acknowledged in laws and dispute resolution processes concerning children.

Moreover, in child custody law reform, it is fathers' rights advocates who have famously sought formal legal equality, or equal treatment with mothers. Dating from the 1970s, they have demanded legal presumptions of joint custody which, they say, will provide equal treatment of fathers as equal parents. Their argument is that the law is biased in favour of mothers and rests on problematic gender stereotypes. To this extent, their argument resonates with early liberal feminist discourse, a point that they sometimes make. Partly due to fathers' rightists' successful invocation of the attractive discourse of formal equality, child custody law has also become a major site of backlash against feminism. Feminists are portrayed as arguing for women's equality in the workplace but resisting men's equality in the family[11] and are said to be selfish in wanting to have their cake and eat it too. They are charged with reverse discrimination. It may be damaging for feminism to be perceived as resisting men's efforts to be equally involved with their children, or to argue for women's autonomy in a field where children's interests are supposed to be the central question.

Indeed, this area of law might be said to provide an example of a rather spectacular failure of feminist substantive equality arguments, perhaps because they are complex and can be misunderstood as reinforcing gendered roles within the family. Despite the ongoing highly gendered realities of family life and related issues such as intimate violence, government discourse in this field in Canada has become strictly gender neutral.[12] In part, gender neutrality has been implemented in order to accommodate the increasing legal recognition of same sex relationships in Canada. Moreover the 'rise and rise of shared parenting'[13] as a norm is evident internationally. To argue against gender neutral parenting law is to run against the tide, with the persuasive force of formal equality behind it.

---

[11] See, eg Boyd, SB, 'Backlash', above n 7; Boyd, SB and Young, CFL, 'Feminism, Fathers' Rights, and Family Catastrophes: Parliamentary Discourses on Post-Separation Parenting, 1966–2003' in Chunn, DE, Boyd, SB and Lessard, H (eds), *(Re)Action and Resistance: Feminism, Law, and Social Change* (Vancouver, UBC Press, 2007).

[12] Boyd, SB, '"Robbed of Their Families?" Fathers' Rights Discourses in Canadian Parenting Law Reform Processes' in Collier and Sheldon (eds), *Fathers' Rights Activism*, above n 10.

[13] Rhoades, H, 'The Rise and Rise of Shared Parenting Laws: A Critical Reflection' (2002) 19 *Canadian Journal of Family Law* 75.

Fathers' Rights Equality Advocacy

It is well established that fathers' rightists have tended to draw on a formal approach to equality and rights, their recommendation for joint custody being the quintessential example.[14] As Lessard has explained, liberal concepts of formal equality and universalism reinforce, rather than challenge, social relations of oppression in the family.[15] Early empirical research found that while the rhetoric of equality may characterise the public fathers' rights stance, individual members may be more concerned with instrumental gains, for instance, in relation to access or diminishing payment of child support.[16]

Not all Canadian groups taking fathers' rights positions in the Committee hearings referred directly to 'equality' but their discourse revolved predominantly around complaints about unfair treatment of fathers (by judges or government or police) or gender bias against them, and most made the case for enhancing men's equality in family law. A few referred explicitly to equality or equality-related concepts in their names (eg Fathers for Equality), while others invoked concepts such as justice (eg Fathers for Justice[17]). Several advocates challenged essentialist stereotypes about the respective capacities of women and men to care for children (eg Victoria Men's Centre). The Men's Educational Support Association similarly argued that '[w]e have two populations of parents with equal distributions of parenting skills'.

Fathers' equality claims were compared to those that women have made in relation to economic power and the labour market:

> At the turn of the [twentieth] century, women began to want to share the economic power that men held. Since the 1970s, women have entered the labour market en masse and fathers are much more involved with their children than previously (*Groupe d'entraide aux pères et de soutien a l'enfant*).

New Vocal Man Inc said (ignoring women's economic inequality):

> Women want equality. Okay, then let's have equality right across the board, not that men have to pay this much and women don't even have to pay an iota. They make an absolute sham of the whole justice system and the family law.

---

[14]   See Collier and Sheldon (eds), above n 10; Kaye, M and Tolmie, J, 'Discoursing Dads: The Rhetorical Devices of Fathers' Rights Groups' (1998) 22 *Melbourne University Law Review* 162.

[15]   Lessard, H, 'Mothers, Fathers, and Naming: Reflections on the *Law* Equality Framework and *Trociuk v British Columbia (Attorney General)*' (2004) 16 *Canadian Journal of Women and the Law* 165, esp 177–81.

[16]   Bertoia, C and Drakich, J, 'The Fathers' Rights Movement: Contradictions in Rhetoric and Practice' (1993) 14 *Journal of Family Issues* 592, 596.

[17]   Not to be confused with Fathers 4 Justice, which began in the UK and has branches in other countries, including Canada.

Fathers' rightists were not always clear about whether equality meant equal time with children or equal decision-making authority. Some seemed to want equal time (eg Men's Equal Access Society) while others such as the Dick Freeman Society seemed to focus more on equal authority based on a bio-genetic relationship. This group, like a few others, demonstrated an anti-state, libertarian bias, resisting the notion that the legislature or the courts should define parental responsibilities (though it did want the state to amend the Divorce Act to respect each parent's equality right). For Family Forum, equality meant that both parents should be on the birth certificate, even if a father found out as long as 10 years after a child's birth that he was 'the father'. Fathers' advocates appeared, then, to be inconsistent on whether they sought equal caregiving responsibility or a more traditionalist equal authority in relation to children, the latter interpretation being one that accords men power over the mothers of their children.[18]

The most common themes were improper judicial treatment of fathers and legal and cultural bias against fathers, as a result of which, 'fathers are excluded from the lives of their children' (FatherCraft Canada). Many suggested emotively that bias against fathers resulted in the loss of a parent. The Men's Educational Support Association suggested that judges had been taught that women seeking custody were at a disadvantage in the courtroom and that the government had 'removed gender bias against women only to replace it and make a gender bias against men'. The National Shared Parenting Association (Saskatchewan) said that while the Supreme Court of Canada had taken steps to address women's economic disadvantage during and after marriage, the same recognition had not occurred: 'that the stereotypical role of men in a marriage disadvantages them after divorce'.

Government bias was also a target. For instance, Fathers for Equality complained that women-centred organisations had lawyers to represent them and funding by the government, whereas fathers' groups did not. FED-UP argued for shelters for male victims of violence and abuse. Men's Equalization Inc charged that the:

> government in Manitoba is destroying families, disenfranchising fathers, alienating grandfathers and grandmothers, driving men to the underground economy, and effecting suicide. The same can be said of the government in Ottawa.

A common complaint was that fathers had (financial) responsibilities, whereas mothers had rights (eg Parental Alienation Network). Because of the introduction in Canada of child support guidelines and enhanced enforcement measures, they blamed the state as much as mothers: divorce

---

[18] See Lessard, above n 15; Fineman, MA, 'Fatherhood, Feminism and Family Law' (2001) 32 *McGeorge Law Review* 1031, 1040.

made a father a 'slave of the state' (Men's Equalization Inc). FED-UP complained that this 'materialism' superseded a child's need for love and care from the other parent. *Groupe d'Entraide* labelled this approach the 'single-parent mother/automatic bank teller father approach'. Mississauga Children's Rights noted that fathers go to jail because they don't pay child support as a result of unemployment, bankruptcy, or being on welfare.

Another key refrain was that claims about male violence against women were exaggerated, fathers were being 'criminalized' (FED-UP), and false allegations against fathers were a low risk strategy for mothers in custody disputes (eg FACT National). The equality angle was that '[m]en are victims of violence and abuse too' (FED-UP). That is, fathers' rightists suggested that feminists over-state women's victimisation and that zero-tolerance policies promoted by women's advocacy groups and shelters generate gender bias and unfairness for men and result in men being 'robbed of their families' (Men's Equalization Inc).

The measures recommended to redress men's inequality adopted some strategies analogous to those used to promote women's equality. Fathers for Equality recommended access enforcement programs similar to support enforcement programs, and men's centres similar to women's centres. The Men's Educational Support Association wanted programs to monitor judicial behaviour and 'a program of affirmative action...within the judicial system to encourage awarding of children to fathers'. As well, it felt that a 'legal action fund should be created to enable fathers to legally challenge their longstanding historical disadvantages in family law'.

On the whole, fathers' rightists' submissions either ignored feminism or were anti-feminist. Advocates often adopted a modified version of liberal feminist rights scripts of the second-wave. A few gestured towards feminism, for instance by suggesting that their proposals would benefit women or assist them in balancing careers and children, lest they have to be 'superhuman' (*Entraid pères-enfants separés de L'Outaouais*). Others were more hostile, accusing the organised women's movement of taking the wrong approach, 'stridently demand[ing] all the privileges and rights without any of the responsibilities' and over-emphasising women's victimisation (Vancouver Men). Vancouver Men suggested that feminism was originally on the right track but had lost its way.

WOMEN'S EQUALITY ADVOCACY

Most advocates who made oral submissions to the Special Joint Committee in relation to women's equality[19] emphasised women's social and economic

---

[19]   Most were women's groups, but Montreal Men Against Sexism took a similar position, including a trenchant critique of the fathers' rights movement that no women's group risked.

realities – and needs flowing from these realities – rather than promoting maternal rights per se. A majority had mandates to deal with questions related to violence against women. By and large, their positions resonated with feminist analysis and strategy in relation to equality and issues such as abuse, although 'feminism' was rarely invoked. In trying to explain why recommendations for joint custody norms were misguided, they stressed women's existing *in*equality and their caregiving responsibilities for children.

The trend for women's advocates to adopt a substantive equality approach that stressed women's social inequality and their disproportionate, socially constructed responsibilities for children and caregiving was clear. Several emphasised the need to address 'the systemic inequities faced by children and their primary caregivers'. Many offered a critique of gender neutral approaches:

> If we ignore the inequalities that women and children face in today's society, we are actually increasing the inequality they live with (Individuals).

Moreover, the reason why 'gender-neutral fantasies like shared parenting' should be rejected is that:

> [t]his well-intentioned idea merely obscures gender realities such as women's primary caregiving work and gives the non-custodial parent control and authority without corresponding responsibilities (Individuals).

Women's advocates noted various social realities, including the fact that in the majority of intact families, women do most of the caregiving (eg National Association of Women and the Law) and the existence of domestic abuse, primarily perpetrated by men. Even groups that felt their equality work was towards a world where women and men are equal and share equally in caregiving stressed these gender-based differences. Some groups offered quite a sophisticated appreciation of the difference between formal and substantive equality:

> At one point in time we believed equal treatment was equality. It is now recognized that equal treatment does not necessarily yield equal results. Today the concept of equality acknowledged that different treatment of women and men may sometimes be required to achieve sameness of results (Kamloops Women's Resource Centre).

Advocates further suggested that 'children are not well served when women's equality rights are ignored' (New Brunswick Advisory Council on the Status of Women). The Metis National Council of Women noted that women's lack of power poses a serious problem for women in negotiating a resolution as an equal partner.

A key recommendation made by many women's advocates was that the law should recognise and affirm the 'historical arrangement of care-giving within the family before the marriage or household broke down' (CONNECT). The YWCA noted that:

> [m]arriage breakdown is not an appropriate time to redefine the responsibilities of parents to care for their children in the interests of gender equity.

The Ad Hoc Committee on Custody and Access stressed that:

> [D]ivorce laws should help the primary caregivers of children to provide continuity of care and security for those children as best they can by recognizing the problems they may encounter – for example, economic difficulties, lack of access to legal advice, abuse, and so on.

In contrast, proposals for joint parenting were idealised 'fantasies of what the family should look like' (Battered Women's Support Services).

Fewer women's advocates than father's advocates discussed gender bias per se, but several argued that women's claims were treated less favourably than men's (eg London Coordinating Committee to End Woman Abuse) and that the legal system fails to take account of women's day to day parenting whereas fathers' contributions are glorified (Yew Transition House). It was also claimed that women's experience of abuse was not taken seriously (Manitoba Association of Women's Shelters). Some alleged that battered women were not believed when they told judges and assessors about their fears for the safety of their children (eg Vancouver Coordinating Committee on Violence Against Women in Relationships). Others countered fathers' rightists' allegations that the legal system was biased in favour of mothers by noting that the greater numbers of custody awards to mothers reflected the greater responsibility that women carry for children in intact families (eg YWCA).

By far the most common theme raised by women's advocates was domestic abuse, reflecting the fact that a plurality of the groups appearing before the SJC had a mandate to serve women who suffered abuse. The Ontario Association of Interval and Transition Houses emphasised that 'violence against women is a women's equality rights issue,' while the BC Yukon Society of Transition Houses stated that:

> Treating couples as if they are equal after there has been abuse gives abusive men further opportunity to abuse their ex-partners and to expose their children to the nightmare of violence and threats of violence.

A key theme was that although women are pressured to leave abusive relationships to protect children, when they do leave:

> they're betrayed by the civil justice system, which often forces them back into contact with abusers through mediation and joint parenting and access arrangements that are not safe (Battered Women's Support Services).

Some women's advocates took care to specify that they supported children having contact with each parent, *except* where there is family violence (eg YWCA), thus carving out abusive situations as the key exception to contact (eg Yew Transition House). The Saskatchewan Battered Women's Advocacy Network noted that shared parenting can work where there is mutual respect and loving concern for the children, but that it was dangerous to support this ideal where abuse is even suspected. To put a survivor of abuse into a joint custodial relationship with the other spouse 'continues to perpetuate the abuse' (Muriel McQueen Fergusson Centre for Family Violence Research).

Several groups argued that safety of children and mothers should be prioritised (eg Cumberland County Transition House Association). Others pointed out how power and control issues played out in dispute resolution processes such as mediation (eg London Coordinating Committee to End Woman Abuse). It was noted that abused parents often make decisions with regard to custody and access out of fear, and may, for instance, trade off fair child support settlements to avoid custody battles.

As we saw above, fathers' rightists argued that stereotyped views of women and men dominate this field. But most women's advocates who linked children's interests with those of their mothers did so by pointing to the sexual division of labour that rendered most mothers as primary caregivers of children before and after separation: 'That means children's best interests and well-being cannot be separated from their mothers' (Battered Women's Support Services). The New Brunswick and Nova Scotia Advisory Councils on the Status of Women emphasised that the primary caregiver presumption should not apply where there was evidence of child abuse or neglect by the primary caregiver. The New Brunswick Advisory Council noted that the presumption was gender neutral and that there was nothing to prevent men 'from reversing this alleged bias...easily by assuming half of the parental and family responsibilities during the marriage.' A few indicated that it:

> would be great if there were a revolution in men's psyches and that there was true equality...but we do have a way to go (CONNECT).

Several women's advocates pointed to the financial stress that many women encounter on separation or divorce, as well as the failure of the justice system to provide adequate legal aid to support women in custody disputes (eg West Coast LEAF). Erratic or inadequate child support payments were identified as a contributor to the poverty of single parent families (National Council of Women of Canada). The National Association of Women and the Law referred to the reduction in child support that fathers often expect with a joint custody arrangement. Manitoba Association of Women's Shelters pointed out that:

> [m]en are financially more able to tie up the mothers in court, whereas many
> women are dependent on legal aid

and suggested that some fathers quit jobs and do work privately under the
table for cash in order to avoid support responsibilities and teach women a
lesson. The Inuit Women's Association spoke of women losing houses and
savings due to years of legal battles, as well as the impediments to Inuit
women using the legal system and/or gaining access to legal aid. They
questioned whether child support orders were adequate given the extreme
costs of living in northern Canada. The Saskatchewan Battered Women's
Advocacy Network stated that they saw many emotionally distraught
women who had to represent themselves due to the refusal or inability of
lawyers to represent them during lengthy court proceedings.

Only a few women's groups articulated the limited capacity of law to
make social change in relation to parenting, but this theme implicitly
underpinned many presentations. The Ad Hoc Committee on Custody and
Access noted that while:

> everyone would like to see fathers participate more in raising children and caring
> for children. ... [t]he major impediments to men sharing child care are in fact
> economic, social, and cultural, not legal. ...Law, in other words, cannot do it
> alone.

Women's groups did, however, feel that law could do more to protect
women's interests, so they invoked the power of law[20] to make a
difference, particularly in relation to protection from abuse and ensuring
safety. Overall, they did not demonstrate the anti-state libertarianism that
characterised some fathers' rightists' interventions.

COMPARATIVE ANALYSIS

The most attractive part of the fathers' rights advocacy was their challenging of essentialist cultural stereotypes about the capacities of women and
men to nurture children. Flowing from this challenge, many argued (often
emotively) for equal post-separation parenting rights for fathers, sometimes suggesting that benefits for overworked mothers would flow. It is
difficult to resist fathers' pleas to 'share the task of raising our children'
(Victoria Men's Centre), though perhaps easier to resist claims for paternal
rights based exclusively on genetic ties (Family Forum). Many fathers'
rightists referred to 'both parents', apparently asserting a dyadic heterosex-
ist model of parenthood that limited the force of their challenge to cultural
stereotypes. Several reinforced the notion that feminism has gone too far,
mothers have been given too much power, and balance must be restored.

---

[20] Smart, C, *Feminism and the Power of Law* (London, Routledge, 1989).

Fathers' rightists raised a two-pronged economic complaint, first, that women want equal labour market rights to men but won't share equal rights in relation to children, and second, that men are seen only as financial providers. Many blamed not only mothers but also the state for this problem. Their solution appeared to be a libertarian removal of state rules, or making mothers pay their own way regardless of differential economic means, rather than asking for a state role in providing economic support to parents. Several groups similarly complained about too much state regulation of male violence.

Overall, fathers' rights advocacy did not offer a structural analysis and their strategies did not address the material underpinnings of gendered roles in heterosexual families. Their complaints fit into the paradigm of economic libertarians, who:

> often use the phrase 'the nanny state' to disparage 'liberal' welfare and regulatory policies, thereby suggesting that freedom from government control is linked to the restoration of a 'proper' hierarchy of gender, race, and class.[21]

Their remedies reinscribed the authority model of the sovereign parent (father), which:

> resonates with a socially conservative vision of parental interests drawn from common law conceptions of paternal authority and of the family as a negative sphere of privacy.[22]

Returning to Cooper's questions and tests concerning unfashionable equality-seekers, fathers' rights claims of unequal treatment clearly invoke gender as an organising principle of inequality – which at first glance appears progressive. What weakens their equality claims is that gender is not an 'equal playing-field' organising principle: the very reason feminists identify gender as an organising principle of social inequality is that it involves a gender *hierarchy* between women and men, with women tending to occupy a position lower on the power hierarchy. In the context of heterosexual families, women continue overall to carry greater caregiving responsibilities and they leave relationships with fewer economic resources.[23] Even the power that women are often said to possess in relation to children[24] renders women vulnerable – for instance to threats that their ex-partners will claim custody if the women leave an abusive relationship. Masculinist norms arguably still permeate family relations and family law itself, despite its overwhelming gender neutrality. Family

---

[21] McCluskey, above n 1, at 1299.
[22] Lessard, above n 15, at 168.
[23] See Fineman, above n 18, at 1041–2.
[24] Collier and Sheldon ask whether there is a relationship with, or even a 'power over', children that some women are not prepared to share: above n 10.

life is not a level playing field for mothers and fathers, so simple equalising solutions in child custody law are unlikely to be effective.

Most women's advocates made this point quite effectively and largely without invoking essentialist stereotypes. They offered a sophisticated substantive equality analysis, accompanied by a critique of the problematic impact of gender neutral law reforms on unequal individuals. They pointed to the material factors that engender the sexual division of labour and generate problems for mothers at separation – factors such as poverty, lack of access to legal aid, and masculinist norms within the legal system. They identified the ways in which abuse inhibits women's ability to be equal in intimate relationships and to negotiate their termination. However, although they sometimes linked these problems with economic difficulties experienced by women, by and large women's advocates did not develop a sustained analysis of the political economy of child custody law.

During the late twentieth century in Canada, successful arguments on behalf of mothers tended not to lie in the realm of child custody law, but rather in relation to enhanced child support obligations, typically owed by fathers.[25] These arguments in turn reinforce privatised economic remedies consistent with the impetus within the neo-liberal state to cast responsibility for economic well-being of individuals on the private sphere, including the family.[26] These remedies reinforce not only ideological expectations of women's responsibility for caregiving within the family but also women's economic dependency on former partners. They also result in initiatives to 'find fathers' for children and to encourage women to stay with male partners or find new ones.[27] They thus diminish women's ability to achieve autonomy, both economically and in relation to detaching from intimate relationships.

Both privatisation strategies and familial ideology have been extensively critiqued by feminists.[28] But women's groups and feminists are not consistent on this point, for reasons that are understandable. Intuitively, it appears appropriate for fathers who are generally better off than mothers to pay what they can towards child support. Also, in the current neo-liberal political climate, it seems virtually impossible to imagine a shift in state policy that would generate state support for parents and children that would obviate the necessity of privatised remedies.[29]

---

[25] Boyd and Young, above n 11.

[26] Boyd, above n 1; Cossman, above n 2.

[27] Eg, Fineman, MA, *The Neutered Mother, the Sexual Family, and Other Twentieth Century Tragedies* (London, Routledge, 1996).

[28] Eg, Cossman, above n 2; Lessard, above n 15; Mossman, MJ, 'Child Support or Support for Children? Re-Thinking "Public" and "Private" in Family Law' (1997) 46 *University of New Brunswick Law Journal* 63.

[29] Feminists have often been forced into defensive positions that appear to fall short, debates on support law being classic. Many resist privatised solutions, yet to say no to spousal

RECONSIDERING FEMINIST STRATEGY

Accepting for a moment that women's advocates problematically (if understandably) reinforced both familial ideology and privatisation in their strategies, what alternative would we suggest? Do fathers' rights arguments gain any greater currency when we notice this problem? On Cooper's analysis of equality, the overall objective is to 'undo the social organising principles that currently work to make people's capacity to exercise power unequal'.[30] But how to accomplish this objective? Feminists might support fathers' rightists' resistance to placing onerous financial responsibilities on men – in other words, we might resist privatisation as a flawed means to address female and child poverty. But, do we also want law to encourage the convergence of men and women in relation to parenting and the diminishing of differences between them? If so, should we support joint custody claims? As with many sameness/difference arguments, this overly simplistic question misses the material context constraining the possibilities of social change. I will suggest (as have other feminists and several women's advocates at the SJC) that meaningful equality and social change in the family are not likely to be promoted by empowering paternal parenting claims through equality norms at the time of separation or divorce.

Anne Phillips explores convergence in relation to the importance of considering economic as well as political equality,[31] albeit without specifically considering the child custody context. She argues that while assimilationist strategies are problematic, it is also problematic to suggest, as cultural feminists do, that equality lies not in convergence but in a revaluation of traditionally female qualities or roles. The notion of a women's culture is notoriously problematic, and it is undesirable to treat 'differences that derive from historical inequalities or relationships of power and subordination' as objects of veneration, or differences that should be sustained.[32] Phillips suggests that some convergence *is* a condition for equality, but that a revaluation of the activities or qualities conventionally associated with women is also necessary – for instance, the work of caring for others. Moreover, this revaluation will remain 'partial and superficial until men and women become more genuinely interchangeable in their social *and parenting roles*'(emphasis added).[33]

---

or child support because it reinforces women's dependency and familial ideology denies recognition of women's unpaid labour. See Hough, J, 'Mistaking Liberalism for Feminism: Spousal Support in Canada' (1994) 29 *Journal of Canadian Studies* 147, 158–9.

[30] Cooper, above n 4, at 88.
[31] Phillips, above n 1, at 91–5.
[32] Phillips, above n 1, at 92–3.
[33] Phillips, above n 1, at 92.

At first glance, Phillips's weak convergence argument seems to lend support to the fathers' rights arguments for joint custody. How can feminists resist fathers' rights claims to make parenting interchangeable and for men to embrace caregiving responsibilities? This interpretation is, however, too simplistic. Phillips insists that convergence in material conditions is a necessary grounding for equality of respect. She also asserts that 'even the most rigorous campaign of cultural revaluation is unlikely to make enough difference' to the association of certain categories of people with certain categories of work, which in turn has profound effects on a society's status order.[34] I would further argue that the material conditions for genuine cultural interchangeability of men and women in relation to parenting (including in *intact* families) do not yet exist. For instance, workplace structures and expectations under capitalism continue to favour male norms. Although some men *choose* to abandon this model and some women are in a position to *choose* to adopt it, these exceptions to the rule do not challenge the material framework for the sexual division of labour. Phillips points out:

> Given the markedly different treatment of boys and girls as they grow up, not to mention the markedly different roles then allocated to them in carework, relationships and employment, it would be distinctly odd if both sexes turned out to be the same.[35]

Our economic and workplace structures still reinforce these differences. Despite its apparent agnosticism as to gender, neo-liberalism renders women's carework more onerous and their ability to 'balance' work and family responsibilities more difficult.[36] Consequently, efforts towards cultural convergence of men and women as parents via law reform directed at post-separation behaviour are fundamentally flawed:

> If, because caretaking is devalued, men can leave the marriage relationship with the future benefits gained by their investment in themselves intact, as well as realize the benefits of their wife's investment in the marital children, why should they change their behaviour?[37]

If fathers are given equal rights despite failing to sacrifice their market skill development to care for children, the economic differential between fathers and mothers is retained, and, perversely, rendered even less visible.

---

[34]   Phillips, above n 1, at 98.
[35]   Phillips, above n 1, at 92.
[36]   Eg Mosher, JE, 'Welfare Reform and the Re-Making of the Model Citizen' in M Young et al (eds), *Poverty: Rights, Social Citizenship, and Legal Activism* (Vancouver, UBC Press, 2007).
[37]   Fineman, above n 18, at 1043.

This analysis underpinned much women's advocacy at the SJC. It was clearest in their remarks about the difference between formal and substantive equality, and the problems with treating fathers and mothers as the same when the social and economic conditions under which they operate reinforce women's systemic inequality. Yew Transition House spoke critically of a gender-neutral approach 'disguised in a child-centred cloak', noting that mothers and fathers were perceived as interchangeable in spite of the different roles they played prior to separation. Some groups also astutely pointed out that using law to promote male parenting at the time of separation or divorce is flawed. In other words, genuine promotion of male parenting must happen at a much deeper level that tackles the material conditions still reinforcing gender differences in relation to children and child care.

Why was women's advocacy so unpopular at the SJC and, to a lesser degree, at subsequent House of Commons Debates on a bill that would have changed child custody law had Parliament not been prorogued? Women's groups were cast as conservative defenders of the status quo, at the same time as they were cast as feminist (anti-male) radicals. They were erroneously constructed as having 'urged the government to make no changes to the custody and access regime' whereas 'father's rights organizations campaigned tirelessly...for the inclusion of a presumption in the law that each parent had equal access to children,' as one MP put it.[38] In fact, although women's groups protested moves towards a shared parenting regime, they typically asked for changes that would enhance the safety of women and children and recognise the gendered nature of parenting. These requests were hardly radical and were often grounded in research, yet they were constructed as extreme anti-male arguments. Fathers' rightists successfully suggested that the status quo favoured women and that the only change that would radically address this gender bias against men would be joint custody or shared parenting.

Researchers have shown that the success of political arguments often has less to do with the empirical reality underpinning them than with the cultural resonance of the argument with dominant ideologies.[39] The illusion that women have achieved equality[40] seems to have dominated Canadian parliamentary and government reactions to the SJC hearings.

---

[38] *House of Commons Debates* 2003, 64, 20 Feb, 3792–4 (Grewal).

[39] Graycar, R, 'Law Reform by Frozen Chook: Family Law Reform for the New Millenium?' (2000) 24 *Melbourne University Law Review* 737; Haltom, W and McCann, M, *Distorting the Law: Politics, Media, and the Litigation Crisis* (Chicago, The University of Chicago Press, 2004).

[40] Gwen Brodsky and Shelagh Day begin *Canadian Charter Equality Rights for Women: One Step Forward or Two Steps Back?* (Canadian Advisory Council on the Status of Women, 1989) with this quote: 'The illusion that women have achieved equality is almost as pervasive as the reality of oppression' (at 11). See also Fineman, above n 9.

This illusion fuelled the rise of father's rights arguments, and governmental response appears to have been a diminishing of space for feminist analyses of the sexual division of labour, women's poverty, violence against women, and gendered power dynamics within the family. The governmental retreat into gender neutral responses and proposals in relation to family law constricts the opportunity for feminist engagement with law reform.

In the House of Commons, a lone MP suggested that the strong lobby of men's groups had impeded the expression of views by women's advocates. Diane Bourgeois identified the diminishing of public space for feminist arguments and that serious issues such as the systemic conditions generating poverty were not being canvassed:

> I remind the House that Canada...does not have a policy promoting women's equality and the well-being of their children within the family.[41]

Bourgeois also captured the dynamic of cultural/political reforms that appear to respond to social problems, but in fact leave them intact or aggravate them, noting that changes that might have enhanced women's material equality had not been proposed:

> The bill insists on formal equality between women and men and does not in any way do anything to ensure material equality for women. Nor does it assure divorcing or separating women of legal aid, representation services or social and economic programs and services.[42]

CONCLUSION: BEYOND SUBSTANTIVE EQUALITY?

Given the apparent failure of substantive equality arguments to win the day in child custody law reform, might it be useful to shift the focus of feminist critique towards more structural issues such as providing greater economic support for women (and men) who assume caregiving responsibilities and measures that support women's ability to live autonomously from men? Is it possible for feminists to leave a defensive position behind in this field of law, and articulate an agenda for reform?

Collier and Sheldon suggest that a fruitful feminist response might be the promotion of a more nuanced and rounded concept of equality than that advanced by fathers' rightists.[43] That is, we might offer an account that allows for the complexity of women's agency whilst contextualising their agency within broader patterns of economic and social factors. These patterns put particular, if different, pressures on both women and men and, in so doing, reinforce a heteronormative framework.[44] For instance, the

---

[41]   *House of Commons Debates* 2003, 52, 4 Feb, 3129
[42]   *Ibid*, at 3144
[43]   Collier and Sheldon, above n 10.
[44]   Boyd, above n 12.

processes of privatisation and economic restructuring within neo-liberal states exacerbate women's already onerous responsibilities for carework at the same time as they position men as carrying a primary responsibility for the costs of childhood and ex-spouses. These dynamics in turn create difficulties for women who are economically disadvantaged *and* groups of men already disadvantaged in terms of class – which some (though certainly not all) fathers' rightists are.

This approach might assist in resisting the common characterisation of this field of law reform as the 'gender wars', which sets up the key players as men and women, or fathers and mothers, with culturally oppositional interests.[45] Drawing on interviews with mothers and fathers in contact disputes in the UK, Kaganas and Day Sclater suggest that the gender war construction is not surprising 'because contact is seen by parents of both sexes as being about parenting, and parenting remains a strongly gendered activity.'[46] Mothers resist the way in which gender neutral laws effectively silenced talk about gender politics (eg the weightier responsibilities that accompany motherhood) by ascribing equal value to mothering and fathering. Fathers tend to invoke the image of the vengeful woman to explain to themselves any unwillingness by their children to maintain contact. These oppositional positions in relation to the gender wars metaphor are articulated from very different social locations.

Yet the oppositional metaphor of gender wars is inadequate in offering an understanding of the complex power dynamics at issue. At the very least, it is essentialist, assuming that the interests of all women (and all men) are identical. In fact, women's experiences of the family law system vary significantly in relation to their race, class, ability, and sexual orientation, as do men's. The metaphor also collapses when one learns that supporters of fathers' rights include second wives of men's rights activists (Second Spouses of Canada), as well as neo-conservative women's groups such as REAL Women of Canada and the Alberta Federation of Women United for Families. To this extent, the political stance of the advocacy group is more significant than its gender composition.

Cooper similarly suggests that looking at inequalities only in terms of the binaries of social location (oppressor and oppressed) is insufficient;[47] rather, we must also look to normative principles that create subordinate positions occupied by those who fail or refuse to live in accordance with prevailing norms. Thinking about this lesson in relation to fathers' rights and women's advocacy, we can see that a discourse that claims that fathers should be treated equally to mothers in relation to children is not sufficient

---

[45] See also Graycar, above n 39.

[46] Kaganas, F and Day Sclater, S, 'Contact Disputes: Narrative Constructions of "Good" Parents' (2004) 12 *Feminist Legal Studies* 1, 16.

[47] Cooper, above n 4, at 116.

because it does not question the (hetero)normative principles that shape paternal and maternal behaviour. Nor does it look to the structural location of a particular group such as fathers, or mothers. It does not help us to understand how modern child custody law discourses that impose responsibility on mothers to ensure that children have relationships with fathers gloss over the inequalities – economic and otherwise – that complicate these relationships.

However, even a substantive equality analysis such as that offered by the women's advocates before the SJC might be inadequate to the task set by Cooper. Lessard has made this point in her detailed examination of the successful formal equality claim taken by a genetic father to the Supreme Court of Canada to be listed on a birth registration and play a role in naming a child, regardless of his lack of social parenting or a relationship with the child's mother.[48] Lessard agrees that:

> a substantive equality analysis would elicit a more textured and thus more nuanced analysis of the social inequalities that differentiate the experience of motherhood from that of fatherhood[49]

but she argues that:

> the fundamentally dyadic structure of both formal and substantive versions of equality rights obscures the investment of the state in ordering familial relations[50]

typically 'in recognizable nuclear units centred on the heterosexual conjugal dyad'.[51]

In order to break free of these dyadic structures, which too often constrain women's autonomy and are reinforced in equality arguments, feminist strategy needs to make the privatised family and neo-liberal re-privatisation strategies of the state a more central target – not an easy task, but one that more feminist voices are raising in one way or another.[52] Some strands of women's advocacy before the SJC hint in this direction – for instance those that highlighted the economic hardships experienced by mothers when faced with family law disputes, lack of legal aid, and lack of support for their caregiving labour. These strands might be usefully linked with the advocacy by anti-poverty activists, which often focuses on single mothers.

---

[48]   *Trociuk v. British Columbia* [2003] 1 SCR 835.
[49]   Lessard, above n 15, at 208.
[50]   *Ibid.*
[51]   *Ibid.*
[52]   Eg Cossman, above n 2; Fineman, MA, 'Cracking the Foundational Myths: Independence, Autonomy, and Self-Sufficiency' (2000) 8 *American University Journal of Gender, Social Policy & Law* 13.

As well, the dyadic nature of family and parenting can be challenged by asking what policies would genuinely promote women's autonomy in relation to parenting and the well-being of children. Almost inevitably these policies will have to address, and redress, women's economic inequality – not only within heterosexual families but within society as a whole. Such policies will swim against the tide of state initiatives that tend to tie women to men – to the fathers of their children and to other men who may be in a position to provide financially for them.

Moreover, it is unpopular to suggest that women's autonomy interests should be affirmed when children's interests are at issue, or when a woman appears to have chosen to produce a child with a known father or father figure. It is very easy to suggest that promoting women's autonomy interests is a selfish manoeuvre. But feminists have perhaps conceded too much in the custody field: women's advocates tend to argue that contact with fathers is a worthy goal as long as abuse is not an issue. They may have drawn this exception to contact too narrowly, meaning that once a woman has involved a man in her parenting scenario, she can never be free of him. No matter how responsible a parent she may be, her parenting is incomplete without involvement of a father figure. Economic autonomy would almost certainly allow women to make parenting choices more freely, and allow legal imaginations to configure parenting regimes that allow women some space for self-determination.

4

Alternatives to Equality

ROSEMARY HUNTER

INTRODUCTION

WHEN FEMINISTS ARGUE that women are *unequal* in some respect, this appeal to the value of equality can be seen to have three aspects. First, there is a rhetorical or strategic element. In liberal societies, equality is taken to be a good, while inequality is taken to be unfair or unjust. Thus, a claim to inequality carries these rhetorical connotations. Secondly, the deployment of the term 'unequal' involves a descriptive claim: that the arrangement in question, and the particular distribution of resources, benefits and burdens it entails, is correctly named, and hence may correctly be understood, as an instance of a specific kind of problem, namely one of inequality. Thirdly, the argument incorporates a normative claim: that the arrangement in question ought to be revised or remedied so as to produce (greater) equality. These three aspects are clearly intertwined (for example, the normative claim to a remedy flows from both the descriptive and rhetorical claims that the arrangement is unequal and unjust). Nevertheless, it is possible to disentangle the three elements and consider them separately for the purposes of analysis.

This chapter argues that the appeal to women's in/equality has been, for feminism, useful as a rhetorical strategy but problematic as a descriptive, and hence as a normative, claim. The contention that women are treated unequally functions as an effective protest slogan. As rhetoric, who can disagree that women's inequality is a bad thing and ought to be eliminated? Equality is a core liberal value and even within neo-liberalism, the value of (individual) equality continues to exert some legitimating force. The problem lies with the descriptive aspect of feminist claims about women's inequality. Clearly, since the advent of second-wave feminism, many instances of anti-woman prejudice, gender stereotyping and direct sex discrimination have been named and challenged as forms of unequal treatment, and have been addressed as such and to a significant extent eliminated. Equally clearly, however, this activity has by no means produced a situation in which women enjoy the same degrees of economic independence, social freedom, bodily autonomy, political power or legal visibility as men. But at this point, disagreements begin to emerge about the content of the term 'equality', and what counts as an instance of inequality. Feminists have developed sophisticated conceptions of in/equality, to encompass, for example, substantive in/equalities, parité,[1] equality of power,[2] equality of condition,[3] and 'equal protection of the imaginary domain'.[4] Yet in practice, these expansive understandings of what in/equality means tend not to be generally comprehended or accepted. And if there is no agreement that a particular arrangement constitutes an instance of inequality, then no normative imperative to remedy it arises. Moreover, some applications of the label of (formal) 'inequality', and the remedies that have followed, have been positively detrimental for (some) women (for example the institution of equal division of marital property on divorce resulted in poverty for many divorced women[5]).

This phenomenon of powerful rhetorical value versus descriptive (and hence normative) limitations is not confined to equality claims, but is also found in relation to other liberal values such as 'human rights', 'justice' and 'fairness'. The scope of all of these notions is indeterminate, giving rise to inevitable contestation over their content. Progressives and reformers tend to interpret them broadly, and to believe that they hold out the promise of extensive remedies, yet in practice, conservative interpretations tend to prevail and remedies either fail to materialise or prove to be disappointing. While this problem can never entirely be resolved, since all language is inherently indeterminate, it may be preferable for feminists, rather than attempting to appropriate liberal concepts in the pursuit of our causes, to introduce new descriptions of women's disadvantages – concepts of our own that may be more persuasive of the existence of a problem, and hence more normatively effective.

This project is not, of course, a new one. Feminists have already coined some well-known terms that do just this. 'Sexual harassment', for example, could be described as an instance of women's inequality in the workplace, but as 'sexual harassment' it graphically specifies what is involved, connotes injustice, and presses for intervention both to end the practice

---

[1] See Scott, JW, 'French Universalism in the Nineties' (2004) 15(2) *differences: A Journal of Feminist Cultural Studies* 32.

[2] Cooper, D, '"And You Can't Find Me Nowhere": Relocating Identity and Structure Within Equality Jurisprudence' (2000) 27 *Journal of Law and Society* 249.

[3] Baker, J, Lynch, K, Cantillon, S and Walsh, J, *Equality: From Theory to Action* (Basingstoke, Palgrave Macmillan, 2004).

[4] Cornell, D, *At the Heart of Freedom: Feminism, Sex, and Equality* (Princeton, Princeton University Press, 1998) 23.

[5] Weitzman, L, *The Divorce Revolution* (New York, Free Press, 1985); Fineman, M, *The Illusion of Equality: The Rhetoric and Reality of Divorce Reform* (Chicago, Chicago University Press, 1991).

and to provide compensation for those who have been harassed. The same is true of terms such as 'marital rape', 'date rape', and 'violence against women',[6] although the latter phrase shares some of the descriptive limitations of 'inequality', as broad feminist interpretations of the concept of 'violence' are not necessarily widely accepted.[7] I would argue, however, that the project of feminist conceptualisation needs to be extended further, for two reasons. First, the terms coined to date have tended to proceed from radical feminist theorising, and to address situations of male abuse of power over women's bodies. In the sphere of material/economic relations, and relations between women and the state, useful alternatives to in/equality are much less in evidence. Secondly, the broader political and discursive context for feminist claims has changed. In the current conjuncture of neo-liberalism, the kinds of words, concepts and problems that connote injustice and generate normative imperatives for change are different from those that might have 'worked' as claims against the liberal state. Now, even if arguments about inequality are descriptively accepted, 'equality' may be reaching its rhetorical or strategic use-by date. We need to be aware of this changing context and adjust our strategies accordingly.

Concepts such as 'sexual harassment' and 'date rape' describe particular phenomena – elements of women's experience – rather than providing overarching analyses of women's position in law and society. Similarly, in considering alternative concepts to equality in this chapter, I propose to work at the phenomenological level rather than suggesting any grand theoretical substitutes for in/equality, such as Catharine MacKinnon's dominance/subordination approach,[8] or the 'disadvantage' analysis advocated by Deborah Rhode.[9] I will make suggestions in relation to two specific areas that have posed descriptive problems for feminism. One is the issue of pay inequity between men and women; the other is the issue of inequitable provision of state services and funding between men and women – in the latter instance focusing particularly on legal aid funding. In each case, I will reflect on the difficulties and limitations of describing the problem as one of inequality, and ask whether there is a better way for

[6] As noted by Fraser, N, 'Talking About Needs: Interpretive Contests as Political Conflicts in Welfare-State Societies' (1989) 99 *Ethics* 291, 303.

[7] For a detailed analysis of the difference between feminist and popular understandings of domestic violence, see Hunter, R, 'Narratives of Domestic Violence' (2006) 28 *Sydney Law Review* 733.

[8] MacKinnon, C, 'Differerence and Dominance: On Sex Discrimination', in *Feminism Unmodified: Discourses on Life and Law* (Cambridge, Mass, Harvard University Press, 1987).

[9] Rhode, DL, *Justice and Gender: Sex Discrimination and the Law* (Cambridge, Mass, Harvard University Press, 1989) 82–6 (although Rhode claims that this is not a 'grand theory', she argues that it will be useful in most, if not all, contexts).

feminists to think and speak about the issue, which is more persuasive of the existence of a problem, and which packs a rhetorical and normative punch.

Ideally, too, alternative concepts should avoid some of the pitfalls of equality analysis. For example, in order to establish a claim to sex inequality, it has usually been necessary to argue or impute both women's sameness to men, and their sameness to each other. Yet as noted earlier and in other chapters of this volume, on the one hand this may mean that equality claims fail because women are not in the same position as men, while on the other hand, treating women as if they are the same and ignoring differences can result in serious disadvantages for (some) women. Concepts that do not require comparisons or equivalence between men and women or among all women would be an improvement on this situation. At the same time, one notable strength of equality analysis is that it has the capacity to represent social disadvantages and inequities as systemic – ie as resulting from structural conditions rather than individual choices or misfortunes.[10] Ideally, again, this is a virtue that alternative concepts ought to retain.

PAY EQUITY

Feminist concerns about pay equity are generally animated by the fact that at national level, women's average weekly earnings represent only some fraction (usually in the range of 60–80 per cent) of men's average weekly earnings. Whether this statistical difference is evidence of *inequality* has been contested from the outset. Human capital theorists have argued that there is no issue of equality here. Rather, different economic outcomes between men and women are a product of women's rational choices to specialise in childrearing, and hence to invest less in human capital, to have lesser attachments to the labour market, and to undertake paid work that provides sufficient flexibilities to enable them to discharge their family responsibilities. Even in its own terms, this argument does not dispose of the issue, because it is usually possible to show that after controlling for differences in educational levels, hours worked, and so forth, there remains an unexplained gender wages 'gap', which must be attributed to some form of 'discrimination'.[11] Feminists have also rejected the human capital argument per se, either on the basis that women would make different

---

[10]   See Christensen, B, 'Equality and Justice: Remarks on a Necessary Relationship' (2005) 20 *Hypatia* 155.

[11]   See, eg Grimshaw, D and Rubery, J, *Undervaluing Women's Work* (Manchester, Equal Opportunities Commission, 2007) 5, 29–31, 35. See also the discussion of 'Statistical and Economic Analysis of Male and Female Wage Differentials', in Industrial Relations Commission of NSW, *Pay Equity Inquiry: Report to the Minister, Volume I* (Dec 1998) 87–146.

'choices' about work and child care if the labour market – and the family – were structured differently, or because they believe in the ultimate objective of women's economic independence, which can only be achieved if women have broadly similar wages outcomes to men. So they have persisted in describing the wages gap in terms of inequality between men and women or discrimination against women in relation to rewards for their labour.

The limitations of equality/discrimination claims in the pay equity context became very clear to me, however, when I was invited to be an expert witness in a Pay Equity Inquiry conducted by the Industrial Relations Commission in the Australian State of New South Wales (NSW) in 1998. I was called as an expert in anti-discrimination law, and my evidence was directed towards establishing that anti-discrimination legislation was *not* an appropriate vehicle for the delivery of pay equity for women. Feminist strategists involved in the Inquiry were concerned to achieve an outcome in which there was a clear separation between the concepts of sex discrimination and pay inequity, so that the former was not seen as a necessary cause of the latter in order to establish entitlement to a remedy.

Part of the background to this position was the fact that in Australia, equal pay was historically dealt with in the industrial relations system rather than under anti-discrimination law. Australia's formerly centralised, collective industrial relations structures allowed for the making of awards which applied to all employees in a particular industry or occupation rather than being confined to individual workplaces. They provided a vehicle for the establishment of minimum conditions through test cases, which would then be inserted into all awards, thus enabling them to apply generally without the need for legislation. The principle of equal pay for equal work was first adopted at national level in this way in 1969,[12] and was extended to incorporate equal pay for work of equal value in 1972.[13] This was some time before the first sex discrimination legislation was enacted at State level in 1977,[14] and at national level in 1984.[15]

When sex discrimination legislation did eventuate, it had limited application in relation to pay equity. It did not contain specific provisions for equal pay claims, but simply enabled complaints of direct or indirect sex discrimination in employment. Under this regime, claims for pay equity could effectively only be made by an individual woman whose remuneration package was inferior to that of a comparable man working for the

---

[12] *Equal Pay Cases* (1969) 127 CAR 1142.
[13] *National Wage and Equal Pay Cases 1972* (1972) 147 CAR 172.
[14] Sex Discrimination Act 1975 (SA), Anti-Discrimination Act 1977 (NSW), Equal Opportunity Act 1977 (Vic).
[15] Sex Discrimination Act 1984 (Aust).

same employer, or where an employer's pay system contained an unreasonable requirement with which a higher proportion of men than of women could comply. In practice, there have been very few pay equity claims brought under anti-discrimination legislation,[16] partly because of the opacity of pay systems, so that it is difficult for women to know if they are being remunerated less than their male counterparts, but also because in a highly gender segregated labour market, many women simply do not have male comparators to refer to. They are either working for different employers or doing different work from men, or if they are doing the same work, the main problem is not that they are paid any less than men, but that the work as a whole is low paid.

The other key part of the background to the strategy adopted in the Pay Equity Inquiry was the *HPM Case*, an equal pay case which had been running in the Australian Industrial Relations Commission (AIRC) since 1995. In 1993, the federal government had legislated several guaranteed minimum industrial conditions and procedures,[17] including provisions on equal pay which enabled the AIRC to make an 'equal remuneration order' where it was satisfied that there was not equal remuneration for men and women workers for work of equal value.[18] The expression 'equal remuneration for men and women workers for work of equal value' was stated to have the same meaning as in the ILO Equal Remuneration Convention No 100 (1951).[19] The ILO Convention defines that phrase to mean 'rates of remuneration established without discrimination based on sex'.[20]

In *HPM*, an application was brought on behalf of a group of female process workers and packers employed by HPM Industries in Sydney, arguing that these women performed work of equal or greater value to that performed by male storemen and general hands employed by the company, yet were paid less, and did not have access to a graded classification structure as the men did. The major issue in the case was the question of how the comparative value of the (dissimilar) work performed by the two groups of workers should be assessed. In a preliminary decision, Commissioner Simmonds rejected the method of comparison contended for by the applicants, and consequently held that he was not satisfied that the pay differential between the two groups arose in circumstances that were sufficiently similar as to amount to discrimination based on sex. Nor was

---

[16]   And those cases are not always successful. Most recently, the High Court held there was no indirect discrimination in a pay system which provided an inferior salary structure for casual teachers (a higher proportion of whom are women) than for permanent teachers (a higher proportion of whom are men): *State of NSW v Amery* [2006] HCA 14 (13 Apr 2006).

[17]   Industrial Relations Reform Act 1993 (Aust). These were retained in the subsequent Workplace Relations Act 1996 (Aust).

[18]   Workplace Relations Act 1996, then ss170BC(3)(a), 170BB(1).

[19]   Workplace Relations Act 1996, then s 170BB(2).

[20]   Equal Remuneration Convention, art 1(b).

he satisfied that there was sufficient evidence to establish that the differential pay rates resulted from indirect sex discrimination.[21] In other words, the focus of the inquiry shifted from the question of whether the women were being paid less for work of equal value, to the question of whether the current pay rates had been set in a manner that involved discrimination on the ground of sex – a higher threshold for the applicants to meet.[22] Although this decision was clearly open to question, and arguably involved a misinterpretation of the statutory provisions and the ILO Convention, it nevertheless served as a salutary warning of the potential pitfalls of conceiving pay inequity within the framework of sex discrimination law. Clearly, sex discrimination may be one of the reasons for pay inequities, but it is by no means the only possible reason for such inequities.

This point was, in fact, accepted by the NSW Pay Equity Inquiry. While the Inquiry heard a great deal of general evidence (such as mine) on the causes and potential remedies for pay inequity between men and women, the core of the inquiry involved a series of case studies in which the existence and reasons for pay inequities between groups of female and male workers were examined in detail. The case studies looked at child care workers in private sector long day care centres, whose work was compared with engineering associates in the metal industry;[23] hairdressers and beauty therapists, who were compared with motor mechanics;[24] public sector librarians, who were compared with public sector geoscientists;[25] female trimmers and male butchers in a major seafood processing enterprise;[26] and outworkers in the clothing industry, who were compared with male machinists in the metal industry.[27] Notably, all of the case studies involved so-called 'women's work', that is, occupations which were exclusively or almost exclusively female, and in which, therefore, there were no readily available male comparators against whose treatment the question of equal remuneration could be determined. Consequently, male comparators were chosen from male-dominated occupations, and efforts were made to show that the work performed by the women was of equal or comparable value to that of the men, having regard to skill, training, education, job content, and so forth. In effect, each case study involved a comparable worth exercise.

---

[21] *AMWU v HPM Industries* [1998] IRCommA 292 (4 Mar 1998).

[22] Similarly, in the subsequent case of *AMWU v David Syme & Co Ltd*, Print R3273 (23 Mar 1999), Ross VP held that the first step in an equal remuneration claim would be for the applicant to show that the rates of remuneration in question had been established as a result of discrimination based on sex, ie 'having regard to the gender of the employees concerned' (para 41).

[23] Industrial Relations Commission of NSW, above n 11, at 156–286.

[24] *Ibid*, at 287–389.

[25] *Ibid*, at 390–496.

[26] *Ibid*, at 648–709.

[27] *Ibid*, at 523–647.

Ultimately, however, the Inquiry did not focus on whether the women in each of the case studies were receiving less remuneration than men for work of equal value, and thus its findings did not hinge on the validity and cogency of the comparisons drawn between the women's and men's work. Rather, the key concept adopted by the Inquiry was that of 'undervaluation', so that it looked in each case at whether the women's work was objectively undervalued. This could, but did not have to, be demonstrated by reference to comparisons with men undertaking comparable work. Undervaluation could also be shown by reference to the fact that current wage rates were depressed by the fact that the work was historically performed by women, or by comparison with the pay received by other women, or by the fact that skills, responsibilities and qualifications associated with the work or within different grades of the work were not reflected or adequately rewarded in the remuneration structure.[28]

Although this approach was derived from a series of case studies, and its application would also necessarily involve case by case analysis, the Inquiry identified a set of profile indicators of undervaluation, including: female-dominated employment, female characterisation of work, new industries and occupations, service industries, home-based occupations, absence of any work value exercise conducted by an industrial tribunal, inadequate application of previous equal pay principles, a weak union or few union members, small workplaces, a large component of casual workers, lack of or inadequate recognition of qualifications, and lack of access to training or career paths.[29] It might be observed that these indicators cover a very wide range of women's employment.

The strategic importance of making 'undervaluation' rather than 'equal remuneration' the central question of the Inquiry was that it enabled the Inquiry to sidestep a host of difficult issues that arise when attempting to apply an equality framework – are the relevant women workers sufficiently similarly situated to the chosen male comparators? how should the relative value of their work be compared, in a way that avoids gender bias? what if the women's work is found to be of lesser or greater value than the men's work? if the women's work is judged to be of equal value but paid less, is there nevertheless a good reason to maintain the status quo? 'Undervaluation' describes the situation in such a way that it can be recognised as a problem, rhetorically connotes injustice, and generates a normative imperative that the situation be remedied. It clearly identifies a systemic rather than individual cause, and points to a solution – proper valuation of

---

[28] For a more extensive discussion of the findings of each case study, see Hunter, R, *The Beauty Therapist, the Mechanic, the Geoscientist and the Librarian: Addressing Undervaluation of Women's Work* (Sydney, ATN WEXDEV, 2000) 17–21.

[29] Industrial Relations Commission of NSW, above n 11, at 46–7.

women's work, addressing the particular causes of undervaluation in the relevant case – that is not limited simply to getting for women the same as some men have.

Evidently, the descriptive power of the concept of undervaluation depends upon the question of how work is valued and by whom. If the value ascribed to particular work is seen as being a result of market forces, then in a neo-liberal context it will be unassailable; there would be no such thing as 'undervaluation'. But the very fact that men and women workers receive different returns for their investments in human capital, as noted above, suggests that something more than market forces is at play. The case studies examined as part of the NSW Pay Equity Inquiry clearly demonstrated that work value is socially constructed. As a consequence, the Inquiry report insisted that when determining whether women's work has been undervalued, the valuation process must be free of gender bias – that is, the various ways in which job evaluation systems have been shown to undervalue women's work[30] need to be challenged and addressed, not perpetuated. In the UK context, Grimshaw and Rubery have also identified a range of non-market factors contributing to gender-based undervaluation, including organisational practices, the design and implementation of remuneration systems, and employers' unwillingness rather than inability to pay higher wages to women, particularly associated with public sector monopsony.[31] The (under)valuation of women's work may thus be seen not as an inevitable and unquestionable result of the operation of market forces, but as a consequence of market *failure*, hence as something that ought to be addressed and remedied within neo-liberal ideology.

Following the NSW Pay Equity Inquiry, similar inquiries were held in most other Australian States,[32] and several States adopted principles and procedures within their industrial relations systems to allow for the making of claims for gender-based undervaluation.[33] All of the cases brought under the new procedures to date – involving librarians, child care workers, local government community services and children's services professionals, and

---

[30] See, eg Burton, C, *Gender Bias in Job Evaluation* (Canberra, AGPS, 1988); Equal Opportunities Commission, 'Good Practice Guide – Job evaluation schemes free of sex bias', at http://www.eoc.org.uk/Default.aspx?page=15381.

[31] Grimshaw and Rubery, above n 11, at 2–3, 54–5, 72–3.

[32] Queensland Industrial Relations Commission, *Worth Valuing: A Report of the Pay Equity Inquiry* (Brisbane, QIRC, Mar 2001); Todd, T and Eveline, J, *Report on the Review of the Gender Pay Gap in Western Australia* (Perth, Department of Consumer and Employment Protection, Nov 2004); Victorian Pay Equity Working Party, *Advancing Pay Equity* (Melbourne, Department for Industrial Relations, Feb 2005).

[33] *Re Equal Remuneration Principle* (2000) 97 IR 177 (NSW IRC); *State Wage Case and Review of Wage Fixing Principles 2000* (Tasmanian Industrial Commission, 6 Jul 2000); *Equal Remuneration Principle* (2002) 170 QGIG 15 (Queensland IRC, 29 Apr 2002). By contrast, two unsuccessful attempts have been made to have an Equal Remuneration Principle inserted into the Western Australian Wage Fixing Principles: Todd and Eveline, *ibid*, at 58.

dental nurses – have been successful, resulting in significant pay increases and improved career structures for the women workers concerned.[34] But it must also be acknowledged that there are definite limits to the potential of undervaluation claims. Relatively few cases have been brought. Case by case studies of how wage rates for women's work have historically been set require considerable research and resources, and cases tend to be contested at considerable length because of their potentially significant impact on the employers' bottom line. In effect, then, undervaluation cases require union backing, which raises the perennial problem of getting women's issues onto union agendas. In the recent neo-liberal climate in Australia, with union membership falling and a federal government intent on rendering them industrially irrelevant, unions could be somewhat forgiven for being otherwise preoccupied. In further bad news, federal industrial relations legislation enacted in 2005 aimed to abolish State industrial relations systems for the bulk of private sector employees,[35] which would have meant the end of the State equal remuneration principles and undervaluation claims.

Nevertheless, the concept of undervaluation has taken some women workers in Australia further than equal pay principles ever did, and I would argue that it remains a useful one. For example, the UK Equal Opportunities Commission (EOC) recently issued two publications on the undervaluation of women's work[36] which demonstrate the strength of the concept. They define undervaluation as 'a higher quality of labour for a given wage',[37] and argue that pay should reflect job requirements, 'not the position of the employee in the organisation's value chain'.[38] Again, this does not require a woman to show that she is doing work that is of equal value to that performed by a male comparator who is paid at a higher rate. The EOC publications also extend the neo-liberal arguments for addressing

---

[34]   *Re Crown Librarians, Library Officers and Archivists Award Proceedings – Applications Under the Equal Remuneration Principle* [2002] NSWIRComm 55 (28 Mar 2002); *Re Miscellaneous Workers Kindergartens and Child Care Centres etc (State) Award* [2006] NSWIRComm 64 (7 Mar 2006); *Re Local Government (State) Award 2001* [2004] NSWIRComm 24 (16 Feb 2004) (by consent); *LHMU v Australian Dental Association (Queensland Branch) Union of Employers* [2005] QIRComm 139 (7 Sep 2005); *LHMU v Children's Services Employers Association* [2006] QIRComm 50 (24 Mar 2006) (interim decision).

[35]   Workplace Relations Amendment (Work Choices) Act 2005 (Aust). This aspect of the legislation survived constitutional challenge in *New South Wales v Commonwealth; Western Australia v Commonwealth* [2006] HCA 52 (14 Nov 2006). However the election of a new federal government in November 2007, with a policy of repealing many of the previous government's industrial relations reforms, may signal a reprieve for the State systems.

[36]   Grimshaw and Rubery, above n 11; Equal Opportunities Commission, *Labourers of Love? The Cost of Undervaluing Women's Work* (May 2007). Note that the Equal Opportunities Commission ceased to exist in October 2007. Its functions have been subsumed into the new UK Equality and Human Rights Commission.

[37]   Grimshaw and Rubery, *ibid*, at 1.

[38]   *Ibid*, at 148.

the undervaluation of women's work, contending, for example, that undervaluation matters because it: damages Britain's productivity and contributes to the national skills gap by discouraging women from gaining accredited skills and qualifications if they will not be rewarded for them; undermines the quality of public services due to high staff turnover; and contributes to child poverty and pensioner poverty due to women's low earnings, which in turn create burdens for the state and for tax payers.[39] And they propose a multi-faceted policy approach to combating under-valuation, including the reform of equal pay legislation.[40] At bottom, the concept of undervaluation currently offers greater political and practical possibilities than the concept of equality for achieving any further narrow-ing of the gender pay gap.

LEGAL AID FUNDING

The issue of women's inequitable access to state funding and services is harder to address than that of pay inequity, since it is more difficult to construct claims of injustice and normative arguments when dealing with the operations of the state than when dealing with the operations of the (labour) market. Within a neo-liberal framework, the state is understood as a residual rather than universal provider, entitled to decide where to target its limited resources, to interpret the needs of claimants in order to determine who is deserving and undeserving, and to specify how identified needs will be met (regardless of what claimants may actually want).[41] Of course, this is one of the reasons why feminist claims of women's substantive inequality in the receipt of funding and services have become descriptively impotent, but it also poses a more serious challenge for potential alternative conceptualisations. One consequence is that, unlike the case of 'undervaluation', there do not appear to be any ready-made alternatives to draw upon. The discussion in this section, therefore, is necessarily more speculative than that in the previous section. Among other things, I cannot demonstrate the practical application or real-world success of the concepts I suggest, but rather offer them as potential advances that fulfil theoretical criteria and hence might be worth taking further in feminist strategies.

As noted earlier, the particular example of state funding and services on which I will focus in this section is the provision of legal aid. Again, in this case, feminist concerns have been animated by a national statistical gap

[39] Equal Opportunities Commission, above n 36, at 4–5.
[40] Grimshaw and Rubery, above n 11, at 148; Equal Opportunities Commission, *ibid*, at 10.
[41] See, in particular, Fraser, above n 6; Fraser, N, 'Women, Welfare and the Politics of Needs Interpretation' (1987) 2 *Hypatia* 103.

between women and men in the receipt of legal aid funding. In Australia, for example, a 1994 report on *Gender Bias in Litigation Legal Aid* found that in 1992–93, women received only 37 per cent of net legal aid expenditure on representation services, and that the success rate of women's applications for legal aid was lower then men's.[42] Eleven years later, in 2005, Legal Aid Queensland's *Gender Equity Report* similarly observed that in 2003–04, women received only 35 per cent of legal aid grants, and again had a lower success rate in their applications (70 per cent) than did men (78 per cent).[43] Historical figures provided in the *Gender Equity Report* indicated that at no stage in the years 1997–98 to 2003–04 was women's share of legal aid applications matched by their share of grants for legal representation.[44]

   The 1994 *Gender Bias in Litigation Legal Aid* report made it clear that the gender bias found in litigation legal aid was a product of indirect rather than direct discrimination against women.[45] That is, legal aid policies and guidelines did not overtly distinguish between men's and women's applications. Rather, the adverse outcomes for women resulted from the differential treatment of legal aid applications relating to criminal law and family law matters. Women enjoyed an equal success rate with men in relation to criminal matters, and an equal or slightly higher success rate than men in relation to family law matters.[46] But legal aid guidelines gave priority to criminal matters in which the defendant was potentially threatened with loss of liberty, criminal law applications outnumbered family law applications, criminal law applications had a higher approval rate than family law applications, and men made the majority of criminal law applications (over 80 per cent), while women made the majority of family law applications (over 70 per cent).[47] Thus, in 1992–93, 72 per cent of all litigation legal aid grants were made in the area of criminal law, consuming 43 per cent of the total legal aid budget. By contrast, only 21 per cent of legal aid grants were made in the area of family law, consuming only 32 per cent of the legal aid budget.[48] Similarly, the 2005 *Gender Equity Report* explained that it remains easier to obtain legal aid for criminal law because the majority of offences are not merit-tested,[49] whereas all applications for

---

[42]   Office of Legal Aid and Family Services (OLAFS), *Gender Bias in Litigation Legal Aid* (Canberra, Commonwealth Attorney-General's Department, 1994) 8–9, 14, 25.
[43]   Women's Legal Aid, *Gender Equity Report 2005: A Profile of Women and Legal Aid Queensland* (Brisbane, Legal Aid Queensland, 2005) 2, 7, 21.
[44]   *Ibid*, at 20–21.
[45]   OLAFS, above n 42, at 40.
[46]   *Ibid*, at 19–21; Australian Law Reform Commission (ALRC), *Report No 69, Part I – Equality Before the Law: Justice for Women* (Sydney, ALRC, 1994) para 4.11.
[47]   OLAFS, *ibid*, at 19–21, 34; ALRC, *ibid*, at paras 4.11–4.12.
[48]   OLAFS, *ibid*, at 24.
[49]   Women's Legal Aid, above n 43, at 7.

family law are subject to both means and merit tests. Legal Aid Queensland made 27,324 legal aid grants in 2003–04, 64 per cent of which were in criminal law, compared to 24 per cent in family law.[50]

The justifications for prioritising criminal law in the expenditure of legal aid budgets are first, that criminal defendants face the overwhelming power and resources of the state, and therefore have the greatest need for legal representation; and secondly, the serious consequences of being found guilty of many criminal offences, ie imprisonment. In Australia, these justifications were reinforced by a 1992 High Court decision, *Dietrich v R*,[51] which held that the right to a fair trial for a person accused of a serious criminal offence includes a right to legal representation, and if the accused is unable to afford such representation, either it must be provided at public expense, or the trial should be stayed. By contrast, the High Court has never characterised lack of legal representation in family law cases as a breach of human rights, and while the Family Court has repeatedly made statements about the iniquities and serious consequences of lack of legal aid funding for family law matters,[52] those statements have had no practical effect on legal aid grants policy.

The justifications for prioritising criminal law in the distribution of legal aid funds came under attack from feminists in the mid-1990s. Some of these attacks were launched under the banner of the need to eliminate discrimination and ensure substantive equality for women. They included positive arguments for women's equality of access to legal aid, for example:

> If legal aid was allocated solely on the basis of relative poverty, it could be expected that more women would receive it than men, given their inferior economic status.[53]

There were also direct counter-arguments to the standard justifications, pointing out (among other things) the potentially serious consequences for women of losing family law disputes and the significant inequality of resources often experienced by women in those disputes, and questioning policies which gave legal aid funding to the perpetrators of violent crimes

---

[50] *Ibid*, at 21. Note that the *Gender Equity Report* reports only on numbers of grant applications and approvals, but does not include any information on budget shares.

[51] (1992) 177 CLR 292. The High Court sits at the pinnacle of the Australian court hierarchy.

[52] Eg *McOwan and McOwan* (1994) FLC 92–451; *T v S* (2001) 28 Fam LR 342; *In the Marriage of S* (1997) 22 Fam LR 112. In *Re K* (1994) 17 Fam LR 537, the father initially argued, relying on *Dietrich*, that the trial had miscarried because he had been refused legal aid, however this ground of appeal was withdrawn. Note also that in the case of *Re JTT; ex parte Victoria Legal Aid* [1998] HCA 44, the High Court held that the Family Court had no power to order that a Legal Aid Commission bear the future costs of a children's representative (or presumably any other party) in family law proceedings.

[53] ALRC, above n 46, at para 4.10.

but not to their victims.[54] Regina Graycar and Jenny Morgan took a slightly different angle in harnessing their argument for women's greater access to legal aid to the concept of citizenship – a concept that received some feminist attention in the mid-late 1990s. Graycar and Morgan used the rhetorically powerful notion of 'civil death' to describe women's inability to invoke the legal system to redress the harms they have suffered, and hence their lack of full enjoyment of citizenship.[55]

However neither equality-based nor citizenship-based arguments have made any dent in the legal aid policies prioritising criminal law which, as noted above, continue to operate to the detriment of women. The failure in this instance appears to have been not so much descriptive as normative. That is, even if the situation was accepted as being one of inequality (or the denial of equal citizenship), this did not generate any normative imperative for change, because in the liberal hierarchy of rights, the liberty of the subject and rights to freedom and a fair trial – in other words the rights of criminal defendants – trump all others. Thus, women's inequality, even if acknowledged, was seen as something to be tolerated, because in a zero-sum competition for resources, (men's) liberty exerted a more compelling normative claim than (women's) equality.

If that was the case in the 1990s, the currently dominant, neo-liberal construction of welfare makes it even more difficult for equality arguments to gain any purchase in relation to legal aid. Legal aid (especially for family and civil law) has come to be seen – at least in Australia – not as an element of citizenship, or even as a facilitator of social inclusion (as in UK discourse),[56] but as something more like a form of charity dispensed to the deserving poor. The normative force of equality arguments presupposes some form of entitlement, whereas as other commentators have noted, there has been a widespread retreat from ideas of universalism and equal access to justice in the legal aid field, in favour of concerns about targeting and efficiency.[57] And this shift has tended to reinforce the conceptual division between criminal and civil law, so that:

[54] *Ibid*, at para 4.17; Mossman, MJ, 'Gender Equality and Legal Aid Services: A Research Agenda for Institutional Change' (1993) 15 *Sydney Law Review* 30, 47–50. See also Mossman, MJ, 'Gender Equality, Family Law and Access to Justice' (1994) 8 *International Journal of Law and the Family* 357; Mossman, MJ, '"Shoulder to Shoulder": Gender and Access to Justice' (1990) 10 *Windsor Yearbook of Access to Justice* 351, 362.

[55] Graycar, R and Morgan, J, 'Disabling Citizenship: Civil Death for Women in the 1990s' (1995) 17 *Adelaide Law Review* 49, 76.

[56] See, eg Social Exclusion Unit, *Preventing Social Exclusion* (London, Cabinet Office, 2001); Lord Chancellor's Department and Law Centres Federation, *Legal and Advice Services: A Pathway Out of Social Exclusion* (2001).

[57] Moorhead, R and Pleasence, P, 'Access to Justice After Universalism: Introduction', in R Moorhead and P Pleasence (eds), *After Universalism: Re-engineering Access to Justice* (Oxford, Blackwell, 2003) 1.

In the context of criminal law, the language of access to legal services is [still] that of equality and rights. However, in the general field of civil justice...an instrumentalist imprint, centred on relative need, and measured through impact and efficiency, has emerged (footnotes omitted).[58]

Several alternative approaches to conceptualising the basis for legal aid grants and organising legal aid provision have been put forward in the past. An early Australian idea was the 'social indicator' approach, which proposed that legal aid should be provided to those who had both a need for legal services, and a reduced capacity to purchase those services in the private market. Reduced capacity in turn would be identified by reference to indicators of social deprivation such as unemployment, geographical isolation, ethnicity, and welfare dependency.[59] It is by no means clear that such an approach would necessarily even out the gender bias in legal aid distribution, but more importantly, by now it is clear that legal aid budgets would not be sufficient to fund all of those who might qualify under this approach, which is considerably broader than current means and merit tests. A second, and somewhat related, proposal would be for legal aid provision to target 'disadvantage', which might bring the needs of poor women trying to access the legal system more squarely into the frame.[60] Again, however, this concept seems too broad to be of much practical value, and could also be interpreted by reference to perceived degrees of disadvantage and in ways entirely consistent with the current arrangements for the distribution of legal aid. For example, while Legal Aid Queensland describes itself as an organisation which 'provides legal assistance to financially and socially disadvantaged Queenslanders', it tolerates the gender disparities in legal aid provision mentioned earlier, and indeed, tolerates lower than average success rates in their legal aid applications for groups who would unquestionably count as disadvantaged in access to legal assistance, such as women from non-English speaking backgrounds (NESB), women living in rural and regional areas, and women with a disability.[61]

A more potentially promising approach has emerged recently out of a series of 'legal needs' studies undertaken primarily in the UK.[62] These

---

[58] *Ibid*, at 10.
[59] Hanks, P, *Social Indicators and the Delivery of Legal Services* (1987) 49, cited in Mossman, 'Gender Equality and Legal Aid Services', above n 54, at 52.
[60] Eg Mossman, *ibid*, drawing on Rhode, above n 9.
[61] Women's Legal Aid, above n 43, at 2–3, 14, 17.
[62] See Genn, H, *Paths to Justice: What People Do and Think About Going to Law* (Oxford, Hart Publishing, 1999); Genn, H and Paterson, A, *Paths to Justice Scotland: What People in Scotland Do and Think About Going to Law* (Oxford, Hart Publishing, 2001); Pleasence, P, Buck, A, Balmer, N, O'Grady, A, Genn, H and Smith, M, *Causes of Action: Civil Law and Social Justice* (London, Legal Services Research Centre Research Paper No 11, 2004); Pleasence, P, with Balmer, N and Buck, A, *Causes of Action: Civil Law and Social Justice*, 2nd edn (London, Legal Services Research Centre Research Paper No 14, Mar 2006).

studies have tried to assess the level of demand for legal aid by conducting large-scale population surveys asking about the incidence of 'justiciable problems' in the community, and what people tend to do when faced with such problems. The most interesting findings for present purposes suggest that people tend to experience clusters of legal problems,[63] and that particular groups of people are more vulnerable to particular clusters of problems than others.

The most advanced examples of this kind of analysis are two studies of civil legal problems published in 2004 and 2006 by the UK Legal Services Research Centre. They found that people with long-standing ill-health or disabilities, lone parents, the unemployed, those living in rented or temporary accommodation, and victims of crime, were more likely than average to report one or more justiciable problems.[64] Those with a chronic illness or disability, lone parents and welfare benefit recipients were more likely than others to experience multiple problems.[65] For example in relation to lone parents, the 2004 study noted that:

> the change in personal circumstances that results from relationship breakdown, especially for those with whom any children of the relationship come to reside, leaves lone parents vulnerable to a range of further problems[66]

including problems with housing, money/debts, welfare benefits (particularly for female lone parents), domestic violence, discrimination, mental health, children and neighbours.[67]

In addition, some problem types were relatively unlikely to be reported in isolation, but rather tended to become more prevalent as the number of reported problems increased. These included domestic violence, problems ancillary to relationship breakdown, and problems related to homelessness.[68] Indeed, experiences of domestic violence and/or divorce were likely to lead to other types of problems, including issues ancillary to the breakdown of the relationship, money/debt problems, problems with rented housing, and problems with children.[69]

In Australia, the Law and Justice Foundation of NSW is engaged in a similar study of Access to Justice and Legal Needs. See the publications listed at http://www.lawfoundation.net.au/publications. For a Canadian study, see Currie, A, 'Civil Justice Problems and the Disability and Health Status of Canadians', in P Pleasence, A Buck and N Balmer (eds), *Transforming Lives: Law and Social Process* (London, TSO, 2007).

[63] Genn, *ibid*, at 31–6.

[64] *Causes of Action*, above n 62, at 10–13; *Causes of Action*, 2nd edn, above n 62, at 19–21. 'Temporary accommodation' included hostels, boarding houses, bed and breakfast lodgings and hotels, but did not specifically include women's refuges (*Causes of Action*, at 6).

[65] *Causes of Action*, *ibid*, at 31–2; *Causes of Action*, 2nd edn, *ibid*, at 54.

[66] *Causes of Action*, *ibid*, at 25.

[67] *Causes of Action*, *ibid*, at 26–7; *Causes of Action*, 2nd edn, *ibid*, at 43–6.

[68] *Causes of Action*, *ibid*, at 33–4; *Causes of Action*, 2nd edn, *ibid*, at 55.

[69] *Causes of Action*, *ibid*, at 35–6; see also *Causes of Action*, 2nd edn, *ibid*, at 58, 64.

The studies identified three particular clusters of problems: the 'family cluster' (comprising domestic violence, divorce, and problems related to relationship breakdown), the 'housing cluster' (involving a cycle of problems with rented housing and homelessness), and the 'economic cluster' (consisting of problems with consumer transactions, money/debts, employment and neighbours).[70] Problems in the family cluster tended to last for longer than other problem types before being resolved.[71] Lone parents, respondents reporting a chronic illness or disability and respondents living in rented housing had a high likelihood of experiencing multiple problems in the family cluster.[72]

Thus, the 2004 report concluded that 'the experience of problems was far from randomly distributed across the survey population',[73] and that 'socially excluded groups' were particularly vulnerable to experiencing multiple legal problems.[74] The 2006 report also noted that as well as socially excluded groups being vulnerable to justiciable problems, such problems can themselves result from social exclusion.[75] The 2004 report called for 'joined up solutions to joined up problems',[76] and in particular suggested a need for coordinated advice and other services so that problems would not be dealt with in isolation, and the likelihood of them leading to further problems could be reduced through early, preventative action.[77] The 2006 report further argued that promoting access to justice was an important means of tackling social exclusion.[78]

Along similar lines, an Australian study of civil and criminal law problems in six socio-economically disadvantaged areas of NSW found a high level of legal need within disadvantaged communities,[79] a wide range of problems experienced by individuals with a chronic illness or disability,[80] and a cluster of problems relating to family law and domestic violence.[81] It also found that Indigenous people experienced a higher than average incidence of problems relating to credit/debt, employment and

---

[70] *Causes of Action, ibid*, at 37–40; *Causes of Action*, 2nd edn, *ibid*, at 66–70. A similar 'family cluster' of problems was found in Genn, *ibid*.

[71] *Causes of Action, ibid*, at 98; *Causes of Action*, 2nd edn, *ibid*, at 146.

[72] *Causes of Action, ibid*, at 43–4; *Causes of Action*, 2nd edn, *ibid*, at 73.

[73] *Causes of Action, ibid*, at 44.

[74] *Ibid*, at 45.

[75] *Causes of Action*, 2nd edn, *ibid*, at 155.

[76] *Causes of Action*, above n 62, at 115.

[77] *Ibid*, at 105.

[78] *Causes of Action*, 2nd edn, above n 62, at 155.

[79] Coumarelos, C, Wei, Z and Zhou, AZ, *Justice Made to Measure: NSW Legal Needs Survey in Disadvantaged Areas* (Sydney, Law & Justice Foundation of NSW, Mar 2006) xix (this study found more than two thirds of participants reporting one or more legal problem events in the previous 12 months, compared to 36–40% in the British surveys).

[80] *Ibid*, at xviii.

[81] *Ibid*, at 77–8.

family law,[82] and that certain problems had a tendency not just to cluster but to recur – including problems relating to employment, family law, human rights, general crime, credit/debt, government, consumer issues and education.[83] The study concluded with the argument that:

> legal services need to have the capacity for resolving the complex situations faced by some individuals involving multiple, concurrent, interconnected legal problems.[84]

None of the legal needs studies has found gender difference per se to be a factor in the incidence of justiciable problems,[85] but the 2006 UK study acknowledged that there were significant differences in the types of problems experienced by men and women, and also by different racial and ethnic groups.[86] Moreover, groups such as lone parents are clearly female-dominated. Neither have any of the studies systematically reported gender breakdowns within the other groups experiencing high levels of problems, such as those with a chronic illness or disability, Indigenous people, those living in rented housing and temporary accommodation, and welfare benefit recipients, whereas from a feminist perspective, we might expect to find quite different gendered experiences within these groups.

This is borne out to an extent by the findings of a recent Australian study of women refused legal aid.[87] The study looked specifically at Indigenous women, NESB women, women with a disability, older women (aged 60+), and women living in rural and regional areas, together with a comparison group of women who did not fall into any of these groups, who were refused legal aid for family law, domestic violence, or discrimination matters between July 2001 and June 2003. Strikingly, almost *all* of these women (87 per cent) had a history of seeking free legal advice and/or applying for legal aid, particularly in relation to family law and domestic violence issues, but also covering a wide range of other civil and criminal matters. The family law–domestic violence pattern of advice seeking and legal aid applications was particularly marked with the NESB women – almost 100 per cent in both instances.

---

[82] *Ibid*, at xx.

[83] *Ibid*, at 162.

[84] *Ibid*, at 164.

[85] Genn, above n 62, at 28; *Causes of Action*, above n 62, at 12; Coumarelos et al, *ibid,* at 26.

[86] *Causes of Action*, 2nd edn, above n 62, at 35, 37. Women were more likely to report being victims of domestic violence and problems with neighbours; men were more likely to report unfair treatment by the police, money/debt problems and employment problems; non-white respondents were more likely to report problems with discrimination and immigration.

[87] Hunter, R, De Simone, T and Whitaker, L, with Bathgate, J and Svensson, A, *Women and Legal Aid: Identifying Disadvantage* (Brisbane, Socio-Legal Research Centre, Griffith University and Legal Aid Queensland, Aug 2006), available at http://www.griffith.edu.au/centre/slrc.

Some of these women's previous applications for legal aid had been successful, but it was clear that the previous legal aid grants (which are generally limited in scope and confined to addressing the immediate issue raised by the applicant) had not fully resolved their legal problems, and so they kept returning to seek further advice and make further applications. Domestic violence matters were particularly likely to recur. Clearly, this pattern of repeated returns for assistance is neither effective for clients, nor efficient for the funding body. If an effort was made to deal with the client's family law/domestic violence/related issues holistically when they first seek assistance, and thereby to prevent problems from escalating or further problems from developing, this would be both more satisfactory for the client, and probably more cost-effective for the legal aid fund.

The 'problem' here, then, is not so much (all) women's inequitable access to legal aid funding, but the failure of legal aid agencies to respond adequately to the cluster of family law, domestic violence, and interconnected civil and criminal law issues that some women experience. This problem might be described as something like 'response failure' or, perhaps better, 'policy neglect'. This description captures the nature of the problem (that a particular and distinctive set of legal difficulties experienced by a group of women has been ignored in legal aid policy-making), rhetorically connotes injustice ('neglect' is a bad thing), and suggests that the situation ought to be remedied (by means of an appropriate policy response). The solution in this instance should be a heightened level of attention when women with children seek legal advice or make a legal aid application in relation to domestic violence, or a family law matter involving domestic violence. The aim should be not simply to achieve an immediate legal solution with minimum expense, but to uncover and address the range of legal and related problems the woman is facing, with the objective of solving those problems holistically and preventing any need for further intervention.

Further, the research suggests that not only are women experiencing family law/domestic violence problems, but both women and men with disabilities, Indigenous people, and people who are homeless or in temporary housing, may also experience policy neglect in this context, and thus the same kind of heightened attention should be paid to them when they seek legal advice or a grant of legal aid. As with the pay equity case studies, too, there is clearly a need for further, local research in relation to the clusters of legal problems experienced by different social groups. Evidently, an argument about 'policy neglect' does not require comparisons between men and women, or ignore differences among women, but may apply to different groups of women and/or men depending upon the particular circumstances. Further, in order to make an argument about 'policy neglect', some form of systemic, group disadvantage must be in evidence (thus demanding a policy response), rather than simply individual choices or misfortunes.

The concept of policy neglect also has the capacity to address the difficulties noted earlier of making normative arguments about the way in which state resources are distributed. Although the state is entitled to set priorities in the provision of services and funding, this is not generally taken to include the notion that it is free to ignore or neglect any groups in the process. And although the state has the power to interpret needs and specify how they will be met, this presumably should be in accordance with and not contrary to empirical evidence about the existence and nature of particular needs. In the case of legal aid provision, the normative force of the policy neglect argument is further strengthened by the fact that it can be shown that the current distribution of resources is inefficient, and that an alternative distribution that more effectively addressed empirically identified needs would also be a more efficient use of public funds.

Another context in which the concept of policy neglect might work would be in relation to women prisoners. Here again, equality arguments have proved of limited value in addressing the fact that women prisoners have access to a more restricted range of services and facilities than male prisoners, and that prison policies often have a severely adverse impact on women – such as the repeated strip-searching of women who are survivors of sexual assault, and the failure adequately to cater for women prisoners with dependent children. A recent Australian report on *Women in Prison*[88] was publicly dismissed by the relevant State government on the basis that there was 'no discrimination' against women prisoners. But there is no question that women prisoners are a neglected group in government policy, and perhaps that might be a more compelling way of attempting to address the issue.

CONCLUSION

The need to find alternative concepts to equality for advancing feminist claims is driven by the descriptive and, increasingly, normative failures of equality in a neo-liberal climate. The two areas examined in this chapter suggest that different issues arise, and hence different descriptors are required, in relation to claims directed at the market and claims directed at the state. Conceivably, too, further differences would arise in relation to women's position in the family, and their position as democratic citizens as

[88] *Women in Prison: A Report by the Anti-Discrimination Commission Queensland* (Mar 2006).

opposed to welfare recipients. It appears, then, that the development of new strategic concepts needs to proceed on a case by case basis.

The two concepts suggested here – undervaluation and policy neglect – are not free of weaknesses. They both rely on research or at least investigation to establish, first, that the particular situation falls within the descriptive scope of the relevant concept, and secondly, what systemic issues underlie women's needs or disadvantages in that situation, which will determine the appropriate normative response. This requires a commitment of resources to undertake the necessary investigation, and an intellectual commitment to undertake it in a way that is open, sympathetic, and free from gender bias.[89] It also requires an investment of faith in research expertise and the production of specialist knowledge which might be seen as elitist and removed from more democratic feminist methods, although the same could be said of the production of sophisticated, feminist understandings of equality referred to at the beginning of this chapter. More positively, any approach that requires particularised inquiries into the circumstances of particular cases will raise the same issues of identification and specialist knowledge. That is how a system of justice as opposed to a system of bureaucratic processing inevitably operates.

Secondly, the appeal to neo-liberal values embodied in both concepts, while having strategic advantages, may also carry some of the same disadvantages as the appeal to liberal values embodied in the concept of equality. That is, there is a risk of co-optation into the dominant political discourse, and the consequent deradicalisation and domestication of feminist claims. And it is likely that these concepts, too, will ultimately lose their rhetorical value with further shifts in political and economic paradigms. Yet these strategic considerations will be present whatever options feminists choose to pursue.

Finally, both concepts require the commitment of resources in creating remedies. Feminist advocates may have the capacity to undertake or to contribute to the research function, but the remedial function requires input from less interested actors, ie private employers and/or the state. But this drawback, again, is not unique to the concepts of undervaluation and policy neglect. Any approach that calls for an improvement in women's material conditions will require resources. The failure of liberal concepts such as (in)equality to mobilise resources, and the need to find new concepts that are capable of generating an imperative for such mobilisation, is the very issue to be addressed.

---

[89] In relation to the risks of determination of needs by the state in an unsympathetic and decontextualised way, see Fraser, above n 6, at 294, 306–7.

Part II

Constitutional Equality Projects

5

Equality Rights: What's Wrong?

REG GRAYCAR AND JENNY MORGAN*

INTRODUCTION

THERE IS SOMETHING a little strange about reflecting on the theme of equality in law coming from Australia, one of the very few Western democracies that has not enacted a Bill of Rights or any other kind of formal recognition of a right to equality.[1] Yet, despite this lacuna in the formal legal framework, we find that our work over the years as feminist legal scholars has been centrally concerned with issues of equality.[2] We have found no shortage of ways in which equality is deeply implicated as a value in the Australian legal system, despite the absence of any constitutional guarantee.[3] In this discussion, we reflect on whether there may be some advantages that flow from the lacuna created by the absence of a constitutional equality guarantee. Could it be that this absence may in some contexts leave room for flexibility and more creative responses for those who have been left outside the mainstream of the legal community? In order to consider this issue, we introduce some of the traditional critiques of rights and touch on the persistence of formal equality as the apparently preferred model of equality. We then consider two specific case studies. First, we look at debates about the recognition of gay and lesbian familial relationships where equality guarantees may constrain rather than enable the development of creative responses to

* Thanks to Kristie Dunn, Tiffany Hambley and Anthea Vogl for their various contributions.
    [1] Though, as discussed below, there has been some activity at State and Territory level.
    [2] See, eg Graycar, R and Morgan, J, *The Hidden Gender of Law* (Sydney, The Federation Press, 1990); Graycar, R and Morgan, J, *The Hidden Gender of Law*, 2nd edn (Sydney, The Federation Press, 2002); Graycar, R and Morgan, J, 'Examining Understandings of Equality: One Step Forward, Two Steps Back?' (2004) 20 *Australian Feminist Law Journal* 23.
    [3] See Galligan, B and Morton, T, 'Australian Exceptionalism: Rights Protection Without a Bill of Rights' in T Campbell, J Goldsworthy and A Stone (eds), *Protecting Rights Without a Bill of Rights: Institutional Performance and Reform in Australia* (Aldershot, Ashgate, 2006), for a discussion of the Australian context and what they term a 'rights revolution by mainly political means' (at 20).

disadvantage. Secondly, we ask whether the absence of an equality right might have allowed more room for an equality discourse about abortion to develop. Finally, we speculate as to whether a way to move the equality debate forward is to focus on carefully defining equality so that the very definition recognises structural disadvantage.

EQUALITY IN AUSTRALIAN LAW

In a recent reflection on the period of time between the publication of the two editions of our book, *The Hidden Gender of Law* (1990 and 2002), we were forced to confront whether or not there was any validity in the notion of a progress narrative.[4] It is often assumed that the effluxion of time brings about some inevitable progression; that things always get better.[5] An analogous proposition, and one we hear frequently in the world of legal practice, is that it is only a matter of time before women take a full place in the senior positions in the legal profession. Yet we have seen the latter to be false: women have been graduating from law schools in very high numbers for well over a generation, and still the male-dominated nature of the profession has changed very little.[6] When we reflected on the period between the two editions, we decided that we could not say that the law is inexorably more open to equality claims in 2002 than it was in 1990, but rather, what we found was very much a situation of 'on the one hand and on the other', or 'one step forward and two steps back'. As part

---

[4] Graycar and Morgan, 'Examining Understandings of Equality', above n 2.

[5] For critical views on this proposition, see generally Smart, C, 'Feminism and Law: Some Problems of Analysis and Strategy' (1986) 14 *International Journal of the Sociology of Law* 109; Thornton, M, 'Feminism and the Contradictions of Law Reform' (1991) 19 *International Journal of the Sociology of Law* 453. See more generally, Graycar, R and Morgan, J, 'Law Reform: What's in it for Women?' (2005) 23 *Windsor Yearbook on Access to Justice* 393.

[6] Hunter, R, 'Women in the Legal Profession: The Australian Profile' in U Schultz and G Shaw (eds), *Women in the World's Legal Professions* (Oxford, Hart Publishing, 2003) 87. See also Urbis Keys Young, *The Solicitors of New South Wales in 2015* (Report prepared for the Law Society of New South Wales, 2003) 4, available at: <http://www.lawsociety.com.au/uploads/filelibrary/1106097418251_0.4707530669071349.pdf> (accessed 31 Aug 2006); Urbis Keys Young, *2005 Profile of Solicitors of NSW* (Report prepared for the Law Society of New South Wales, 2006) 6, available at: <http://www.lawsociety.com.au/uploads/files/1151459771531_0.5626301848610452.pdf> (accessed 31 Aug 2006); New South Wales Bar Association, *Statistical Profile of the NSW Bar: Members of the NSW Bar Association* (2005) 4: available at: <http://www.nswbar.asn.au/Public/About%20us/statistics/vol4/documents/Statssect1.pdf> (accessed 31 Aug 2006). See also Victorian Bar Council, *Equality of Opportunity for Women at the Victorian Bar* (Melbourne, Victorian Bar Council, 1998); Law Society of NSW, *Profile of the Solicitors of NSW 1998* (Research Report 2, Sydney, Law Society of NSW, 1998); Keys Young, *Research on Gender Bias and Women Working in the Legal Profession* (Sydney, NSW Department for Women, 1995); NSW Ministry for the Status and Advancement of Women, *Gender Bias and the Law: Women Working in the Legal Profession in NSW* (Summary Report, 1995).

of this process, we pondered why, on the one hand, there has developed a very sophisticated discourse of equality in feminist and other critical scholarly literature, but on the other hand, that sophisticated understanding of equality has had very limited purchase in Australian courts (or indeed, in debates in this country about Bills of Rights).

At the time we started writing *The Hidden Gender of Law*, scholarly work had already begun critiquing formal equality – the principle that likes should be treated alike, usually according to established norms. Catharine MacKinnon's book *Feminism Unmodified* had been published, with its clear rejection of both the 'sameness' and 'difference' understandings of equality;[7] Canadian legal scholar Elizabeth Sheehy had published an influential analysis which focused on substantive rather than formal equality;[8] and in 1988 the Supreme Court of Canada decided the *Andrews* case, laying the framework for what would come to be seen as a jurisprudence of substantive equality[9] – a jurisprudence that recognises structural differences and dis/advantages between groups, and requires that the experience of non-dominant groups be incorporated into the formulation of legal norms, in order to overcome disadvantages and produce substantively fair results. Yet while substantive equality has been articulated by courts in Canada[10] and subsequently, South Africa,[11] formal

---

[7] MacKinnon, C, *Feminism Unmodified: Discourses on Life and Law* (Cambridge, Mass, Harvard University Press, 1987).

[8] Sheehy, E, *Personal Autonomy and the Criminal Law: Emerging Issues for Women*, Background Paper (Ottawa, Canadian Advisory Council on the Status of Women, 1987).

[9] *Andrews v Law Society of British Columbia* [1989] 1 SCR 143. In this case, the Supreme Court first set out its substantive view of 'equality', subsequently reaffirmed in a number of cases: see in particular, *Law v Canada (Minister of Employment and Immigration)* [1999] 1 SCR 497.

[10] Some of the significant 'post-Andrews' jurisprudence includes: *Symes v Canada* [1993] 4 SCR 695; *Egan v Canada* [1995] 2 SCR 513; *Miron v Trudel* [1995] 2 SCR 418; *Thibaudeau v Canada* [1995] 2 SCR 627; *Eldridge v British Columbia (Attorney General)* [1997] 3 SCR 624; *Vriend v Alberta* [1998] 1 SCR 493. However, see more recently *Trociuk v British Columbia (Attorney General)* [2003] 1 SCR 835; *Gosselin v Quebec (Attorney General)* [2002] 4 SCR 429. Note, though, suggestions by a number of feminist scholars that the Canadian Charter, and interpretations of it by the Supreme Court of Canada, remain wedded to notions of formal equality. See Majury, D, 'The Charter, Equality Rights and Women: Equivocation and Celebration' (2002) 40 *Osgoode Hall Law Journal* 297; and see also Lessard, H, 'Mothers, Fathers, and Naming: Reflections on the *Law* Equality Framework and *Trociuk v British Columbia (Attorney General)*' (2004) 16 *Canadian Journal of Women and the Law* 165; Young, M, 'Blissed Out: Section 15 at Twenty' (2006) 33 *Supreme Court Law Review* 45; Gavigan, SAM, 'Equal Families, Equal Parents, Equal Spouses, Equal Marriage: The Case of the Missing Patriarch' (2006) 33 *Supreme Court Law Review* 317. On South Africa, see Jagwanth, S and Murray, C, 'Ten Years of Transformation: How Has Gender Equality in South Africa Fared?' (2002) 14 *Canadian Journal of Women & the Law* 255.

[11] See, eg *Harksen v Lane NO* (1998) 1 SA 300 (CC); *National Coalition for Gay and Lesbian Equality and Another v Minister of Justice and Others* (1999) 1 SA 6 (CC); *Du Toit and De Vos v Minister for Welfare and Others*, CCT 40/01 (10 Sep 2002); *Minister of Home Affairs and Another v Fourie and Another* (2005) 60 SA 1 (CC); although see also the critique

equality continues to hold sway in Australia.[12] A recent example is the first use of the State of Western Australia's racial vilification law.[13] Enacted, presumably, in response to the endemic existence of racism, the Act has been used to charge three young Aboriginal women who are accused of vilifying a young white woman. The legislation subjects those convicted to imprisonment.[14]

Why, in Australia, does formal equality dominate the jurisprudential understanding of equality? Why are the academic critiques of equality, and substantive understandings of equality applied in other jurisdictions, seemingly not part of the Australian jurisprudential debate? We do not purport to have 'the answers', but proffer a few observations. First, a scan of the footnotes of the Commonwealth Law Reports would suggest that the Australian judiciary does not read much beyond the curial utterances of their 'fellow' judges. This lack of exploration of scholarly and contextual literature could be a partial explanation for the persistence of formal equality. Secondly, we must remember that formal equality has the great advantage of being simple – it does not take a lot of effort to understand and does not require any disruption in the current distribution of power. Thirdly, it could be argued that the absence of a Bill of Rights, or any constitutionally based equality rights, has decreased the opportunities for the development of a complex public discourse in Australia about equality. By contrast the jurisprudence of both Canada and South Africa has incorporated substantive equality. Before urging the adoption of a Bill of Rights in Australia, however, some countervailing arguments need to be taken into account.

ARE RIGHTS ALWAYS RIGHT? FEMINIST CRITIQUES OF RIGHTS

Rights claims have, in fact, been the subject of persistent criticism by some feminist scholars in countries that, unlike Australia, have well established constitutional Bills of Rights (in particular, the USA and Canada).

First, it has been argued that rights are indeterminate and incoherent. One now quite old, but still very interesting, illustration of this argument comes from Fran Olsen questioning what might be involved in a 'right to

by Jagwanth and Murray in Jagwanth, S and Murray, C, 'No Nation Can Be Free When One Half of it is Enslaved: Constitutional Equality for Women in South Africa' in B Baines and R Rubio-Marin (eds), *The Gender of Constitutional Jurisprudence* (New York, Cambridge University Press, 2004).

[12] For an explicit acknowledgement of this context by a senior Australian judge, see Hon Justice Keith Mason, 'Unconscious Judicial Prejudice' (2001) 75 *Australian Law Journal* 676, 678–9.

[13] Criminal Code (WA), ss 80A-80B.

[14] See Higgins, E and Buckley-Car, A, 'Aboriginal Girl First to Face Race-Hate Law', *The Australian* (1 Jun 2006).

(family) privacy'.[15] Does a law that requires that a minor's parents be informed before she is prescribed contraception, uphold or breach family privacy? On the one hand, it could be argued that such a law is upholding family privacy – the family makes the decision about the young woman's contraceptive treatment rather than the state. On the other hand, Olsen argues, it could be seen as a breach of family privacy as the state is interfering in the communications between a parent and child by mandating a particular form and content to that communication.[16]

Secondly, there is a concern that rights discourses sometimes require us to rank rights one against the other. Bills of Rights do not normally prescribe a hierarchy of rights, labelling one as more important than another. Hence, a legal dispute will often involve a competition between rights – for example, laws restricting questions about the sexual history of a complainant in a rape trial might be said to pitch the equality rights of a target of sexual assault against the fair trial rights of the alleged perpetrator – with no predetermined or clear answer as to whose rights will prevail.[17]

The third critique points to the unelected nature of the body that determines rights claims – the judiciary. Is there any reason to suggest that such an unrepresentative group would be more responsive to the interests of disadvantaged groups than an elected parliament?[18] In a related critique, the entrenchment of a Bill of Rights may lead to the 'legalisation of politics': it is argued that political questions are turned into legal questions, with a consequent narrowing of the terms of the debate, problems of access to legal fora and an inflation of the importance of law as opposed to other sites for progressive intervention.

Finally, it has also been argued that Bills of Rights treat people as isolated individuals, divorced from a social context, and therefore they cannot properly recognise group rights.[19]

---

[15] Olsen, F, 'The Myth of State Intervention in the Family' (1985) 18 *Journal of Law Reform* 835.

[16] *Ibid*, at 860.

[17] See *R v Seaboyer; R v Gayme* [1991] 2 SCR 577; *Darrach v R* [2000] 2 SCR 443; see also Sheehy, E, 'Feminist Argumentation Before the Supreme Court of Canada in *R v Seaboyer; R v Gayme*: The Sound of One Hand Clapping' (1991) 18 *Melbourne University Law Review* 450. The same issue has arisen in the UK following enactment of the Human Rights Act 1998: see *R v A (No 2)* [2002] 1 AC 45; and see Samuels, H, 'Feminist Activism, Third Party Interventions and the Courts' (2005) 13 *Feminist Legal Studies* 15. In her chapter in this volume, however, Rosemary Hunter suggests that there is a fairly clear answer to the question of whose rights will prevail.

[18] See Hanks, P, 'Moving Towards the Legalisation of Politics' (1988) 6 *Law in Context* 80.

[19] See Kingdom, E, *What's Wrong with Rights: Problems for Feminist Politics of Law* (Edinburgh, Edinburgh University Press, 1991); Bakan, J, *Just Words* (Toronto, University of Toronto Press, 1997).

These criticisms are not, of course, unanswerable. While there will always be a level of indeterminacy in the legal language of rights, there may be ways to be somewhat more specific, at least in relation to some rights, and we return to this issue in the context of our discussion of a definition of equality below. If we could agree that some rights, for example, a right to equality, were more central than others, we could also expressly provide for that in any Bill of Rights.

Theorists such as Patricia Williams and Elizabeth Schneider have responded to the critiques of rights by pointing out that it is easy for those who have always had rights to criticise their politically enervating effect.[20] For those who have not been rights-bearers, or who have only recently been conceded rights, the language of rights not only *seems* more powerful than it might to those who have long held rights and can take them for granted, but it also *is* more powerful. And, as Didi Herman has pointed out, some of the criticism of rights-claiming assumes (perhaps somewhat patronisingly) that those who are fighting in the language of rights (and she is specifically considering here those people fighting for lesbian and gay rights) are doing so naively:

> [F]ew if any people believe that winning human rights will achieve equality, much less liberation. The acquisition of formal rights was always one strategy among many. ... The discourse deployed was strategic and hopeful, not indicative of a wilful, trusting, submissive approach to law or belief in law's neutrality, objectivity and so on.[21]

In other words, she argues that however limited the gains from 'rights claims' might be, there is an important rhetorical purchase to their invocation.

Finally, some of the criticisms of rights seem to rest on an over-inflated view of the positive nature of elected bodies – the focus on their democratic nature by contrast with that of courts often overlooks the fact that they, too, are not always 'representative'. And while access to justice is an ongoing problem, it could (but probably would not be) addressed with proper funding of appropriate cases, such as via the establishment of something along the lines of the (now defunct) Court Challenges program in Canada.[22] Nor is there any necessary reason why the courts would become the singular forum for political engagement.

---

[20]   See Williams, P, *The Alchemy of Race and Rights: Diary of a Law Professor* (Harvard, Harvard University Press, 1991); Schneider, E, 'The Dialectics of Rights and Politics: Perspectives from the Women's Movement' (1986) 17 *New York University Law Review* 589.

[21]   Herman, D, 'Beyond the Rights Debate' (1993) 2 *Social and Legal Studies* 25, 33.

[22]   In its enquiry on 'Equality Before the Law', the Australian Law Reform Commission (ALRC) proposed that such a fund be established as part of a National Women's Justice Program: see ALRC, *Equality Before the Law: Women's Equality, Report No 69, Part II* (Sydney, ALRC, 1994) 133, Recommendation 7.3. However, such funding is always subject to political vagaries: in September 2006, the conservative government in Canada abolished

In this essay, however, we focus on critical responses to the argument that adoption of a Bill of Rights would necessarily result in a more sophisticated discourse about equality in Australian law.

Australia's lack of a constitutionally entrenched equality right can clearly only be a partial explanation for the general failure of the judicial branch to engage with substantive equality – the US has a longstanding Bill of Rights and its constitutional jurisprudence has also not moved much beyond formal equality.[23] However, while Australia does not have a constitutional Bill of Rights, that does not mean that there is not almost constant pressure from some quarters for one — particularly during a period of long-lasting conservative government, as we had from 1996–2007, that was intent on winding back many of the progressive gains of previous decades. For that reason, there have been moves toward the enactment of State and Territory statutory Bills of Rights, even though they have no legal effect in relation to Commonwealth activities and could perhaps be overridden by federal legislation.

Thus far, the Australian Capital Territory (ACT) and Victoria have each adopted local Bills of Rights.[24] While both these Acts refer to sex discrimination, they do not explicitly address the problem of gender inequality. For example, the ACT's equality provision is in the following terms:

8 Recognition and equality before the law

(1) Everyone has the right to recognition as a person before the law.

(2) Everyone has the right to enjoy his or her human rights without distinction or discrimination of any kind.

(3) Everyone is equal before the law and is entitled to the equal protection of the law without discrimination. In particular, everyone has the right to equal and effective protection against discrimination on any ground.[25]

---

funding for the Law Commission of Canada, Status of Women Canada, and the Court Challenges program (which had been established in 1979), all seen as a way of silencing opposition to its programs and policies: see Schmitz, C, 'Court Challenges Program Cancelled' (2006) 26(21) *The Lawyers Weekly* (Oct 6 (news)). That article cites University of Ottawa law professor Martha Jackman as saying '[A] constitutional democracy requires access to justice by groups that are not part of the political majority. The Charter, without funding to ensure access to justice, becomes a pretty hollow instrument'.

[23] See generally MacKinnon, C, *Sex Equality* (New York, Foundation Press, 2001); Siegel, R, 'Gender and the United States Constitution: Equal Protection, Privacy, and Federalism' in Baines and Rubio-Marin (eds), above n 11, at 306.

[24] Human Rights Act 2004 (ACT); Charter of Human Rights and Responsibilities Act 2006 (Vic).

[25] Human Rights Act 2004 (ACT) s 8. The equality provision in the Victorian Act is identical, except that there is an additional sub-s 4 which states that: 'Measures taken for the purpose of assisting or advancing persons or groups of persons disadvantaged because of discrimination do not constitute discrimination'.

The only express reference to *inequality* in the ACT Act is in s 27, which deals with the rights of minorities. That provision accords to any member of 'an ethnic, religious or linguistic minority' the right to:

> enjoy his or her culture, to declare and practise his or her religion, or to use his or her language.[26]

It is early days yet in the interpretation of these provisions, but we do not consider that they have had, nor will have, much impact on the issue of substantive equality rights for women (though they may well serve other important political and discursive functions). In one of the first published commentaries on the ACT's Bill of Rights, however, Poole expressed the concern that s 27:

> may be said to detract from the ideal of equal republican citizenship, the affirmation of which ought to provide the rationale behind every domestic bill of rights.[27]

This suggests once again that formal equality is very firmly entrenched in Australia.

Yet despite the fact that formal equality remains dominant, not only in jurisprudential contexts but also in many of the debates about Bills of Rights, we suggest that there is nonetheless some (albeit limited) space within which Australian debates have been able to move beyond formal equality. We look at this via our two case studies, both of which show a more nuanced understanding of equality; this, in turn, leads us to consider whether equality guarantees might, in some circumstances, impede or limit the development of effective responses to inequality.

THE ABSENCE OF AN EQUALITY RIGHT – ARE THERE ANY ADVANTAGES?

The two concrete examples we explore with a view to considering whether there might be some advantages in the absence of a constitutional guarantee of equality are first, the quest for legal recognition of familial relationships by gay men and lesbians, and secondly, the area of access to abortion (or more broadly, women's rights to reproductive autonomy).

---

[26] Human Rights Act 2004 (ACT), s 27. A similar provision exists in the Victorian Charter, which recognises the right of all persons with a particular cultural, religious, racial or linguistic background to enjoy his or her culture. This section also recognises the 'distinct cultural rights' of Aboriginal people in particular: Charter of Human Rights and Responsibilities Act 2006 (Vic) s 19.

[27] Poole, T, 'Bills of Rights in Australia' (2004) 4 *Oxford University Commonwealth Law Journal* 197, 210.

Relationship Recognition

High Court of Australia Justice Michael Kirby has suggested that if there had been a constitutional Bill of Rights in Australia, we would have seen more speedy (and less grudging) recognition of the equality rights of homosexual Australians by the courts than we have seen with our reliance on parliaments.[28] We are not quite so convinced of this. In the United States, where there is a long standing constitutional Bill of Rights, the debate on relationship recognition has largely been dominated by a call for what is usually termed 'gay marriage'. While Massachusetts is the only state that permits gay and lesbian couples to marry (after a successful 'equality' challenge), the federal government has passed a Defense of Marriage Act (DOMA) and many of the States have followed suit in the form of what are known as 'baby domas'.[29] A smaller number of States have legislated to permit the registration of civil or domestic partnerships.[30] By contrast, in a number of other countries marriage has played less of a role. In these countries, both informal relationships between same sex partners and more formal (opt in) forms of recognition are available (whether marriage or civil unions).[31]

However, the legal changes that have taken place in all States and Territories of Australia suggest the possibility of a different approach. State and Territory laws (though not Federal laws) provide some substantive

---

[28] Kirby, M, 'Beyond the Ballot Box', *The Age* (27 March 2001) 13.

[29] See *Goodridge v Department of Public Health* 798 NE 2d 941 (Mass 2003). See also Defense of Marriage Act, Pub L No 104–199, 110 Stat 2419 (1996). The DOMA defines marriage as 'a union exclusively between one man and one woman for the purpose of all federal laws' and provides that the federal government must not recognise a marriage between persons of the same sex. The DOMA also provides that no State government need recognise a same-sex marriage, even if the marriage was concluded or recognised in another US State. For a list of the States that have adopted similar measures, see 'The Marriage Map', available at: <http://www.thetaskforce.org/downloads/reports/issue_maps/Marriage_Map_06_Nov.pdf > (accessed 30 Mar 2007). As at the start of 2007, more than half of the US States had passed either a constitutional amendment or a statute banning marriage between same sex partners.

[30] As at January 2007, the States that recognise civil unions or domestic partnerships are Vermont, Hawaii, New Jersey, Maine, Connecticut, District of Columbia and California. See Human Rights Campaign, 'Map: Relationship Recognition in the US' (Jan 2007), available at: http://hrc.org/Template.cfm?Section=Center&CONTENTID=26860&TEMPLATE=/ ContentManagement/ContentDisplay.cfm (accessed 30 Mar 2007).

[31] For Canada, see Civil Marriage Act 2005, c 33 (following the decision of the Supreme Court of Canada in *Reference re Same Sex Marriage* [2004] SCC 79). While same-sex partners may marry in Canada, there are also a range of forms of informal recognition that do not require any form of opting in. In New Zealand, the Civil Union Act 2004 provided for both same sex and opposite-sex civil unions. On the same day this Act came into effect in April 2005, the Relationships (Statutory References) Act 2005 amended about 100 statutes and regulations to provide for the same treatment of marriages and civil unions in most areas. For further discussion, see Graycar, R and Millbank, J, 'From Functional Family To Spinster Sisters: Australia's Distinctive Path To Relationship Recognition' (2007) 23 *Washington University Journal of Law & Policy* 121.

forms of recognition not only to unmarried heterosexual and same sex couples, but to a limited set of others in non-marital relationships (usually relations of care and mutual interdependence).[32] Where marriage in Massachusetts allows for the highly symbolic act of a public affirmation of a relationship, it does not affect any of the rights and obligations controlled by federal law, nor is that status likely, on current law, to be recognised by the laws of other States.[33] By contrast, while the symbolic status of marriage is unavailable to gay men and lesbians in Australia,[34] in all States and Territories, the law has been amended to recognise and attach substantive rights to both heterosexual and same sex de facto partnerships in a fairly comprehensive manner.[35]

One possible reason for this difference is that where same sex relationship rights/recognition results from equality litigation, it is almost inevitable that marriage will be the benchmark; the standard against which 'inequality' will be judged. This is because of the ways in which litigation, particularly litigation based on claims about equality, relies so frequently on a comparator.[36] So, the argument will go, if heterosexual couples have access to some benefits (here, the right to marry), then equality demands that same sex couples can marry too. An interesting illustration of this is the Massachusetts litigation in *Goodridge* in which the Supreme Judicial Court of Massachusetts held in 2003 that it was a denial of equality for

[32] For the amending legislation see Property (Relationships) Legislation Amendment Act 1999 (NSW); Statute Law Amendment (Relationships) Act 2001 (Vic); Discrimination Law Amendment Act 2002 (Qld); Acts Amendment (Lesbian and Gay Law Reform) Act 2002 (WA); Acts Amendment (Equality of Status) Act 2003 (WA); Law Reform (Gender, Sexuality and De Facto Relationships) Act 2003 (NT); Relationships Act 2003 (Tas); Relationships (Consequential Amendments) Act 2003 (Tas); Legislation (Gay, Lesbian and Transgender) Amendment Act 2003 (ACT); Sexuality Discrimination Legislation Amendment Act 2004 (ACT); Statutes Amendment (Domestic Partners) Act 2006 (SA). In contrast to these developments in State and Territory law, the Australian federal government has not amended laws to recognise same-sex relationships in areas within its exclusive power, however, it has purported to 'ban' same sex marriage: see Marriage Amendment Act 2004 (Aust). See also Millbank, J, 'Recognition of Lesbian and Gay Families in Australian Law – Part One: Couples' (2006) 34 *Federal Law Review* 1, 3; Graycar and Millbank, *ibid.*

[33] The New York Court of Appeals recently upheld an appeal against a judgment that had recognised a Vermont Civil Union for the purpose of the deceased's partner's bringing a wrongful death action in New York: see *Langan v St Vincent's Hospital of New York* 25 AD 3d 90, 802 NYS 2d 476 (2005), reversing 765 NYS 2d 411 (2003). The plaintiff's appeal from the Court of Appeal's decision was dismissed: 817 NYS 2d 625 (2006).

[34] See Marriage Amendment Act 2004 (Aust). Ironically, the government's enactment of a law to this effect may well be seen to have led to a campaign amongst gay men and lesbians in favour of marriage: see Graycar and Millbank, above n 31.

[35] See n 32 above for details of the amending legislation; and see also Millbank, above n 32, and Graycar and Millbank, above n 31.

[36] Note that this is also possible in a jurisdiction, such as Canada, that has developed a substantive equality definition of 'equality': for a clear example, see *Trociuk v British Columbia (Attorney General)* [2003] 1 SCR 835, where the SCC upheld an equality-based claim from a man whose 'right to equality' had been denied by his being excluded from naming his child (with whom he did not live).

same sex couples not to be able to marry.[37] As a remedy, the Court ordered the government of the State of Massachusetts to act to ensure that the identified violation of the state's equal protection clause was remedied. However the legislature then sought an advisory opinion from the Court as to whether enacting a scheme for the introduction of civil unions would be an appropriate remedy. A majority of the sharply divided court rejected this, holding that only marriage could equate the legal status of same sex couples with heterosexual couples.[38]

In South Africa, while the Constitutional Court's decision in *Fourie*, which recognised the rights of gay men and lesbians to marry, has been 'warmly welcomed',[39] it has also been described as using 'a formal equality framework that easily allows gays and lesbians the full benefits of an existing institution'.[40] Beth Goldblatt contrasts this with another recent decision of the Constitutional Court, where that court refused to recognise non-formalised domestic partnerships, something which she argues disadvantages many South African women living in those relationships, who 'remain an underrepresented vulnerable group'.[41] Goldblatt suggests that extending marriage to same sex couples is a much more limited approach than what she suggests would be the 'substantive equality framework' that would be necessary to recognise a group such as disadvantaged cohabiting women, as part of a 'new form of legal regulation of the family'. And, while the UK's Civil Partnership Act 2004 is not the direct result of equality litigation, it was enacted in the wake of that country's adoption of a Human Rights Act. Carl Stychin's compelling critique of the Civil Partnership Act, which he describes as a 'victory for the politics of

---

[37] *Goodridge v Department of Public Health* 798 NE 2d 941 (Mass, 2003).

[38] See *Opinions of the Justices to the Senate* 802 NE2d 565 (Mass, 2004). By contrast, in *Minister of Home Affairs and Another v Fourie and Another* (2005) 60 SA 1 (CC), the Constitutional Court of South Africa unanimously found that the exclusion of same sex couples from marriage was a violation of the equality guarantee of the Constitution. The majority of the Court (O'Regan J dissenting) held that the proper remedy was to give the legislature one year to remedy the situation. O'Regan J would simply have amended the common law definition to include same sex couples within the existing framework of marriage. However, when the South African government responded, they enacted a separate Civil Union Act rather than making any amendments to the Marriage Act. While the Civil Union Act allows for a 'civil union' to be solemnised either as a 'marriage' or as a 'civil partnership', this status is still separate from that under the Marriage Act 1961 (SA), although the rights accorded to each are expressly equated. See Civil Union Act 2006 (SA), ss 2, 8, 13.

[39] Goldblatt, B, 'Case Note: Same Sex Marriage in South Africa: the Constitutional Court's Judgment' (2006) 14 *Feminist Legal Studies* 261, 262.

[40] *Ibid*, at 268.

[41] *Ibid*. Goldblatt is referring here to the decision in *Volks v Robinson and Others* (2005) 5 BCLR 446 (CC).

compromise',[42] notes that it leaves out of account recognition of other forms of excluded relationships, including those involving heterosexual cohabitants:

> Rather than taking the opportunity to create a substantively new relationship form, the Act (virtually) replicates the institution of marriage in all but name.[43]

Stychin continues:

> [T]here is virtually no space for a critical interrogation of the institution of marriage, or the need for an alternative model of legal recognition available to all. There is certainly no acknowledgment…of the various feminist critiques of marriage. Instead a perception of the 'sameness' of same sex relationships overwhelmingly dominates. Inclusion, rather than social change is the message.[44]

But if, instead of litigating via an equality rights framework, or relying on a Human Rights Act modelled on formal equality, the matter is left to community activism, there seem to be other possibilities.[45] A community initiated law reform process in NSW, which resulted in the discussion paper *The Bride Wore Pink*, provides a clear illustration of an approach that bypassed the heterosexual comparator approach (ie, marriage as benchmark).[46] The authors of the discussion paper started from the premise that lesbian and gay relationships were not just queer versions of heterosexual marriage but might instead have some significant features that distinguish them. For example, these relationships exist within a context of homophobia where heterosexual privilege is taken for granted.[47] For these reasons, many gay men and lesbians, whether partnered or not, have found themselves forced to make their own (new) families/ communities, where relationships with their birth families may have soured. For example, irrespective of their couple status, they might have

---

[42]   Stychin, C, 'Not (Quite) a Horse and Carriage: The Civil Partnership Act 2004' (2006) 14 *Feminist Legal Studies* 79, 79.

[43]   *Ibid.*

[44]   *Ibid,* at 81. Note that in July 2006, Susan Wilkinson and Celia Kitzinger sought a declaration in the High Court that their Canadian marriage should be recognised in the UK, but Sir Mark Potter, President of the Family Division, rejected the application: see *Wilkinson v Kitzinger* [2006] EWHC 2022 (Fam).

[45]   This is not to suggest that community activism or other forms of political action in the absence of a Bill of Rights will always be successful strategies for equality-seeking groups, but rather that they may have a greater capacity to transcend formal equality.

[46]   Katzen, H and Shaw, M, *The Bride Wore Pink* (1993), reproduced in (1993) 3 *Australasian Gay & Lesbian Law Journal* 67. A revised version of the paper was produced the following year: see Katzen, H and Shaw, M, *The Bride Wore Pink—Legal Recognition of our Relationships,* 2nd edn (1994), available at: <http://www.glrl.org.au/pdf/major_reports/bride_wore_pink.pdf> (accessed 3 Aug 2006). For further discussion, see Graycar, R and Millbank, J, 'The Bride Wore Pink…To the *Property (Relationships) Legislation Amendment Act 1999*: Relationships Law Reform in New South Wales' (2000) 17 *Canadian Journal of Family Law* 227.

[47]   Katzen and Shaw, 2nd edn, *ibid,* at 34.

close relationships of interdependence with friends whom they might want to recognise for purposes such as medical treatment decision making or as beneficiaries of retirement benefit funds, etc.[48]

The Bride Wore Pink, the discussion paper published by the Gay and Lesbian Rights Lobby, the community organisation that initiated the process, raised questions about issues such as why certain rights and obligations automatically flow from marriage (and, in some cases, other relationships), and why marriage is always presumed to be the benchmark or standard against which other relationships are compared. An underlying theme was a suspicion, clearly grounded in feminism, of marriage as the model upon which other forms of relationship should be modelled. *The Bride Wore Pink* canvassed both the advantages and disadvantages of relationship recognition. For example, the authors questioned why welfare payments presume that people in heterosexual couples share their income and assets, a policy that would disadvantage those cohabiting same-sex couples who choose not to share their income and assets. They were concerned that, as same sex couples had traditionally been marginalised, it was important to ensure that any new regime of recognition supported by the lesbian and gay communities did not replicate and reinforce other exclusions. They also noted that recognition is often welcomed by governments (or courts) only insofar as it shifts financial burdens away from the public toward private obligations, and acknowledged that those who might benefit most from recognition might be those most privileged, ie, those with property.

The Bride Wore Pink proposed the establishment of a presumptive (or opt out) approach: the relationship is recognised if you meet certain criteria unless you opt out by contract, rather than an opt-in approach where a couple has to choose to be registered (the more common registration system that has developed in Europe and North America). This involved a recognition that those most vulnerable are those least likely to formalise their relationships and legal affairs.[49] The overarching guiding principle was that the basis for relationship recognition should be purposive. The kinds of relationships that laws should regulate ought to depend upon the purpose of the law in question. As these purposes vary, so should the type of recognition and obligation. For example, some laws that recognise relationships point to financial dependence or interdependence between the partners, while others are more concerned with emotional connection. Live-in sexual relationships are not the only relationships to give rise to such ties, but they are the relationships that are most likely to give rise to many of them.

---

[48] *Ibid,* at 5, 26.
[49] *Ibid,* at 4–7.

Therefore, it was proposed that live-in partner relationship recognition should be broad based and presumptive. In addition, other forms of close relationships that may give rise to emotional or financial ties in certain circumstances, also warranted some limited recognition, but it was considered that those situations may not be so predictable, nor so widespread. The government in effect implemented these recommendations in 1999,[50] and the outcome is that NSW law now recognises same sex couples in the same way as married or heterosexual non-married couples for most purposes, and in addition, others who are not in couples but in a defined 'close personal relationship' have a more limited range of rights and obligations under some (but not as many) NSW laws.[51]

The developments in NSW, and ultimately, in all the Australian States and Territories, seem to be an example of what Galligan and Morton refer to as a 'rights revolution by mainly political means'.[52] We cannot say that this broad form of recognition of diverse relationships could only have happened in a jurisdiction without a Bill of Rights: after all, France has developed the *Pacte Civil de Solidarité* (PaCS), a limited form of registered partnership for both same sex and opposite sex couples, and France has a long history of recognition of formal equality.[53] But the argument may nonetheless apply to those jurisdictions where rights debates have taken place in courts and through litigation relying on a constitutional or

---

[50] The implementation of these proposals followed an election in which the governing Australian Labor Party was returned with an increased majority, and resolved to legislate without there being any significant period of debate or discussion. For a detailed account of the passage of the bill through Parliament (where it was not opposed by the main opposition party), see Graycar and Millbank, above n 46. See also Millbank, J and Sant, K, 'A Bride in Her Every-Day Clothes: Same Sex Relationship Recognition in NSW' (2000) 22 *Sydney Law Review* 181; Shaw, J, 'Law Reform Happens' (1999) 24 *Alternative Law Journal* 247; Millbank, J and Morgan, W, 'Let Them Eat Cake and Ice Cream: Wanting Something "More" From the Relationship Recognition Menu' in R Wintemute and M Andenaes (eds), *Legal Recognition Of Same-Sex Partnerships: A Study of National, European, and International Law* (Oxford, Hart Publishing, 2001).

[51] See Property (Relationships) Act 1984 (NSW). Section 4(1) defines a 'de facto relationship' as two adult persons who 'live together as a couple' and are not married to one another or related by family. The interdependent category is defined by s 5(1) as a 'close personal relationship' between 'two adult persons, whether or not related by family, who are living together, one or each of whom provides the other with domestic support and personal care', where that care is not provided for a fee or reward. While the ACT was the first to have legislation that recognised people in non-conjugal relationships, and included non-cohabiting couples for limited purposes (see Domestic Relationships Act 1994), other States that have followed suit (and extended the form of recognition considerably) are Victoria (some categories of benefit require cohabitation while others do not) and Tasmania: see Millbank, above n 32.

[52] See Galligan and Morton, above n 3.

[53] For a historical discussion of the PaCS, see Martin, C and Théry, I, 'The PaCS and Marriage and Cohabitation in France' (2001) 15 *International Journal of Law, Policy and the Family* 135; and for a more recent discussion of the limitations of PaCS, see Borrillo, D, 'Who is Breaking with Tradition? The Legal Recognition of Same-Sex Partnership in France and the Question of Modernity' (2005) 17 *Yale Journal of Law and Feminism* 89, esp 90–92.

statutory right to equality (of which the United States is the prime example), rather than through political and legislative processes.

Abortion

A second example that we canvass, and one that continues to be an issue in many countries, including those with Bills of Rights or equality guarantees, is abortion. Access to safe, publicly funded, termination services has been a fundamental goal for feminists over many years. An examination of the legal and political debate about such access provides an opportunity for some interesting reflections on the role of constitutionally entrenched rights. How have constitutionally entrenched rights assisted or hindered access to abortion? What is the role of equality rights in articulating the right to safe termination in both the judicial and political arenas?

In the United States, abortion is treated as a privacy issue[54] and is almost constantly under siege by the vocal anti-choice minority. In Canada, constitutional litigation led to the criminal prohibition on abortion being lifted in 1988, relying on the right to 'life, liberty and security of the person', with little or no attempt to recriminalise it since.[55] In Australia, while abortion is not a matter of constitutional or statutory equality law, there are a number of different contexts in which legal issues about abortion arise, and via which the practice is regulated.[56] In any event, abortion is quite a common procedure in Australia: the national health insurance system pays for about 80,000 terminations per year.[57]

Until recently, most Australian States retained some form of criminal prohibition on abortion, the gist of which was that an 'unlawful' abortion is an offence.[58] However, an abortion is 'not unlawful' when it is considered necessary for the woman's health (which has been very broadly interpreted to include both medical and socio-economic issues).[59] This is

---

[54] See *Roe v Wade* 410 US 113 (1973) and the case law that has followed it, including *Planned Parenthood v Casey* 505 US 833 (1992).

[55] *R v Morgentaler* [1988] 1 SCR 30.

[56] See *The Hidden Gender of Law*, 2nd edn, above n 2, ch 8.

[57] National Health and Medical Research Council, *An Information Paper on Termination of Pregnancy in Australia* (Canberra, NH&MRC, 1996) 3; see also Pratt, A, Biggs, A and Buckmaster, L, *How Many Abortions Are There in Australia? A Discussion of Abortion Statistics, Their Limitations, and Options for Improved Statistical Collection* (Canberra, Social Policy Section, Department of Parliamentary Services, Research Brief No 9, 2005), available at: <http://www.aph.gov.au/library/pubs/rb/2004–05/05rb09.pdf> (accessed 10 Aug 2006).

[58] See, eg Crimes Act 1900 (NSW), ss 82–83; Crimes Act 1958 (Vic) ss 65–66.

[59] See the case law discussed in *The Hidden Gender of Law*, 2nd edn, above n 2, at 201–2.

based on the use of the common law defence of necessity.[60] Prosecutions have been rare: until August 2006, it was probably 30 years since anyone in NSW or Victoria was prosecuted solely for the reason that they performed an abortion.[61] However, in Western Australia, two doctors were prosecuted for performing an unlawful abortion in 1998,[62] and this led a politician, the Hon Cheryl Davenport, a long time advocate of equality for women, to use the opportunity to try to remove the offence from that state's criminal laws.[63] Her campaign succeeded and Western Australian law now provides that informed consent of the woman is the sole legal requirement for an abortion under 20 weeks (a more regulated process operates for later than 20 weeks).[64] Around the same time, the ACT adopted a law that placed a number of severe restrictions on the availability of abortion, but only two years later (2002), the criminal prohibition was removed entirely and abortion taken out of the Crimes Act.[65]

Most recently, early in 2006, an effective ban on the use of RU486 (a drug used in the non-surgical termination of pregnancy) was lifted after women from all the parties represented in the national Parliament got together and organised a conscience vote (ie, members were not obliged to vote in line with their party).[66] What we want to draw attention to is the extent to which a discourse of women's right to substantive equality was used in the parliamentary debates surrounding all these changes; that is, notwithstanding the absence of a constitutional equality right, the language

---

[60] For many years, the law had been considered governed by the decisions of the courts respectively in *R v Davidson* [1969] VR 667, and *R v Wald* (1971) DCR (NSW) 25, which both elaborated on the use of the defence of necessity in the determination of whether an abortion is 'unlawful'.

[61] In August 2006, a Dr Sood was convicted of performing an unlawful abortion, the first case of its kind in 25 years (see *Sydney Morning Herald* (24 Aug 2006) 1). The jury found Sood had administered an abortifacient and sent the five-months-pregnant woman home, to return the next day. The woman went into labour and delivered a still born foetus. The prosecution seems to have been motivated by this doctor's practices, rather than by the fact that she performed an abortion. Nonetheless, she has now become the first person convicted in NSW, the most populous state, of performing an unlawful abortion in many years. For a history of abortion law in Australia see Teasdale, L, 'Confronting the Fear of Being "Caught": Discourses on Abortion in Western Australia' (1999) 22 *University of New South Wales Law Journal* 60, 65. And see also, more generally, Graycar and Morgan, *The Hidden Gender of Law*, 2nd edn, above n 2, at 200–02.

[62] For a discussion of the circumstances in which this occurred, see Teasdale, *ibid*.

[63] This campaign is described in Teasdale, *ibid*, at 63.

[64] Acts Amendment (Abortion) Act 1998 (WA).

[65] Health Regulation (Maternal Health Information) Act 1998 (ACT). The Crimes (Abolition of Offence of Abortion) Act 2002 (ACT) removed the offence of abortion from the Territory's Crimes Act 1900 (ACT).

[66] Therapeutic Goods Amendment (Repeal of Ministerial Responsibility for Approval of RU486) Act 2006 (Aust). For a detailed account of the history of this, in particular from the perspective of its being presented as a cross party women's coalition, see Allison, L, ABC Radio National Perspective (28 Mar 2007), available at: http://www.abc.net.au/rn/perspective/stories/2007/1881868.htm#transcript.

of equality can still be politically salient. In the RU486 debate, some members relied explicitly on a discourse of equality, others did so more implicitly. So, for example, arguing in favour of lifting the ban on RU486 in Australia, one member of parliament noted:

> What today's abortion debate really centres on is how much weight is given to the rights of the woman over the rights of the unborn child. So it is a rights debate — complete rights, unfettered rights, limited rights, equal rights and so on, but it is a rights debate. And that is exactly what we are debating here today: the rights of women to have abortions by yet another method.[67]

Similarly, parliamentary debates surrounding the decriminalisation of abortion in the ACT centred on the reproductive rights of women and women's equality as requiring gender-specific rights and protections. Often the arguments in favour of decriminalisation explicitly rejected formalist approaches to equality, in order to argue in favour of women's rights to reproductive freedom:

> Responsibility in parenthood is still one of the fundamental differences between the roles of men and women in life. Whatever view you hold on that point – whether you believe that women must be primary caregivers...the responsibilities of parenthood have, on the whole, a much greater impact on women than on men.[68]

> My view has always been that access to safe, legal abortion is a human rights issue for women. ... Women must have the right to make reproductive decisions for themselves and the community should respect and support such decisions.[69]

> Against the blind inertia of a systemic oppression, women have had to construct their own positive view of what it means to be a woman, and then to change hearts and minds – and we are still doing it. One of the battles we continue to fight is for the right of self-determination over our bodies. We have laws that say that it is illegal to discriminate on the basis of gender. ... It is completely unacceptable that a woman seeking to exercise her right to decide when to have a child faces the possibility of 10 years in prison as a consequence.[70]

We suggest that there may be some advantages in the absence of a formal constitutional right to equality (or, indeed, privacy or due process), which, first of all allows the language of equality to be used in discussion of access to abortion, and in particular, allows, indeed requires, a move beyond formal equality.

---

[67] McGauran, J (Liberal), Senate, *Parliamentary Debates (Hansard)* (8 Feb 2006) 142.

[68] Tucker, K (Greens), ACT Legislative Assembly, *Parliamentary Debates (Hansard)* (21 Aug 2002) 2512.

[69] Stanhope, J (Labor), ACT Legislative Assembly, *Parliamentary Debates (Hansard)* (21 Aug 2002) 2544, 2546.

[70] Dundas, R (Australian Democrats), ACT Legislative Assembly, *Parliamentary Debates (Hansard)* (21 Augt 2002) 2547–8. The equality rhetoric in Western Australia is canvassed in Teasdale, above n 61.

TALKING ABOUT EQUALITY IN A LAW REFORM CONTEXT

The question remains as to whether a substantive equality analysis can be expressly articulated in formal Bills of Rights. This was raised in the Australian Law Reform Commission's reference on Equality Before the Law in the early 1990s,[71] to which we were both appointed as part-time Commissioners. The recommendations made by the Commission contemplated the possibility of a Bill of Rights that would successfully foster the idea of substantive equality, rather than consigning all constitutional equality instruments to being comparison-based or guaranteeing nothing more than formal 'equal treatment' – as is the case in both the ACT and Victorian Bills.

The Commission recommended that the Federal Parliament enact an Equality Act.[72] This was meant to be a mid-stage strategy, prior to considering the enactment of an entrenched equality guarantee. The Commission was unanimous in its view that in recommending an Equality Act, it was essential to define what was meant by that concept. To that end, the Commission adopted a definition of equality in the following terms:

> [I]n assessing whether a law, policy, program, practice or decision is inconsistent with equality in law, regard must be had to
>
> —the historical and current social, economic and legal inequalities experienced on the ground of gender
>
> —the historical and current practices of the body challenged and the extent to which those practices have contributed to or perpetuate the inequalities experienced
>
> —the history of the rule or practice being challenged.[73]

We hoped that having an understanding of equality in these terms, ie, a contextualised approach that drew on the substantive equality jurisprudence of the Supreme Court of Canada,[74] would discourage a court from unthinkingly adopting a formal equality approach. So, for example, such a

---

[71] ALRC, *Equality Before the Law: Women's Access to the Legal System, Interim Report No 67* (Sydney, ALRC, 1994); ALRC, *Equality Before the Law: Justice for Women, Report No 69, Part I* (Sydney, ALRC, 1994); ALRC 69 Part II, above n 22.

[72] See ALRC 69 Part II, *ibid*.

[73] *Ibid*, at 66.

[74] Compare *Andrews v Law Society of British Columbia* [1989] 1 SCR 143; Majury, D, 'Equality and Discrimination According to the Supreme Court of Canada' (1991) 4 *Canadian Journal of Women and the Law* 407.

definition would hopefully mean that programs designed to redress the disadvantage of women in a particular area were not declared invalid as a breach of men's equality rights.[75]

However, while all members of the Commission agreed on the definition of equality, with our colleague Hilary Charlesworth, we disagreed with the other Commissioners on the final recommendations. We dissented on two crucial issues.[76] We argued that the proposed Equality Act should extend to equality-denying actions that occurred in the 'private' sphere,[77] and that it should *not* be gender-neutral. We had no illusions that any Parliament was likely to enact a gender specific law directed at women's inequality – a law that on its face sought to protect only the equality rights of women – but we did think it necessary to identify clearly the problem that needed to be addressed, to name it, and to generate a debate about it.[78] The problem was (and remains) that women experience inequality; this is not a gender-neutral problem and a gender-neutral response is not likely to address that problem effectively. We were also concerned that there was some inconsistency between the majority's adoption of a substantive definition of equality in the recommended Equality Act, and the Act's proposed application to women and men on a gender-neutral basis, as we believed that this obscured the issue to which we were responding: women's inequality. We questioned the extent to which men were disadvantaged by reference to their sex, as opposed, say to their class or racialised status, and we took the view that men already had the opportunity to challenge laws for 'discrimination' under the Sex Discrimination Act 1984, which, under the Commission's proposals, would have remained operative.[79] In terms of international human rights law, we sought support for our position from the CEDAW convention which expressly targets the

---

[75] Compare, eg *Proudfoot v ACT Board of Health* (1992) EOC 92–417; and see generally *The Hidden Gender of Law*, 2nd edn, above n 2, at 35–40.

[76] See ALRC, above n 22, at ch 16: 'Minority View with Respect to Certain Aspects of the Equality Act'.

[77] Compare the South African constitution which eschews the more common 'state action' or 'government action' limit and applies to natural persons as well: Constitution of the Republic of South Africa, s 8(2). For a more general discussion of the South African constitution, see Jagwanth and Murray, above n 10. See also Jagwanth and Murray, above n 11. For a critique of how the state/government action doctrine has affected the availability of abortion, see Lessard, H, 'The Construction of Health Care and the Ideology of the Private in Canadian Constitutional Law' (1993) 2 *Annals of Health Law* 121; and see more generally *The Hidden Gender of Law*, 2nd edn, above n 2, at ch 2.

[78] We reflected on this some years later at a Women's Constitutional Convention: see Graycar, R, Morgan, J and Charlesworth, H, 'Equality for Women Under the Constitution?', paper presented at the Women's Constitutional Convention (Jan 1998), archived at: http://pandora.nla.gov.au/nph-arch/H1998-Sep-2/http://www.womensconv.dynamite.com.au/threept.htm.

[79] It is well documented that men use this Act quite frequently to challenge services designed expressly for women: see, eg the cases noted in *The Hidden Gender of Law*, 2nd edn, above n 2, at 38, n 45.

problems of women's inequality.[80] We regret that we were unable to convince our fellow Commissioners to join with us in that approach.

CONCLUDING THOUGHTS

We have tried to illustrate ways in which one can meaningfully engage with the notion of equality for women without necessarily doing so via a constitutional/statutory equality provision. Perhaps more controversially, we are also interested in exploring whether we can be sure that women and other outsider groups are necessarily worse off in the absence of a (formal) right to equality. As noted above, we do not have much confidence that the statutory Bills of Rights adopted in the ACT and Victoria are likely to deliver substantive equality. Yet the absence of such constitutional guarantees does not seem to impede the ability to conduct debates about concrete issues of women's equality such as abortion, and other issues important to equality-seeking groups such as those demanding recognition of alternative family forms, in ways that eschew formal equality altogether and that provide discursive spaces in which to articulate concerns about substantive inequality.

---

[80] Compare *Aldridge v Booth* (1988) EOC 92–222.

6

Haunting (In)Equalities

KARIN VAN MARLE

There is always the danger, for the white liberal imagination, that politics simply spoils matters.[1]

INTRODUCTION

IN THIS CHAPTER I critically investigate the concept of equality. Taking into account the limits of the law, law's inherent tendency to reduce and exclude, but importantly also its tendency to self-destruct, I consider to what extent, if any, legal or constitutional protection of equality can address the issue of women's subordination, exclusion and inequality. The contemplation goes wider than merely the protection of equality, but turns on law's capacity to partake in political and social transformation in a way that does not merely affirm the status quo and reduce transformation to mere repetition and reproduction of the past and the present. I reflect on equality against the background also of Jacques Derrida's writings on friendship – his insight that all friendships turn on exclusion should make us cautious towards the promise of equality. Added to that, his exposure of autoimmunity in democracy, in other words its tendency to self-destruct, to destroy itself from within, problematises the very notion and discourse of equality.

The specific context for this consideration is equality as it has been entrenched in the South African Constitution of 1996. It is generally accepted that the South African Constitution not only protects formal equality but goes further to protect substantive equality by addressing material circumstances of South Africa's past and present.[2] The connection

---

[1] Rose, L, 'A Use For the Stones' *London Review of Books* (20 Apr 2006) 22.
[2] Albertyn, A and Kentridge, J, 'Introducing the Right to Equality in the Interim Constitution' (1994) 10 *South African Journal on Human Rights* 149; L'Heureux-Dubé, C, 'Making a Difference: The Pursuit of Equality and a Compassionate Justice' (1997) 13 *South African Journal on Human Rights* 335.

between substantive equality and the notion of 'transformative constitutionalism' should be noted.[3] Transformative constitutionalism means different things to different people. The term was coined in a 1998 article by US critical legal scholar, Karl Klare,[4] and since then the notion of transformative constitutionalism has been central to post-apartheid constitutional and jurisprudential discourse. Klare published his article as a tribute to the late Etienne Mureinik, a South African administrative law scholar, who called for the Constitution to be seen as a 'bridge' that would enable the democratic transition from authoritarianism to a culture of justification.[5] Klare defines transformative constitutionalism as follows:

> By transformative constitutionalism I mean a long-term project of constitutional enactment, interpretation, and enforcement committed (not in isolation of course, but in a historical context of conducive political developments) to transform a country's political and social institutions and power relationships in a democratic, participatory, and egalitarian direction...it connotes an enterprise of inducing large-scale social change through nonviolent political processes grounded in law.[6]

According to Klare, the South Africa constitution is not a traditional liberal document, but rather post-liberal, because of features like the inclusion of social rights and substantive equality, affirmative state duties, horizontality, participatory governance, multiculturalism and historical self-consciousness. Klare calls for a progressive politics to be followed by South African legal scholars. He challenges South African Constitutional Court judges by saying that:

> Future generations will judge the Constitutional Court by the contribution it makes to achieving equality, advancing social justice, and deepening the culture of democracy, multiracialism, and respect for human dignity. *How tightly the Court squares its arguments with textbook canons and maxims will be far less important at the end of the day.* (emphasis added)[7]

However, we should stop and ask to what extent, if at all, law and legal practices in general, but in particular South African law and legal practices, can be, as Klare argues, 'a foundation of democratic and responsive social transformation'.[8] Isn't law as a structure too limited, too conservative to have the capacity for this envisioned transformation? For Klare, the law could be a tool of social transformation if we give an 'updated, politicized

---

[3] Klare, K, 'Legal Culture and Transformative Constitutionalism' (1998) 14 *South African Journal on Human Rights* 146.
[4] *Ibid.*
[5] See Mureinik, E, 'A Bridge to Where? Introducing the Interim Bill of Rights' (1994) 10 *South African Journal on Human Rights* 31.
[6] Klare, above n 3, at 150.
[7] *Ibid*, at 171–2.
[8] *Ibid*, at 188.

account of the rule of law'.[9] As he and others have noted, the South African Constitution has 'massively egalitarian commitments', but these are superimposed on a 'formalistic legal culture without a strong tradition of substantive political discussion and contestation through the medium of legal discourses'.[10] Even if law as a system can sustain such transformative efforts (and I shall be questioning that capacity), South African legal culture presently is one based on legal formalism and accordingly a law/politics divide. Not only the limits of the law but also the limits of legal culture, and more specifically the participants within the formalist South African legal culture, might hinder the optimistic ideals of transformative constitutionalism.

One could highlight (at least) two diverse accounts of transformative constitutionalism in current South African legal discourse. One is a more or less instrumental/functionalist account that focuses on the creation of an egalitarian society and is strongly connected to substantive equality.[11] Another account takes a critical distance from such a linear understanding and argues for an approach that treats the notion of transformative constitutionalism itself as unstable and indeterminate, open for continuous change and contestation.[12] For the purposes of this chapter, the connection between transformative constitutionalism and substantive equality is significant, as well as the two accounts of transformative constitutionalism as they bear on the understanding and application of equality.

Legal scholars have criticised the South African Constitutional Court for placing dignity at the heart of South African equality jurisprudence.[13] One line of critique originates from the connection between substantive equality and transformative constitutionalism and argues that the emphasis on dignity might deviate from the centrality of material change; another is closer to the more tentative approach to transformative constitutionalism and argues for a complex understanding of equality that could take multiple values into account. I regard the understanding of transformative constitutionalism and substantive equality as solely focused on material reform as a functionalist/instrumentalist understanding of equality and

---

[9] *Ibid.*

[10] *Ibid*, at 153.

[11] Albertyn, A and Goldblatt, B, 'Facing the Challenge of Transformation: Difficulties in the Development of an Indigenous Jurisprudence of Equality' (1998) 14 *South African Journal on Human Rights* 248; De Vos, P, 'Grootboom, the Rights of Access to Housing and Substantive Equality as Contextual Fairness' (2001) 17 *South African Journal on Human Rights* 258; Pieterse, M, 'What Do We Mean When We Talk About Transformative Constitutionalism?' (2005) 20 *South African Public Law* 155.

[12] Van der Walt, AJ, 'Dancing with Codes – Protecting, Developing and Deconstructing Property Rights in a Constitutional State' (2001) 18 *South African Law Journal* 258; Botha, H, 'Metaphoric Reasoning and Transformative Constitutionalism' (2002) *Journal for South African Law* 612 (pt 1) and (2003) *Journal for South African Law* 20 (pt 2).

[13] Albertyn and Goldblatt, above n 11; De Vos, above n 11.

transformative constitutionalism.[14] To counter this approach I consider the approach of 'complex equality' put forward by South African legal scholar Henk Botha,[15] as well as an 'ethical' approach to equality.[16] The argument for 'complex equality' entails, amongst other things, that a multiplicity of values and rights must come into play in the interpretation of equality. Botha argues that in some cases dignity might be the best value to enhance equality, but in other cases not.

An ethical interpretation of equality takes the limits of the law, the distinction between law and justice, as a starting point. At the heart of ethical equality lies the recognition of the impossibility of law, and in this context, equality (formal and substantive), to serve justice fully. The recognition of this impossibility is not nihilistic or defeatist, but rather an incentive actively to pursue better ways of serving equality. The argument for ethical equality rests on the necessity of a vibrant public sphere, active politics and a thick version of democracy. Politics, or rather the notion of the political,[17] is central to an ethical understanding of equality. Connections and disconnections between equality, democracy and difference need to be analysed. Coming back to the notion of transformative constitutionalism, my view is that equality should not only go beyond a formal protection, but should also entail more than a functionalist/instrumental aim of creating an egalitarian society. This ideal is of course tempered by the concern about law's capacity to encompass politics, in other words to play an active part in social transformation. I agree accordingly with a more tentative reading of transformative constitutionalism and am cautious about the potential of substantive equality to make a radical difference to women's lives. Drucilla Cornell's distinction between evolution and transformation must be recalled in this context. For Cornell, transformation must also mean a change of subjects themselves and not merely the change of a system.[18] Law, because of its incapacity to engage in reflexivity, cannot achieve such radical transformation of subjects. I reconsider the discourse on dignity in light of a recent article of Cornell's in which she considers the 'politics of the heart'.[19] Although I agree with the critiques of the Constitutional Court's negation of politics, some of the

---

[14] Pieterse, above n 11. See also Schlag, P, 'Rights in the Postmodern Condition' in A Sarat and TJ Kearns (eds), *Legal Rights. Historical and Philosophical Perspectives* (Ann Arbor, University of Michigan Press, 1997) 263, for a discussion of what he calls 'an instrumental aesthetic'.

[15] Botha, H, 'Equality, Dignity and the Politics of Interpretation' (2004) 19 *South African Public Law* 724.

[16] Van Marle, K, 'Equality: An Ethical Interpretation' (2000) 3 *Journal for Contemporary Roman Dutch Law* 595.

[17] Lacoue Labarthe, P and Nancy, JL, *Retreating the Political* (London, Routledge, 1997); Van der Walt, JWG, *Law and Sacrifice* (London, Birkbeck Press, 2005).

[18] Cornell, D, *Transformations* (New York, Routledge, 1993).

[19] Cornell, D, 'The Solace of Resonance' (2005) 20 *Hypatia* 215.

stark critiques of dignity in favour of material concerns to my mind sometimes evade the reality of hurt and loneliness – non-material concerns that are also affected when our equality is infringed. To my mind, Cornell captures these concerns accurately with the phrase, the 'politics of the heart'.

I situate these reflections on equality within the context of a wider discourse on legal memory, the memorial and the monumental constitution and the idea of slowness, which I also connect with the two approaches to transformative constitutionalism and approaches to equality.[20] I have previously argued for an approach of slowness to law and legal interpretation as an approach that would be more attentive to particularities, to context and lived experience. I have contrasted this approach with traditional/formalist approaches to law – that an emphasis on law's generality and universality will result in speedy decisions that negate the complexities and nuances of life. In that context I have distinguished between two divergent approaches to language and memory. The one, by being aware of the materiality of life, recognises the multiple meanings of words and holds the past as something that will always be open for reinterpretation – remembering and memory ask for slow contemplation in order to notice the specificity, the detail and therefore the complexity of meaning and of events. The other approach, by focusing more on abstract ideas and grand notions of the past, monumentalises in a quick and solid fashion, fixing and closing further reflection.

My initial reflection on slowness was followed by an engagement with writings that connected the distinction between memorial and monumental to South African political memory and also to the South African constitution. My earlier writings highlighted the monumental and memorial aspects of the constitution and constitutional decisions. My initial reflections showed stronger support for memorial constitutionalism in contrast to monumental, celebratory and optimistic constitutionalism. Memorial and monument thus came to be used as metaphors for not only the South African constitution, but for constitutionalism as such. I extend their metaphoric use here to the notion of equality and distinguish between monumental and memorial equality, which is connected also to the distinction between monumental and memorial constitutionalism. I argue below that not only formal equality but, quite ironically, also the project of

---

[20] Van Marle, K, 'Law's Time, Particularity and Slowness' (2003) 19 *South African Journal on Human Rights* 245; 'Lives of Action, Thinking and Revolt – A Feminist Call for Politics and Becoming in Post-Apartheid South Africa' (2004) 19 *South African Pubic Law* 605; 'Constitution as Archive' in Veitch, S (ed) *Law and the Politics of Reconciliation* (Aldershot, Ashgate, 2007) 215.

substantive equality and transformative constitutionalism can be associated with approaches based on chronology and linearity, and thus monumental constitutionalism.

In this chapter, however, I also critically consider the distinction between monumental and memorial itself and question my earlier alliance with memorial in light of the slippage between the two – when does memorial become monumental, monumental memorial? Recalling an argument that focuses on the limits of the law, on law's incapacity to do more than what the formalist or positivist expects, I contemplate the metaphorical use of monument and memorial in light of formal and substantive equality. We should consider if formal equality isn't an approach that is more honest about what law can do (in other words its limits) than the optimism embedded in substantive notions of equality. With reference to the discourse on substantive equality and the critique of dignity jurisprudence, I expose how memorial can slip into monument. Finally, I reconsider equality in light of Derridean notions of friendship and democracy, and ask if equality, like democracy, isn't always already destroying itself from within. Are we not always left with the haunting of inequality?

TRANSFORMATIVE CONSTITUTIONALISM AND THE LIMITS OF THE LAW

I have referred above to Karl Klare's vision of transformative constitutionalism. Klare argues that because of the post-liberal features of the South African Constitution, we need post-liberal/transformative approaches to constitutionalism and human rights. Because the South African constitution is open to a 'new imagination and self-reflection about legal method, analysis and reasoning', 'new conceptions of judicial role and responsibility' should follow.[21] However, Klare is well aware of the conservative state of South African legal culture. With the term 'legal culture' he refers to 'professional sensibilities, habits of mind, and intellectual reflexes'.[22] Participants within a specific legal culture will quite often be unaware of their own situatedness and accept their culture as natural and fixed. It is important to note that with the term 'conservative', Klare does not refer to political ideology, but means a cautious tradition of analysis. He notes that:

> even the most optimistic proponents of progressive social change often display the same jurisprudential habits of mind as shown by their more pessimistic or politically conservative colleagues[23]

---

[21]   Klare, above n 3, at 156.
[22]   *Ibid*, at 168.
[23]   *Ibid*.

and continues to describe legal interpretation in South Africa as 'highly structured, technicist, literal and rule-bound'.[24] It is the combination of a formalist legal culture and commitments to substantive equality that results in the most instrumental versions of transformative constitutionalism where law, even though combined with material reform, is still divorced from that which goes beyond mere accommodation. But then we should ask after law's capacity to go beyond.

Emilios Christodoulidis focuses on the limits of the law and its consequent incapacity to contain politics.[25] His argument is directed primarily at the civic republican argument which holds that the law, and in particular a constitution, contains politics and substantiates community. He shows how civic republicans rely on the notion of indeterminacy as exposed by critical legal scholars, and accordingly also criticises the tendency of critical legal studies to equate law with politics. Arguments pertaining to the ability of a constitution to contain politics and to substantiate community are quite common within the South African context of transforming from an authoritarian past to a democratic future. Certain understandings of transformative constitutionalism and, related to it, substantive equality, share this kind of 'constitutional optimism'.[26]

Christodoulidis highlights two essential requirements that have to be met for the containment thesis to hold true: firstly that the law must be able to 'pick up' all voices without excluding anyone, and secondly that these voices must not be transformed, re-aligned or distorted by their containment in the law.[27] Regarding the first requirement (that the law is able to include all voices), civic republicans believe that the deliberative process is open and attuned to all voices. Regarding the second requirement (that the law must include all voices without re-aligning or transforming them), Christodoulidis notes that individuals can only claim to be self-determinant insofar as they are able to revise and alter the terms of social life.[28] No external constraints should stand in the way of our self-revisionary powers and the institutions that provide for our self-determination should not have any such constraints. An understanding of substantive equality that focuses on the ability of law and a court applying law to take difference and material and political circumstances and factors into account might be seen to rely on an idea of containment, that law is able fully to represent all voices and include the previously excluded.

---

[24] *Ibid.*
[25] Christodoulidis, EA, *Law and Reflexive Politics* (Dordrecht, Kluwer,1998).
[26] See Christodoulidis, EA, 'Constitutional Irresolution: Law and the Framing of Civil Society' (2003) 9 *European Law Journal* 401.
[27] Christodoulidis, above n 25, at 62.
[28] *Ibid*, at 63.

If law provides for the self-revision of a community, the law itself must not prevent the possibilities for change. Civic republicans must then treat law as 'malleable, as open to reflexivity, as capable of self-revision'.[29] Christodoulidis explains that this is the reason for the references in civic republicanism to the work of critical legal studies. Their own argument requires them to treat the law as self-revisionary, open to meet specific, and even competing, political objectives. For civic republicans, legal indeterminacy ensures the space for politics, with immanent critique as the mode of political contestation and action. They argue that, because law is indeterminate, it can accommodate political challenge and in that way it contains the potential for the self-revision of the community.[30] This is more or less critical legal scholar Karl Klare's vision of transformative constitutionalism explained above. Christodoulidis, however, opposes the inter-connections between politics, community and law – the invitation 'to reconceive all that is political as legal'. He stands critical towards the attempt of critical legal scholars (like Karl Klare) to disrupt the legal system's tendency of assimilation and rationalisation by seeking deviations and contradictions as intellectual and political opportunities that can be drawn from the system itself.[31] Christodoulidis distinguishes between what he calls simple inertia and structural inertia. While the former can be transformed from within, the latter cannot.

Legal scholars who follow the framework of civic republicans and critical legal scholars make the mistake of attributing containment and reflexivity to law.[32] Although simple inertia (one source of normalisation) can be countered, deep-seated structural inertia cannot. Because of structural inertia, challenges will always be dealt with so as to accord with:

> already existing or accepted meaning, always already normalised, kept within the confines of what legal expectations can read as conceivable alternatives, always hedged in, always tamed.[33]

Christodoulidis quotes Luhman, stating that in the legal system 'the unknown is assimilated to the known, the new to the old, the surprising to the familiar'.[34] Indeterminacy cannot provide for political contestation as such because the indeterminacy itself is fixed and framed by legal concepts and assumptions. Reflecting on transformative constitutionalism and substantive equality one must ask whether we are not attributing more to

---

[29]   *Ibid.*
[30]   *Ibid*, at 64.
[31]   *Ibid*, at 211–12.
[32]   *Ibid*, at 220.
[33]   *Ibid*, at 222.
[34]   *Ibid*, at 221; Luhman, N, 'Meaning as Sociology's Basic Concept' in *Essays on Self-Reference* (New York, Columbia University Press, 1990) 33.

law's capacity than we should. And in doing this, aren't we merely erecting another monument in order to celebrate, while forgetting the haunting of the excluded, the unequals?

To recapture my argument – I have indicated above that of the many responses and engagements with the notion of transformative constitutionalism, two streams can be highlighted. One line of response to transformative constitutionalism in light of the bridge metaphor is to view it as a linear, chronological process that should strive towards the creation of an egalitarian society in which social justice is served to all.[35] This response shows a narrow interpretation of transformative constitutionalism with an end result in sight and a certain instrumental politics (economics) at play. A danger of this approach is that it places too much emphasis on the public face of transformation and neglects the transformation of private law, with the result of protecting the status quo, for example property law and the law of contract.[36] Another line of response is one that problematises the metaphor of the bridge as a one-way only device and refuses the instrumentality of that version.[37] By ignoring the call for progressive politics, the former response reduces the notion of transformative constitutionalism and limits the potential of the ideal inherent in the notion. Drawing on Christoudoulidis, I ask whether even the latter approach might be making too much of law, by attributing to law the ability to contain politics, aspirations for community, and our ideals for transformation/change.

Following the distinction between monuments and memorials and taking it to transformative constitutionalism, one may argue that the reading of transformative constitutionalism in a linear and instrumental fashion could be coupled with the monumental constitution. The approach calling for more tentativeness and progressive politics could be coupled with the memorial constitution. However, as indicated above, I ask whether the danger of slipping into a monumentalism is also present in this approach. Below I consider whether the distinction between monument and memorial should itself be scrutinised with reference to South African equality jurisprudence, in particular the notion of substantive equality. Before doing that, however, I will refer to Jacques Derrida's reflections on friendship, his problematisation of how we conceive of friendship traditionally and his call for another kind of friendship that he phrases as 'a democracy to come'. Could we hope for an equality to come that could entail more than the failures of all present protections? I also recall Derrida's thoughts on

---

[35] Albertyn and Goldblatt, above n 11.

[36] See, eg Van der Walt, A, 'The Public Aspect of Private Property' (2004) 19 *South African Public Law* 676; Van der Walt, above n 17; Barnard, AJ, *A Critical Legal Argument for Contractual Justice in the South African Law of Contract* (LLD thesis, University of Pretoria, 2005).

[37] Van der Walt, above n 12; Botha, above n 15.

democracy's self-destruction, which can be seen as an extension of his work on democracy developed, amongst others, in *The Politics of Friendship*. I ask whether equality, like democracy, may always be at risk because of a possible self-destructive nature. These insights should inform our thoughts on equality, or at the very least push us toward further and ongoing critique.

THE POLITICS OF FRIENDSHIP AND DEMOCRATIC SUICIDE

In *The Politics of Friendship*, Derrida exposes the betrayal of 'democratic equality' by exposing how all friendships turn on exclusion.[38] All friendships in fact become nothing but relations of fraternity, 'naturalized friendship'.[39] Derrida is concerned with the possibilities of moving beyond the logic of fraternisation and, as Thomson notes, with the question of what kind of political thought can be organised around the category of friendship.[40] Is the impossibility of pure friendships similarly true for equality? If all friendships ultimately become exclusive by choosing/selecting/preferring, are all equalities tainted on account of the same logic? And could one argue that this is true for equality per se, whether one follows formal, substantive, complex or ethical equality? For Derrida, responsibility and judgement come into play only where one is beyond the predictable workings of a specific programme or rule. Fraternity is then nothing but the becoming irresponsible of friendship. Friendship based on a natural bond or allegiance amongst brothers disables responsibility.[41] Isn't equality, when it is based on nothing but a formal protection or an instrumental aim of transformation, similarly disabling of responsibility and judgement?

A crucial issue in *The Politics of Friendship* is the question of the 'sister'.[42] If all friendships become fraternity – a brotherhood amongst men – what about the friendship amongst women and between men and women? Women face a double exclusion – they are absent, excluded by a hegemonic discourse that recognises only the same; but when recognised they are instantly neutralised, generalised, humanised. How can women prevent this? Isn't every act of addressing inequality at the cost of reducing oneself to the hegemonic yardstick – reducing the sister to a brother? Derrida names two options: 1) displace politics and accordingly equality altogether; 2) keep the name of politics and accordingly equality but

---

[38]   Derrida, J, *The Politics of Friendship* (London, Verso, 1997).
[39]   *Ibid*.
[40]   *Ibid*; Thomson, A, *Deconstruction and Democracy* (London, Continuum, 2005) 12.
[41]   Thomson, *ibid*, at 16. See also Thomson, A, 'What's to Become of "Democracy to Come"?' (2005) 15 *Postmodern Culture* 1.
[42]   Derrida, above n 38, at 271–306.

analyse the logic and disrupt it from within.[43] And of course for Derrida there is no choice. As in other examples he holds on to a double strategy. He introduces the notion of 'aimance', which is an experience of friendship between active and passive. He identifies two contradictory moments of friendship, the one being the possibility of having many friends with whom I am in no relation yet (active or passive); the other being the moment when I betray the possibility of having many friends by preferring certain friends and excluding others.[44] It is worthwhile quoting Derrida's call towards the end of *The Politics of Friendship*:

> When will we be ready for an experience of freedom and equality that is capable of respectfully experiencing that friendship, which would at last be just, just beyond the law, and measured up against its measurelessness?[45]

In later writings Derrida introduced the notion of democratic suicide. With this he problematises his earlier call for another kind of friendship, a 'democracy to come'. Democratic suicide refers, firstly, to the fact that democracy is always exposed to the risk of an undemocratic party being democratically elected. But, secondly, it refers to the possibility that, because of autoimmunity, democracy may also self-destruct from within.[46] Thomson defines autoimmunity as:

> a term used in the biomedical sciences to describe a phenomenon in which a body's immune system turns on its own cells, effectively destroying itself from within.[47]

He explains that the link between democracy and autoimmunity lies in describing:

> a threat to democracy that comes from within rather than from without. ... Autoimmunity is the always-possible failure of such a system to distinguish what it protects from what it protects against.[48]

As explained in the discussion of Derrida's notion of friendship above, whenever friendship/democracy is constituted, it excludes, thereby creating not only a particular instance of non-democratic action, but also destroying its own essence, which is precisely not to exclude – destroying, that is, itself.

Extending this suggestion from democracy to equality, we should consider a similar threat – in other words, to what extent is inequality

---

[43] *Ibid.* See also Thomson, above n 40, at 22.
[44] Thomson, *ibid*, at 15.
[45] Derrida, above n 38, at 306.
[46] Derrida, J, *Rogues: Two Essays on Reason* (Stanford, Stanford University Press, 2005); Thomson, A, above n 41.
[47] Thomson, above n 40, at 2.
[48] *Ibid.*

always already threatened from within, or, to be more precise, from its inherent tendencies towards inequality. Thomson notes Derrida's extension of autoimmunity to community – the survival of community depends on its tendency to exclude.[49] My interest in drawing on Derrida's reflections on democratic suicide, and particularly Thomson's interpretation, is to consider to what extent equality, and the legal protection of and/or right to equality, inherently prevents equality, specifically an equality open for difference, equality that does not always result in someone's inequality. Because, whenever equality is constituted between two parties according to a certain standard or approach, it excludes others. The idea of equality, as with democracy, holds the germ of its own destruction. That is, if to constitute equality in a particular instance inevitably excludes, then to constitute equality means inevitably to act unequally, to destroy equality itself. This is similar to the argument of law's limits – law's incapacity to protect radical difference – but also different, in that legal equality does not merely fail because of the structural limits of the legal system as an institutional system, but because of tendencies within the idea of equality itself that threaten equality. Just as Derrida's thoughts in *Rogues* pushed him to proclaim that 'no enemy of democracy can refuse to call himself a democrat',[50] inequality will result from the actions of those who insist on equality.

A central concern for Thomson is whether Derrida shifted in *Rogues* from his earlier understanding of 'democracy to come'. He interprets Derrida as challenging his own earlier use of democracy, and by extension the use of democracy generally, underscoring democracy's 'hegemony'.[51] For Thomson, the implication might be that 'responsible citizenship must mean (at the very least) [that] all those who present themselves as democrats' must be interrogated.[52] The further implication is that anyone involved in the discourse of equality similarly must be interrogated, or deconstructed one might say. Deconstruction, as Derrida has explained, is not a theory, a method or a political programme, but 'a description of "what happens"', 'a sensitivity or patient attention to upheavals and disruptions already underway'.[53] The notion of democracy's disruption from within shows how the blame for the failure of democracy cannot be placed on something outside, by drawing on something that seemingly falls outside of democracy itself. Blame must be cast within; those who profess democracy must be interrogated.

---

[49] *Ibid.*
[50] Cited in *ibid*, at 3.
[51] *Ibid*, at 4.
[52] *Ibid.*
[53] Cited in *ibid*, at 7.

This brings us back to *The Politics of Friendship* and Derrida's association of democracy with equality. I have discussed above how the possibility and impossibility of friendship act in the same moment. It is the desire to have friends that prevents having friends other than mere brothers. As Thomson notes, 'fraternity is naturalised friendship', or:

friendship, which prefers, cannot help becoming brotherhood. Similarly, democracy, which embodies an appeal to equality, can never live up to its name.[54]

Even more pertinently:

All the more or less evident restrictions of equality within a so-called democracy (the *de facto* or *de jure* inequality of women, of the poor, of minorities, of minors, of strangers tolerated only according to a limited hospitality) can and must be criticized in the name of democracy, judged and found wanting against the principle of equality.[55]

For Thomson, Derrida, more than 10 years later, is still calling for 'democracy to come', but he is more cautious. In Thomson's words, 'the terms in which it is phrased have hardened'.[56] Modern democracies are caught up in a cycle in which self-destruction and self-sustenance are inseparable:

Democracy [and I would add equality], the legal and political frameworks of the sovereign state, can secure all kinds of goods, but only at the cost not only of others...but also of its own existence.[57]

Of course, for Derrida, there is no clear distinction between threats to democracy (and for me, to equality) from outside and from within, but instead a disruption between inside and outside. Democracy/equality has a cyclical nature: for example, democracy can be destroyed if an undemocratic party is democratically elected – destroyed by a force from outside – but such a party can only be elected because the very idea of democracy requires that possibility – destruction at the same time from within. This idea of disruption between inside and outside brings us back to the relation between monument and memorial and raises the possibility that a clear distinction between the two is impossible – isn't the memorial always already becoming a monument and vice versa? We return to the ideas of monument and memorial because, in the South African context, memory is embedded within the constitution and therefore also in the protection of substantive equality found in that constitution. And memory necessarily implies forgetting, but also selection, choice and exclusion.

[54] *Ibid.*
[55] *Ibid.*
[56] *Ibid*, at 10.
[57] *Ibid.*

MEMORIAL AND MONUMENTAL EQUALITY

Section 9 of the Constitution of South Africa protects the right to equality.[58] It is generally accepted that this section should be understood as not only protecting formal equality but also substantive equality.[59] In other words, a court will accept that in some instances, individuals must be treated differently in order to protect their right to equality. An approach based on substantive equality supposedly takes the concrete circumstances of an individual into account in contrast to a formal, abstract approach based on sameness. In *President of the Republic of South Africa and another v Hugo*,[60] the court phrased its approach to equality as follows:

> We need...to develop a concept of unfair discrimination which recognises that although a society which affords each human being equal treatment on the basis of equal worth and freedom is our goal, we cannot achieve that goal by insisting upon identical treatment in all circumstances before that goal is achieved. Each case, therefore, will require a careful and thorough understanding of the impact of the discriminatory action upon the particular people concerned to determine whether its overall impact is one which furthers the constitutional goal of equality or not. A classification which is unfair in one context may not necessarily be unfair in a different context.[61]

A year later, in *Harksen v Lane*,[62] the court formulated the 'test' that must be followed in order to determine unfair discrimination. Yet a close look at the court's decision shows how, even given a presumably substantive and transformative aim, the protection of equality can nevertheless result in unjust consequences.[63] The Constitutional Court, by formulating a test to

---

[58] Constitution of the Republic of South Africa, 1996. The section reads as follows:
1. Everyone is equal before the law and has the right to equal protection and benefit of the law.
2. Equality includes the full and equal enjoyment of all rights and freedoms. To promote the achievement of equality, legislative and other measures designed to protect or advance persons, or categories of persons, disadvantaged by unfair discrimination may be taken.
3. The state may not unfairly discriminate directly or indirectly against anyone on one or more grounds, including race, gender, sex, pregnancy, marital status, ethnic or social origin, colour, sexual orientation, age, disability, religion, conscience, belief, culture, language and birth.
4. No person may unfairly discriminate directly or indirectly against anyone on one or more grounds in terms of subsection (3). National legislation must be enacted to prevent or prohibit unfair discrimination.
5. Discrimination on one or more of the grounds listed in subsection (3) is unfair unless it is established that the discrimination is fair.

[59] Albertyn and Kentridge, above n 2; L'Heureux-Dubé, above n 2; Albertyn and Goldblatt, above n 11.

[60] (1997) 6 BCLR 708 (CC).

[61] *Ibid*, at para 1.

[62] (1997) 11 BCLR 1489 (CC).

[63] The court in *Harksen* set the test out as follows: Where someone relies on the equality section to attack a legislative provision or executive conduct, the first question is whether the

be followed when equality is to be considered, has reverted to a generalisation that ultimately does not go far beyond formal equality.[64] Following the distinction between monumental and memorial constitutionalism one could ask if the Constitutional Court's approach can be seen as an example of monumental constitutionalism – another attempt to bring the difficulties of dealing with equality to an end, to make it easy, to reduce.[65]

Another problematic aspect of the current approach to substantive equality is the fact that the Constitutional Court has collapsed the protection of dignity with the protection of equality. Albertyn and Goldblatt note that 'the constitutional court has sought to define equality by placing the value of dignity at the centre of the equality right', adding that 'we don't agree with this'.[66] They support the view that the right to substantive equality should be given a meaning that is independent of the value of dignity and that 'disadvantage and difference are core characteristics of substantive equality'.[67] They also praise the judgment of Constitutional Court justice Kate O'Regan in *President of the Republic of South Africa v Hugo*,[68] for placing the:

idea of systemic discrimination and patterns of group based disadvantage (and material interests) at the centre of the equality right.[69]

For them:

provision *differentiates* between people, or categories of people. If so, the next step is to see if there is a *rational connection* between the differentiation in question and a legitimate governmental purpose. If the rational connection is proved, the court will then determine whether the differentiation amounts to *discrimination* and, if it does, whether the discrimination is *unfair*. The constitution provides for two categories of discrimination: differentiation on one of the *grounds specified* in the equality section, and differentiation on a *ground not specified* but *analogous* to such grounds. The *Harksen* court decided that discrimination on an *unspecified but analogous* ground is differentiation based on attributes or characteristics that have the potential to impair the fundamental dignity of persons as human beings, or to affect them adversely in a comparably serious manner. If the discrimination is on a *specified* ground, unfairness will be *presumed*, but if it is on an unspecified ground, unfairness will have to be *established* by the complainant, considering factors such as: (a) the *position* of the complainants in *society* and whether they have suffered in the *past* from patterns of disadvantage; (b) the *nature* of the provision or power and the purpose achieved by it; (c) any other relevant factors. If the discrimination is held to be unfair, or if there is no rational connection between the differentiation and a legitimate government purpose, the court will then proceed to the limitations clause, to see if the violation may nevertheless be justified (see Van der Walt, A and Botha, H, 'Coming to Grips With the New Constitutional Order: Critical Comments on *Harksen v Lane NO*' (1998) 13 *South African Public Law* 17).

[64] Van Marle, K, Unpublished LLD thesis, *Towards an 'Ethical' Interpretation of Equality*.
[65] Van Marle, above n 20.
[66] Albertyn and Goldblatt, above n 11, at 254.
[67] *Ibid*, at 256.
[68] (1997) 6 BCLR 708 (CC).
[69] Albertyn and Goldblatt, above n 11, at 256–60.

the replacement of disadvantage with dignity returns us to a liberal and individualised concept of the right. The centrality of disadvantage, vulnerability and harm, and their connotation of groups-based prejudice – the essence of the right – is lost.[70]

The Constitutional Court's tendency to place human dignity at the heart of its equality jurisprudence could be seen as another example of monumental constitutionalism in contrast to a concern with material redress that would be closer to the memorial approach described above. As noted above, commentators have criticised the Constitutional Court's dignity approach for being too individualistic and for not sufficiently giving content to a materialist notion of equality.[71] The pro-dignity argument holds that equality is an empty notion that is best filled with reference to dignity. The main problem with the court's reliance on dignity is that it follows, one can say, a classical liberal approach – for the court it is the dignity of the autonomous individual that is at stake, with the effect that a universal, neutral approach to equality is followed.[72] This approach is monumental in the sense that it evades politics, thereby forgetting the memory of the past. More than that, it closes and fixes present understandings of equality, preventing future refigurings. I have alluded in the introduction, however, to the fact that I disagree with an understanding of transformative constitutionalism as entailing nothing but a functional/instrumental approach and that I also have some reservations concerning this applica-tion of substantive equality.[73] The main contention against the court's reliance on dignity is embedded in an understanding of transformation as the achievement of an egalitarian society. Critics oppose the court's reliance on dignity because they understand substantive equality and transforma-tion as processes through which an egalitarian society could be achieved.[74] This is a good example of how a concern with material circumstances, politics and social context – memorial constitutionalism – by being fixated with one project and/or programme, can slip into momumentalism, or to be precise, monumental constitutionalism.

---

[70]   *Ibid*, at 258.
[71]   *Ibid*. See also *National Coalition for Gay and Lesbian Equality v Minister of Justice* (1999) 1 SA 6 (CC).
[72]   Botha, above n 15.
[73]   My concern here is that when we protect the equality and socio-economic rights of one person or group of persons, we should not harm the dignity of others. The point is that the way in which we address inequality and socio-economic rights should be a reflection of a regard for dignity and respect. My aim is not to prevent social and institutional transforma-tion or to protect 'existing rights', but to approach these with a concern for dignity and respect.
[74]   Van Marle, K, '"No Last Word": Reflections on the Imaginary Domain, Dignity and Intrinsic Worth' (2002) 13 *Stellenbosch Law Review* 299; Van Marle, K, '"The Capabilities Approach", "The Imaginary Domain", and "Asymmetrical Reciprocity": Feminist Perspec-tives on Equality and Justice' (2003) 11 *Feminist Legal Studies* 255.

Like all metaphors, the metaphor of the constitution as monument and/or memorial should also be scrutinised. The distinction between monument and memorial, like most distinctions, is not watertight. We are confronted by a fluidity in deciding when we are in the realm of the monumental and when in the realm of the memorial, not only because of the closeness of the two, but also because of the issue of memorial becoming monument and vice versa. We have seen above how ideals that started out with the aim of material concerns, tentativeness and memorial constitutionalism have either slipped or nearly slipped into the realm of the monumental. We should also ask after the potential of the monument: if we expose the cracks in the monument and walk those cracks, the monumental might show even more potential for undermining itself than the memorial.[75] Does this mean that formal equality is to be preferred above substantive equality? If we take the limits of the law seriously, shouldn't we concede that law's application in the realm of social transformation, and in this context equality, has a narrow scope (able to address only what Christodoulidis calls 'simple inertia')?[76] Substantive equality, by claiming to be able to do more than law can do, might create false consciousness and false hopes as regards law's potential. The possible failure also of substantive equality repeats the notion of equality's self-destruction and of the need to interrogate all those claiming to be in support of equality, as in the case of democracy.

RECONSIDERING EQUALITY

Complex Equality

Henk Botha also argues against the court's emphasis on dignity because it assumes neutrality and universality and accordingly ignores the politics involved when addressing equality.[77] He puts forward a concept of 'complex equality' that amounts to the following: A court, when following complex equality, should take account of the interrelatedness between equality and many other values – for example democracy and social justice – in order to reach a better understanding of the 'moral, political and material dimensions of equality'.[78] Complex equality will base its analysis on the type of discrimination that is at issue – in other words it accepts that one would in some cases focus on 'moral harm' and in other cases on

---

[75] See Braidotti, R, *Transpositions* (Oxford, Blackwell Publishing, 2006).
[76] Christodoulidis, above n 25.
[77] Botha, above n 15.
[78] *Ibid*, at 748.

'political disempowerment and material disadvantage'.[79] Complex equality will resist generalisations and pay attention to concrete life experiences, 'the intersectional nature of disadvantage' and different issues like education, employment, welfare and citizenship.[80] According to Botha, complex equality, because it is more open to 'multiple forms of disadvantage', will be in a position to follow a more 'nuanced approach' to equality and discrimination.[81] He argues that it would also 'deepen our understanding of the relation between equality, dignity, democracy and social justice' as well as the understanding of the relationship between equality and difference.[82] Botha contends that complex equality encompasses moral, political and material dimensions without reducing material disadvantage and political disempowerment to moral harm. It recognises how economic disadvantage, political invisibility and moral stigma are connected to unequal relations of power.[83] An important feature of complex equality is that it is informed by an understanding of the politics of law that rejects assumptions of legal neutrality.

Ethical Equality, Plurality and Difference

The notion of an ethical interpretation of equality is an approach that would make the question of the political central to each decision and that would realise the impossibility of ever fully recognising difference and protecting equality.[84] I have previously configured an ethical interpretation of equality as follows: It requires an intersection between public space (the potential of politics), conceptions of equality and the ideal of justice. In other words it holds that equality cannot be thought of without making a vision of a vibrant public space and political action central to it. Within the South African context, where under apartheid the denial of equality went hand in hand with the absence of a democratic public space that allowed for any active politics, this is of particular concern. More than 10 years after the initial change, post-apartheid society and law is still inclined to protect private mindsets and privileges to the detriment of the transformation of a public space. I do not consider public events that merely celebrate and monumentalise the present as true reflections of vibrant public spaces. Another element of ethical equality is the insight that difference can never be understood fully and therefore can never be served fully by law or

---

[79]   *Ibid.*
[80]   *Ibid.*
[81]   *Ibid*, at 749.
[82]   *Ibid.*
[83]   *Ibid*, at 751.
[84]   Van Marle, above n 16; Van Marle, above n 64.

anyone else. Any attempt to provide for difference will produce an excess that lies beyond the formal effort to understand and attempt to encompass difference.

I have previously argued that the 'postmodern' or 'critical' approaches of Drucilla Cornell and Iris Marion Young show more regard and respect for difference and particularity in comparison to the more liberal approach of Martha Nussbaum of focusing on a list of human capabilities to be protected.[85] Cornell's ethical feminism as a way of reflecting on sex, gender, difference and equality is marked by a non-essentialist starting point yet is concerned with new ways of articulating sexual difference.[86] Through the concept of the imaginary domain she wants to protect a space where women (and men) can be evaluated as free and equal persons. For Cornell the requirements for the imaginary domain must be met prior to any formulation of a theory of justice. Liberalism fails because it is only concerned with what 'is'. Iris Marion Young similarly laments the reductionism of modern political theory, positivism and liberalism in their celebration of commonness and sameness over specificity and difference.[87] She argues that theories of justice often conflate moral reflection with scientific knowledge (empirical research) by claiming universalism, comprehensiveness and necessity. Her vision of critical theory entails a normative reflection that is situated historically and socially and rejects the formulation of a universal normative system. She emphasises imagination as 'the faculty of transforming the experience of what is into a projection of what could be'.[88]

In a recent piece, 'The Solace of Resonance', Drucilla Cornell reflects on the phenomenon of loneliness, in particular the loneliness of women of a certain generation.[89] Related to what she calls her 'musings' are the themes of politics, ethics and friendship. With reference to Betty Friedan's earlier writings, she recalls the loneliness of white middle-class women, the isolation of nuclear family life.[90] The slogan, 'the personal is political' is seen by Cornell as partly also a response to the loneliness of women. She explains that early consciousness raising groups perceived 'the ways of the heart' as political and as a reason for women to find ways of loving and sustaining themselves beyond the confines of heterosexual marriage.[91] The

---

[85]   Van Marle, 'The "Capabilities Approach"', above n 74.
[86]   *Ibid*, at 259–60. See Cornell, D, *Beyond Accommodation* (New York, Routledge, 1991); *The Imaginary Domain* (New York, Routledge, 1995); *At the Heart of Freedom* (Princeton, Princeton University Press, 1998).
[87]   Van Marle, *ibid*, at 263; See also Young, IM, *Justice and the Politics of Difference* (Princeton, Princeton University Press, 1990).
[88]   Young, *ibid*, at 5.
[89]   Cornell, above n 19, at 215–22.
[90]   *Ibid*, at 216.
[91]   *Ibid*, at 216–17.

'politics of the heart' is as significant for women today. Cornell laments what she calls the depoliticisation of the matters of the heart. She wants to search for ways and spaces where women can be together, ask questions, and interact as a way of resisting isolation. Responding to a variety of possible feminist critiques referring to the 'professionalization' of feminism, she says, 'White-knuckle feminism brings nothing but white knuckles, and who needs those?'[92] In her musings Cornell is asking for a resonance and an affinity amongst women as a way of political engagement with the matters of the heart. What Cornell calls resonance in this context recalls her earlier reflection on 'sublime affinity'.[93] Through a reading of Kant's analysis of aesthetic judgement she formulates a notion of an imagined community for women where all possible viewpoints can be imagined and each and everyone's intrinsic worth and dignity can be protected. Cornell's notion of a politics of the heart is to my mind significant also when thinking about equality. Equality, as Botha argues, is connected with many other values and rights and the given context will dictate which values and rights are relevant.

In a recent judgment, *Minister of Home Affairs v Fourie*,[94] the South African constitutional court found the section in the Marriage Act that relies on the common law definition of marriage – a union between two members of the opposite sex – unconstitutional. The court gave parliament a year to change the definition or put a new Act on the table, otherwise the common law definition would be deemed to include members of the same sex. Parliament responded by putting forward the Civil Union Bill, which supposedly opens the way for gays and lesbians to get married. This Bill was met with a huge outcry from, amongst others, members of the gay community.[95] The Civil Union Bill, instead of opening the common law definition of marriage to all, insists on making special provision for gay couples who want to get married. As a result:

> it looks like a marriage, it sounds like a marriage, it even feels like a marriage, but section 13 and section 8(2) of the bill makes it abundantly clear it is not a marriage.[96]

What makes this interesting for the development of equality jurisprudence is the emphasis placed on dignity by those people opposing the Bill. If the issue were only about the material realities – to be able to enter into a civilly recognised union – the Bill would have sufficed. However, the issue

---

[92]   *Ibid*, at 220.
[93]   Cornell, D, *Between Women and Generations: Legacies of Dignity* (New York, Palgrave, 2002) 71–94.
[94]   2006 (1) SA 524 (CC).
[95]   See, eg Barnard, J, 'Civil Union Bill Gives Gays No Marriage Choice', *The Sunday Times* (1 Oct 2006).
[96]   *Ibid*.

goes much further; it goes to the need for the inherent dignity of every person to be protected. Scholars have argued that the emphasis on dignity placed by the court in previous cases on gay equality was apt, but that in cases of sex and gender discrimination for example, the emphasis on dignity could be the reason for the evasion of structural and political inequality.[97] As Cornell has noted, however, the moralistic tendencies of the court and its evasion of politics in its approach to dignity might flow from a flawed understanding of dignity rather than being a natural result of a dignity-based approach.[98] This connects with her notion of a politics of the heart – to show a concern with dignity and respect, seeming 'private' protection, is by no means neutral or non-political.

Although the result of the dignity jurisprudence of the constitutional court in the past was an evasion of deeply embedded structural inequality, the ideal of dignity should not be negated, not even when material concerns are prevalent. Because we would like to see equality that is more than mere accommodation, transformation that is more than evolution, and a politics that also involves matters of the heart, our conception of equality should be complex, like Botha argues; ethical; and should resonate with all aspects of our lives. Yet again, we should ask whether the law, given its inherent structural and systemic limits, and also because of its tendency to self-destruct, could allow such a concept?

HAUNTING (IN)EQUALITIES

In this chapter I have situated equality within the wider South African constitutional ideal of transformation. I have referred to the notion of transformative constitutionalism put forward by Karl Klare and some of the engagements with transformative constitutionalism. I have connected transformation with two approaches to the constitution, namely monumental and memorial constitutionalism, and I have linked these two approaches to equality, particularly formal and substantive equality. After constructing these distinctions, however, I considered the impossibility of drawing pure distinctions in light of the slippage between monument and memorial, formal and substantive. Central to my reflections is the notion of the limits of the law, asking after law's capacity to bring about transformation that goes further than formal change. I have also drawn on Derrida's notion of friendship and democratic suicide to expose how every protection of equality always already excludes that which cannot be

---

[97] Botha, above n 15.
[98] *Ibid*, at 747, fn 92.

protected by law. This is not merely a feature of the limits of the law, the legal protection of equality in this context, but of the inherent tendencies of equality to self-destruct.

Within the South African context, Derrida's exposure of fraternity, its logic of exclusion and betrayal, as well as the notion of self-destruction, are significant. His insistence that programmatic change, like natural bonds, disables responsibility and judgement, must be noted. Even more, we should note his description of the inherent tendencies toward self-destruction of democracy and equality. What kind of equality could be thought of while knowing that all attempts at achieving equality disable responsible action; that equality is based on a logic of exclusion in particular for women; and that, because of autoimmunity, equality is turning on itself, self-destructing from within? Like the monument with its cracks exposed, we are left with what I see as a haunting (in)equality – every act of equality will be haunted by its own exclusions. This is also a haunting from within. The haunting, the coming back of the forgotten, the cracks on the wall represent the call of the political and of a radical politics that continues to trouble the liberal imagination, constitutional optimism, human rights activism, gender mainstreaming and other attempts to evade politics, responsibility, judgement and ultimately the call for justice.

Part III

Personal Equality Projects in the Legal Profession

7

Gender Equality and Legal Professionalism: Challenges for the First Women Lawyers

MARY JANE MOSSMAN

INTRODUCTION

La question de la femme-avocat est une face du grand et complexe problème de l'affranchissement du sexe féminin. Non seulement nous souhaitons que toutes les carrières intellectuelles et libérales, y compris le barreau, soient rendues accessibles aux femmes, mais notre désir est de voir disparaître enfin les incapacités injustifiables que frappent encore les femmes.[1]

Modern readers [of biography]…know that women's lives are complex and that region, period, personality and circumstance crucially influence what a subject is able to make of herself. … And modern women lawyers know that the biographies of women who chose to locate their professional lives in the law are likely to be stories of *piecemeal progress and circumscribed success*. (emphasis added)[2]

THESE QUOTATIONS ABOUT the first women lawyers represent quite different perspectives about them. The first comment occurred in the preface to Louis Frank's treatise on the *femme-avocat*, published in Paris in 1898, when women in a number of jurisdictions around the world were beginning to gain admission to the bar. Clearly, Frank envisaged such achievements on the part of women lawyers as part of broader legal and social changes relating to the goals of women's reform

---

[1] Frank, L, *La Femme-Avocat: Exposé Historique et Critique de la Question* (Paris, V Giard et E Brière, 1898) ii.

[2] Sanger, C, 'Curriculum Vitae (Feminae): Biography and Early Women Lawyers' (1994) 46 *Stanford Law Review* 1245, 1257.

movements at the end of the nineteenth century.[3] An admirer of John Stuart Mill and his efforts to reform laws concerning women's unequal status, Frank wrote prolifically on a wide variety of topics concerning the status of women at the end of the nineteenth century.[4] In addition, some women's organisations identified equality goals explicitly: for example, the Declaration of Sentiments, adopted by American women at the Seneca Falls Convention in 1848, included goals of 'equal rights in the universities, [and] in the trades and professions', as well as 'complete equality in marriage', and the right to vote; Canadian women formed an Equal Suffrage League in Montreal in the early twentieth century; and Ethel Benjamin wrote a paper for the National Council of Women at their convention in 1898 in New Zealand on 'The Inequalities of the Law regarding Men and Women'. Thus, ideas about equality were often adopted by reformers, including Frank, as well as women suffragists and lawyers, in their quest to achieve '*l'affranchissement du sexe feminin*'.[5] By contrast with Frank's optimism at the end of the nineteenth century, however, Carol Sanger's assessment in the second quotation was written near the end of the twentieth century, and it offers a more cautious appraisal of the 'equality' achieved by women who first entered the legal profession.[6] Indeed, Sanger's conclusion that the stories of women lawyers generally reveal only 'piecemeal progress and circumscribed success' suggests that the promise of equality for women lawyers remained largely unfulfilled in the century after Frank published his treatise.

This paper explores ideas about gender equality in relation to the aspirations and experiences of some of the first women lawyers. Clearly, some women were successful in gaining admission to the bar at the end of the nineteenth century. In the same period, however, other women's aspirations for admission to the bar were being defeated by judicial conservatism and/or legislative intransigence, so that their ability to work in law was often thwarted completely, or at least defined in terms of narrow, subordinate activities. In spite of such challenges, the 'voices' of

---

[3] Frank, above n 1. See also Bolt, C, *The Women's Movements in the United States and Britain from the 1790s to the 1920s* (Amherst, University of Massachusetts Press, 1993); Kealey, L (ed), *A Not Unreasonable Claim: Women and Reform in Canada 1880s -1920s* (Toronto, Women's Educational Press, 1979).

[4] See, eg Frank, L, *Essai sur la Condition Politique de la Femme: Étude de Sociologie et de Législation* (Paris, Arthur Rosseau, 1892); Frank, L, *Le Grand Catéchisme de la Femme* (Paris, Verviers, 1894); and Frank, L, *Cours sur La Législation Féministe: Notions Élémentaires* (Bruxelles, JH Moreau, 1895).

[5] Bolt, above n 3, at 88; Hoff, J, *Law, Gender, and Injustice: A Legal History of US Women* (New York, New York University Press, 1991) 136; *Montreal Gazette*, 19 Nov 1914; Nicholls, R, *The Women's Parliament: The National Council of the Women of New Zealand 1896–1920* (Wellington, Victoria University Press, 1996) 35.

[6] Sanger, above n 2. See also Morgan, C, '"An Embarrassingly and Severely Masculine Atmosphere": Women, Gender and the Legal Profession at Osgoode Hall, 1920s to 1960s' (1996) 11(2) *Canadian Journal of Women and the Law* 19.

early women lawyers often reflect confidence and enthusiasm about their efforts to gain equal access to the bar.

Yet, even for women who successfully gained admission to the bar at the end of the nineteenth century, difficulties in obtaining legal work and in gaining acceptance as lawyers suggest that they were not always treated as equal members of the traditional 'gentleman's profession' of law.[7] Thus, as Pearson and Sachs argued in relation to the exclusion of women from dinners on the circuit messes in the United Kingdom, 'the removal of legal impediments . . .was not the same as creating equal opportunities'.[8]

Moreover, the rhetoric of gender equality, which was often adopted by women to gain admission to the bar, seems to have become gradually subdued among those who succeeded in working as lawyers. In its place, many of the first women lawyers tended to embrace norms of objectivity and rationality embedded in ideas of professionalism: they became *lawyers*, rather than *women lawyers*. In this context, their stories reveal how the professional context often subtly reshaped the meaning of equality for women who first challenged the 'gentleman's profession' of law.[9] Thus, the stories of the first women lawyers offer important insights about the history of relationships between ideas of gender equality and professionalism in law.[10]

In exploring some of these issues, this paper provides a brief introduction to some of the first women lawyers in different jurisdictions at the end of the nineteenth century. The paper then examines the 'voices' of some of these women lawyers, in their published writings, diaries and letters. Paradoxically, their 'voices' often reflect the hopefulness of Louis Frank's comments about the potential for achieving gender equality, even as their experiences sometimes reflect Sanger's more sanguine assessment of merely 'piecemeal progress and circumscribed success'.

---

[7] See Gidney, RD and Millar, WPJ, *Professional Gentlemen: The Professions in Nineteenth-Century Ontario* (Toronto, University of Toronto Press, 1994); Pue, WW and Sugarman, D (eds), *Lawyers and Vampires: Cultural Histories of Legal Professions* (Oxford, Hart Publishing, 2003).

[8] Pearson, R and Sachs, A, 'Barristers and Gentlemen: A Critical Look at Sexism in the Legal Profession' (1980) 43 *Modern Law Review* 400, 405. See also Thornton, M, *Dissonance and Distrust: Women in the Legal Profession* (Melbourne, Oxford University Press, 1996).

[9] Grossberg, M, 'Institutionalizing Masculinity: The Law as a Masculine Profession' in MC Carnes and C Griffen (eds), *Meanings for Manhood: Constructions of Masculinity in Victorian America* (Chicago, University of Chicago Press, 1990) 133.

[10] Drachman,VG, *Women Lawyers and the Origins of Professional Identity in America: The Letters of the Equity Club 1887–1890* (Ann Arbor, University of Michigan Press, 1993) vii; Mossman, MJ, *The First Women Lawyers: A Comparative Study of Gender, Law and the Legal Professions* (Oxford, Hart Publishing, 2006). See also Eberts, M, 'Women in Law: Retreat and Renewal' in E Sheehy and S McIntyre (eds), *Calling for Change: Women, Law, and the Legal Profession* (Ottawa, University of Ottawa Press, 2006) 83.

AN INTRODUCTION TO THE FIRST WOMEN LAWYERS: A COMPARATIVE CONTEXT

In trying to sort out the reasons for professional women's successes or failures, it is far too facile to say that there were prejudices against women that they had to overcome. The ways in which the prejudice manifested itself were extremely complex and insidious. ... As determined, aspiring professionals, women were not easily deterred. They found a variety of ways to respond to the discrimination they faced.[11]

The late nineteenth century context, in which women began to seek entry to the legal professions in a number of different jurisdictions, was characterised by considerable optimism about legal and social reforms. Two reform movements were particularly important: the 'women's equality movement' and the 'professionalisation' project in law. In relation to the women's equality movement, a number of legal reforms were achieved in the late nineteenth century, which enhanced opportunities for women, including access to university education, reforms of married women's property, and even suffrage in some jurisdictions.[12] In the same period, traditional occupations such as law were also increasingly engaged in 'professionalisation' projects to enhance the status of their members; in law, these reforms resulted in new arrangements for legal education, the establishment of professional associations, and new developments in the nature and organisation of legal work.[13] The intersection of these two reform movements shaped the legal and social context in which women who aspired to join the legal professions presented their claims to courts and legislatures. As will be suggested, this context also created ongoing tensions between goals of gender equality and ideas about (ungendered) professionalism for the first women lawyers. To provide a comparative context in which to examine these tensions, this section briefly introduces the first women lawyers in a number of different jurisdictions at the end of the nineteenth century.

---

[11] Glazer, PM and Slater, M, *Unequal Colleagues: The Entrance of Women into the Professions, 1890–1940* (New Brunswick, Rutgers University Press, 1987) 12.

[12] See *ibid*; Bolt, above n 3; Kealey, above n 3; Harris, BJ, *Beyond Her Sphere: Women and the Professions in American History* (Westport, CT, Greenwood Press, 1978); Albisetti, JC, 'Portia Ante Portas: Women and the Legal Profession in Europe, ca 1870–1925' (2000) 33 *Journal of Social History* 825. Although women in a number of jurisdictions adopted equality language to promote their reform efforts, Rosemary Auchmuty in this volume clearly argues that proponents of married women's property reforms in the UK did not espouse 'equality' in pursuing their goals.

[13] See Abel, R and Lewis, P (eds), *Lawyers in Society* (Berkeley, University of California Press, 1988–9); Schultz, U and Shaw, G (eds), *Women in the World's Legal Professions* (Oxford, Hart Publishing, 2003); Gidney and Millar, above n 7; Halliday, TC and Karpik, L (eds), *Lawyers and the Rise of Western Political Liberalism* (Oxford, Clarendon Press, 1997); Pue and Sugarman, above n 7; Thornton, above n 8.

United States

American women were the first to claim admission to state bars in the USA in the late 1860s and 1870s: they included Arabella Mansfield, who gained admission to the bar in Iowa in 1869,[14] and Ada Kepley, the first American woman to obtain a university law degree (at Union College of Law, now Northwestern) in 1870.[15] However, not all women who wished to become lawyers succeeded in doing so. For example, Myra Bradwell, who petitioned for admission to the bar of Illinois in 1869 (the same year that Mansfield was admitted to the legal profession in Iowa), experienced rejection of her application both by the court in Illinois and by the Supreme Court of the United States in *Bradwell v Illinois* in 1873.[16]

From the perspective of ideas about equality, these early American cases were important in defining legal arguments in women's applications for admission to the bar. In Mansfield's case in 1869, for example, Justice Springer adopted an *inclusive* interpretation of male pronouns in the statutory language, concluding that women were eligible for admission to the legal profession in Iowa; and a legislative amendment confirmed his decision a year later.[17] Thus, this initial decision held the promise of gender equality for women who aspired to enter the legal professions. By contrast, when Bradwell appended constitutional arguments in her appeal to the US Supreme Court, including an argument pursuant to the Fourteenth Amendment (equal protection), all her arguments were rejected. Thus, although Bradwell clearly based her claim for admission to the bar on her right to equality, it seems, as Nancy Gilliam concluded, that Bradwell's use of the Fourteenth Amendment to support her claim was 'generations ahead of her

---

[14] Morello, KB, *The Invisible Bar: The Woman Lawyer in America 1638 to the Present* (New York, Random House, 1986) 12–14. For other histories of women lawyers in the United States, see Drachman, V, *Sisters in Law: Women Lawyers in Modern American History* (Cambridge, Mass, Harvard University Press, 1998); Weisberg, DK, 'Barred from the Bar: Women and Legal Education in the United States 1870–1890' (1977) 28 *Journal of Legal Education* 485; Hoff, above n 5.

[15] See Drachman, above n 10, at 235; Bittenbender, AM, 'Women in Law' in AN Meyer (ed), *Women's Work in America* (New York, Henry Holt and Company, 1891).

[16] *In re Bradwell*, 55 Ill 535 (1869); *Bradwell v Illinois*, 83 US (16 Wallace's Supreme Court Reports) 130 (1873). See also Gilliam, NT, 'A Professional Pioneer: Myra Bradwell's Fight to Practice Law' (1987) 5 *Law and History Review* 105; Friedman, JM, *America's First Woman Lawyer: The Biography of Myra Bradwell* (Buffalo, Prometheus Books, 1993); Hoff, above n 5.

[17] See Hoff, *ibid*, at 162–3. As Hoff noted, the provision of the statute referred to potential candidates for admission to the bar as 'white male' candidates. Amending legislation was adopted in Iowa in 1870, although Hoff argued that the legislature did not intend 'to strike a blow against either racism or sexism in the legal profession'.

time'.[18] In addition, however, Justice Bradley's opinion in this case confirmed that existing societal ideas about 'a woman's place' were enforceable in law. As he explained:

> The natural and proper timidity and delicacy which belongs to the female sex evidently unfits it for many of the occupations of civil life. The constitution of the family organization, which is founded in the divine ordinance, as well as in the nature of things, indicates the domestic sphere as that which properly belongs to the domain and functions of womanhood. The harmony, not to say identity, of interests and views which belong or should belong to the family institution is repugnant to the idea of a woman adopting a distinct and independent career from that of her husband.[19]

As Joan Hoff noted, Justice Bradley conceded that single women were not affected by these same duties and incapacities, but he regarded unmarried women as exceptions to his view of proper social and family structures.[20] Such views reveal how interpretive principles in the law were malleable concepts; when male pronouns and gender-neutral language were interpreted inclusively, women were held to be equally entitled with men to admission to the bar, but when the statutory language and ideas about equality were interpreted more restrictively, women lawyers' claims were rejected. Moreover, as the opinion of Bradley J demonstrated, judges' views about women's social roles often guided their approach to the legal interpretation of statutory language.[21] Thus, legal arguments concerning women's admission to the bar had to confront conceptions of gender inequality that were *both legal and social*.

Yet, in spite of some setbacks, there were enough women lawyers in the United States by the end of the 1880s to establish the 'Equity Club', a correspondence club that provided information and support to women lawyers all over the United States for a few brief years.[22] Significantly, however, women who succeeded in gaining admission to the bar continued to experience conflict in their roles as members of the legal professions. Did equality mean acting exactly like men who were lawyers, or were women lawyers entitled (or required) to act 'like women'? For example, women lawyers faced a pressing issue about hats, as Virginia Drachman explained:

> Here was the burden for the nineteenth-century woman lawyer. As a proper lady of her day, social etiquette required that she wear a hat in public. But as a lawyer, professional etiquette demanded that she remove her hat when she entered the

---

[18] Gilliam, above n 16; see also Hoff, *ibid*.
[19] *Bradwell v Illinois*, 83 US 130 (1873), 141–2.
[20] Hoff, above n 5, at 165–6.
[21] Mossman, MJ, 'Feminism and Legal Method: The Difference it Makes' (1986) 3 *Australian Journal of Law and Society* 30.
[22] Drachman, above n 10.

courtroom. As a result, the question of the hat once again confronted women lawyers with the enduring challenge of reconciling their traditional role as *women* with their new professional identity as *lawyers*.(emphasis added)[23]

In spite of ongoing debates about such challenges, American women continued to seek entry to the legal professions with some success. Indeed, by the end of the nineteenth century, there were 300 women lawyers in the United States; as the *Illustrated London News* reported in 1897, 'the lady lawyer [in the United States] meets us here, there, and everywhere'.[24]

Canada

Interestingly, in spite of geographical proximity to the United States, only one woman, Clara Brett Martin, gained admission to a Provincial bar in Canada before the end of the nineteenth century.[25] However, a number of women's claims for admission to the bar in Canada were litigated in the first two decades of the twentieth century, and courts in Canada frequently relied on American precedents about women's (lack of) eligibility to become lawyers. For example, Mabel Penery French was involved in litigation and legislative lobbying to gain admission to the bar, both in New Brunswick in 1905–06 and then a few years later in British Columbia in 1911–12.[26] Nonetheless, in spite of her pioneering role as a woman lawyer, French's admission to the 'gentleman's profession' was recorded in the minutes of the Law Society of British Columbia as 'the admission of twenty gentlemen, including Mabel Penery French'.[27]

The third litigated claim in Canada occurred in Québec, when Annie Macdonald Langstaff, the first woman to graduate in law at McGill, presented her application for admission to the *barreau* in 1914. Her application was denied, both at the first level and then on appeal.[28] According to one of the partners in the law firm where Langstaff later worked as an administrator (she never achieved her goal of admission to the *barreau* during her lifetime), Langstaff was active in the firm for 67

---

[23] Drachman, above n 14, at 95.

[24] 'Portias of Today', *The Illustrated London News* (13 Nov 1897) 696.

[25] Roth, T, 'Clara Brett Martin – Canada's Pioneer Woman Lawyer' (1984) 18 *The Law Society Gazette* 323; Backhouse, C, 'Lawyering: Clara Brett Martin, Canada's First Woman Lawyer' in C Backhouse, *Petticoats and Prejudice: Women and Law in Nineteenth-Century Canada* (Toronto, The Osgoode Society, 1991).

[26] *In re French* (1905) 37 NBR 359; *Re French* (1910–12) 17 BCLR 1. See also Yorke, LK, 'Mabel Penery French (1881–1955): A Life Re-created' (1993) 42 *University of New Brunswick Law Journal* 3.

[27] Watts, A, *History of the Legal Profession in British Columbia, 1869–1984* (Vancouver, The Law Society of BC, 1984) 134.

[28] *Langstaff v Bar of Québec* (1915) 47 RJQ 131; (1916) 25 RJQ 11.

years, retiring at the age of 88.[29] Although legislation was not enacted to permit women to become lawyers in Québec until 1941,[30] all other Canadian Provinces permitted women to gain admission to the bar by 1918. Significantly, however, the statutes in some Provinces declared women eligible for admission to the bar 'on the same terms as men',[31] language which simultaneously declared women's equality with men who were lawyers, but without at all challenging the fundamental tradition of law as a 'gentleman's profession'.

New Zealand

Women in other parts of the world were also challenging male exclusivity in the legal professions at the end of the nineteenth century. Thus, just a few months after Clara Brett Martin was admitted to the bar of Ontario in 1897, Ethel Benjamin gained admission to the bar of New Zealand. Perhaps because the New Zealand Parliament had already enacted legislation granting women's suffrage as early as 1893, the Parliament also adopted amendments permitting women's admission to the bar, a year *before* Benjamin had fully qualified to petition for admission to the profession.[32] At the time of her admission to the bar, Benjamin was just 22 years old and a member of Dunedin's small Jewish community. Her career combined an advocate's passion with considerable entrepreneurial skills, and she became well known for her advocacy on behalf of women clients in family matters, particularly involving issues of domestic violence. Nonetheless, Benjamin's correspondence reveals that the relative ease with which she achieved admission to the bar contrasted, sometimes sharply, with unequal treatment as a member of the legal profession; it is possible that these experiences prompted her decision, just 10 years after her celebrated admission to the bar, to leave New Zealand with her husband

[29] Letter from Michael Vineberg to Dean John Brierley, McGill University, 16 Dec 1981, in Faculty of Law archives, McGill University. See also Gillett, M, *We Walked Very Warily: A History of Women at McGill* (Montréal, Eden Press Women's Publications, 1981); Pilarczyk, IC, *'A Noble Roster': One Hundred and Fifty Years of Law at McGill* (Montréal, McGill University Faculty of Law, 1999). In September 2006, Langstaff was admitted to the *barreau* posthumously: see Leger, K, 'Woman's Struggle Recognized', *The Gazette* (15 Sep 2006) B3.
[30] Women did not become entitled to admission to the bar in Québec until legislation was enacted in 1941: see Gallichan, G, *Les Québecoises et le Barreau: L'Histoire d'une Difficile Conquête, 1914–1941* (Québec, Septentrion, 1999).
[31] See, eg *An Act to Provide for the Admission of Women to the Study and Practice of Law*, SO 1892, c 32; and *An Act to Amend the Act to Provide for the Admission of Women to the Study and Practice of Law*, SO 1895, c 27. For other Provincial statutes, see Mossman, above n 10, at 68–9.
[32] Brown, C, 'Ethel Benjamin: New Zealand's First Woman Lawyer' (Dunedin, University of Otago BA Hons Thesis, 1985); Gatfield, G, *Without Prejudice: Women in the Law* (Wellington, Brooker's, 1996); Mossman, above n 10, at 166–9.

and to join her family who had moved to Britain a few years earlier.[33] Significantly, women were not yet entitled to practise law in Britain, and even after amending legislation was enacted after World War I, it seems that Benjamin never sought admission to the legal professions there.

Britain

Interestingly, by the time that Benjamin moved to Britain just prior to World War I, Eliza Orme had already retired after nearly 30 years in legal practice as a conveyancer and patent agent.[34] Orme and a woman colleague had established an independent law office in London in the mid-1870s, successfully 'practising law' without ever seeking admission as barristers or solicitors, a feat that is particularly remarkable in the context of a number of unsuccessful challenges on the part of aspiring women lawyers in the decades before the *Sex Disqualification (Removal) Act 1919*.[35] As her published writing reveals, Orme was a formidable professional woman who was appointed by the government to the Royal Commission on Labour in the 1890s. Indeed, Michael Holroyd argued that Orme was the model for Vivie, the cigar-smoking actuary in George Bernard Shaw's play, *Mrs Warren's Profession*, and Shaw's stage directions for Vivie's office bear a quite remarkable resemblance to a contemporary description of Orme's office in Chancery Lane in 1888.[36] At the same time, it seems that Orme retired from law practice in the early twentieth century, two decades before women in Britain became eligible to become barristers and solicitors after World War I.[37]

India

In the context of these new developments for women lawyers, a judge in India exercised discretion in 1896 to permit Cornelia Sorabji to represent an accused in a murder case in a British court in Puna; the relevant statute permitted an accused to be represented by a 'person', and the judge

---

[33] Brown, *ibid*, at 98–9.
[34] Howsam, L, '"Sound-Minded Women": Eliza Orme and the Study and Practice of Law in Late-Victorian England' (1989) 15 *Atlantis* 44; Mossman, above n 10, at 115–21.
[35] 9 &10 Geo 5, c 71.
[36] See Mossman, above n 10, at 131–2, 142–8.
[37] 'Women and the Bar', *The Law Journal* (12 Dec 1903) 620.

interpreted this language to include men and women equally.[38] Although Sorabji had already become the first woman to successfully complete examinations for the BCL degree at Oxford in 1892, her appearance for the defence in a murder case in India occurred nearly three decades before she actually received her BCL degree at Oxford, and before she was formally admitted as a *vakil* and then as a barrister after World War I. In the context of her appearance in this murder case in a British court in 1896, however, it is likely that Sorabji, a Parsi Christian from India, became the 'first woman lawyer' in the British Empire.[39]

At the same time, Sorabji's relationship to British India was complicated: as she stated, she semed to stand:

> midway between [the East and the West]; my birth allotting me to one hemisphere but my education and instincts and friendships allotting me to the other.[40]

Thus, after spending nearly two decades in the imperial post of Lady Assistant to the Court of Wards, a position which required her to supervise women and children who were 'wards' in northern India before and during World War I, Sorabji retained her independent, pro-British views. In the 1930s, she publicly criticised Gandhi, firmly opposing his strategies for achieving Indian independence. As Vera Brittain concluded, Sorabji's contributions are not well known now because, although her life coincided with 'two great and successful struggles for freedom' (equality for women and national liberation for India), her views on both issues were eventually sidelined.[41]

Europe (Italy, Belgium and France)

Beyond these examples in the common law world, there were also a number of litigated challenges in the civil law jurisdictions of western Europe in the late nineteenth century. For example, applications for admission to the bar were presented in Italy by Lydia Poët and in Belgium by Marie Popelin in the 1880s,[42] but both were rejected by the courts. Then, in 1897, Jeanne Chauvin presented an application for admission to the *barreau* in Paris, notably with the enthusiastic support of Louis Frank.

---

[38] Mossman, MJ, 'Cornelia Sorabji: A "Woman in Law" in India in the 1890s' (2004) 16(1) *Canadian Journal of Women and the Law* 54; Mossman, above n 10, at 213–16; and Gooptu, S, *Cornelia Sorabji: India's Pioneer Woman Lawyer* (New Delhi, Oxford University Press, 2006).

[39] Mossman, 'Cornelia Sorabji', *ibid*.

[40] Sorabji Papers, British Library F165/20: letter to Mrs A Darling, 17 Oct 1897.

[41] Brittain, V, *The Women at Oxford: A Fragment of History* (London, George Harrap & Co Ltd, 1960) 84–5.

[42] Mossman, above n 10, at 246–55.

Although Chauvin's application was rejected by the court, the National Assembly in France enacted legislation a few years later in 1900 to permit women to be admitted to the bar in France,[43] almost two decades before similar amending legislation in Britain. Significantly, the arguments presented in these civil law cases in Europe were not substantially different from those adopted in common law jurisdictions, a conclusion which confirms the widespread acceptance of ideas about the law as a 'gentleman's profession' at the end of the nineteenth century. As in common law jurisdictions, women were sometimes successful in gaining equality of access to the legal professions in European jurisdictions, but they often faced challenges in working as equals with men who were lawyers. For example, Chauvin continued to work as a high school teacher after gaining admission to the bar, because she did not receive enough legal work to sustain more than a part time legal practice.

Thus, the overall context at the end of the nineteenth century, in which women were beginning to seek admission to the bar, was quite varied, as were the strategies and choices adopted by individual women who aspired to become lawyers. Moreover, it is clear that some male lawyers actively supported women's aspirations for admission to the bar in the late nineteenth century. Among them, the Belgian barrister Louis Frank is particularly important because, in the context of his efforts to support Chauvin's application to the *barreau* in Paris, Frank corresponded with women lawyers in a number of different parts of the world.[44] As a result, letters written by women lawyers to Frank in the 1890s, as well as some of their published writings on a variety of topics (including women's equality), provide important insights about their perceptions of law and the legal professions, about how they attempted to 'function in [a] male-defined world *on their own terms*',[45] and about how their perceptions of equality shifted in relation to ideas about gender and legal professionalism.

THE CHALLENGES OF EQUALITY AND PROFESSIONALISM: THE
VOICES OF THE FIRST WOMEN LAWYERS

Disjunction – between what she said and did, what she aspired to and achieved, and even between what she most fervently proclaimed at one point and another – is typical of Foltz's life. ... Because of her ambivalence about what women

---

[43] Frank, above n 1. See also Mossman, *ibid*, at 265–8.
[44] *Papiers Frank*, Bibliothèque Royale, Brussels.
[45] Lerner, G, *The Majority Finds its Past: Placing Women in History* (New York, Oxford University Press, 1979) 148–9.

should do and be, and because she tried so many things professionally and personally, her life and thought have a fractured, sometimes even frantic, quality.[46]

In this assessment of Clara Shortridge Foltz, the first woman lawyer in California, Barbara Allen Babcock identified how Foltz's voice shifted during her career, and how her views and actions, as well as her goals and achievements, often seemed discordant. Yet, while Babcock's conclusion that Foltz's life revealed 'disjunction' and 'a fractured, sometimes even frantic, quality' may appear accurate from our perspective, these shifting views in Foltz's life may also point to an ongoing need, on the part of many early women lawyers, to reshape arguments and strategies to achieve specific objectives at different points in time and in differing circumstances. In this context, an examination of how early women lawyers adopted the language of gender equality – or not – and how they identified – or ignored – particular barriers to achieving their goals, may reveal how the rhetoric of equality often, perhaps necessarily, shifted to accommodate the demands of specific contexts, including ideals about (ungendered) legal professionalism. In exploring some of the 'voices' of the first women lawyers, in relation to both their claims about admission to the bar and also with respect to their access to legal work, it is possible to identify some of the tensions they experienced between ideas about gender equality and about professionalism in law.

Gaining Admission to the Bar: Variations on Themes of Equality

Aspiring women lawyers in the late nineteenth century often reflected Louis Frank's optimism about societal changes which increasingly promoted the achievement of women's equality, particularly in relation to access to paid work. For example, in her speech to the university's convocation ceremony in Dunedin in 1897, Ethel Benjamin identified a range of occupations in which women were already achieving 'equality of access', including lady butchers, lady commercial travellers, lady auctioneers, lady opticians, lady dentists, lady watchmakers, and even lady blacksmiths. Full of optimism for the future, she concluded:

> [N]ow women's lives are becoming fuller, freer. They have at last come forward and claimed their right to work as and how they will. The struggle for their rights has not yet ended [but] it is growing keener and keener day by day and year by year. ... For centuries women have submitted to the old unjust order of things, but at last they have rebelled, and as Sarah Grand has it: 'It is the rebels

---

[46] Babcock, BA, 'Reconstructing the Person: The Case of Clara Shortridge Foltz' in SG Bell and M Yarom (eds), *Revealing Lives: Autobiography, Biography and Gender* (Albany, SUNY Press, 1990) 131, 139.

who extend the boundary of the right, little by little narrowing the confines of wrong and crowding it out of existence'.[47]

Benjamin's words reveal how new opportunities for paid work for women represented evidence of significant progress in women's larger struggle for full equality, and her optimism about inevitable success. Similarly, when she began to practise law in late 1897, Benjamin wrote to Frank, commending his efforts on behalf of Chauvin in Paris, and expressing hope that the right of:

all duly qualified women to practise as advocates will before long be recognised by the Courts of France and of all civilized countries.[48]

Benjamin's optimism about the achievement of equality goals was also reflected in Jeanne Chauvin's idealistic letters to Frank, in preparation for submitting her application for admission to the *barreau* in Paris. As she explained in a letter in July 1896, '*Je brûle du désir de me jeter dans la melée, presque certaine d'obtenir de bons résultats*'.[49] Moreover, like Benjamin, Chauvin believed that her application formed part of the larger project of reforming the overall legal status of women, a project in which both Chauvin and Frank had been involved throughout the 1890s:

J'estime de mon devoir de contribuer même ainsi à côté de vous [au] progrès à la grande cause qui parrait l'unique souci de votre vie.[50]

Significantly, when her application was denied by the Paris court, Chauvin turned her attention to Parliament, quoting John Stuart Mill's support for women's liberty and equality, and characterising them as '*principes des civilisations modernes*'.[51]

This optimism about progress in achieving women's equality in the voices of Benjamin and Chauvin was realised, at least initially, since both of them were admitted to the bar within a few short years. By contrast, for women whose efforts to gain entry to the legal professions lasted for decades, or were never realised at all, optimism about goals of gender equality appears more constrained. For example, after more than a decade of unsuccessful efforts to gain admission to the bar, Cornelia Sorabji identified a need to formulate careful strategies to overcome the barriers to women's exclusion from the legal professions. Thus, when she learned about the rejection of Bertha Cave's application for admission to Gray's

---

[47] Brown, above n 32, at 20, citing *Otago Daily Times* (10 Jul 1897) 6.
[48] *Papiers Frank*, above n 44, #7791–6: (typewritten) letter from Benjamin to Frank, 21 Dec 1897.
[49] *Ibid*, #7791–3: letter from Chauvin to Frank, 26 Jul 1896.
[50] *Ibid*, #7791–3: letter from Chauvin to Frank, 27 Aug 1896.
[51] Chauvin, J, '*Féminisme et Antiféminisme*' (1897) *La Revue Blanche* 321, 325.

Inn in 1904 (just a few short months after Cave had completed her qualifications), Sorabji's response suggested anger and frustration rather than optimism:

> How annoying it is to hear of the progress of refusals about women & the Bar! I wish they had not put the question to such unripe test. It bespeaks neither *prudence* nor *tact*: & the possession of either of these gifts seems to be an absolute necessity for the working of any new or forward movement.[52]

In addition, Sorabji's response to Cave's application reveals how one woman's individual strategies for gaining admission to the bar might constrain the equality aspirations of other women. In such a context, equality rhetoric was not at all sufficient to achieve women's goals.

In this context, some aspiring women lawyers eschewed these optimistic claims about the inevitable progress of ideas concerning women's equality. Instead, they grounded their arguments for women's access to the legal professions in economic necessity. For example, in a speech presented by Annie Macdonald Langstaff, who was a single parent while studying law at McGill, equality of access to paid work was the essential goal for women. Langstaff argued that lofty arguments about women's traditional societal roles impeded their ability to earn a decent living; thus, equality of access to paid work, rather than similarly lofty ideals about women's equality, was her primary goal:

> It is all very well to say that women's sole sphere should be the home, but it shows most lamentable blindness to the economic conditions which one would think were potent. The plain fact...is that many women have to earn their living outside the home, if they are to have homes at all ... [All] that is asked for women who desire to practise is that they shall prove [their abilities] as men have to prove them.[53]

Langstaff's focus on access to paid work was similar to arguments published by Eliza Orme in Britain much earlier in 1874, in which Orme had recommended women's access to degrees at the University of London. For Orme, it was clear that women needed access to education to earn a living; thus, she too focused on pragmatic equality in terms of access to paid work:

> It is not a question of whether women are to work or not to work. Many women must work. The question is, are women to have the assistance of a University degree in the work they are obliged to do?[54]

---

[52] Sorabji papers, above n 40, F165/17: letter to Lady Hobhouse, 23 Feb 1904. See also 'Lady Law Students' (Jan 1904) *Englishwoman's Review* 49; *The Times* (3 Dec 1903).

[53] Langstaff, AM, speech to the Insurance Underwriters' Dinner, 1915, cited in Gillett, above n 29, at 306.

[54] Orme, E, 'University Degrees for Women' (May 1874) *The Examiner* 508. Moreover, even in the United States, where women had been becoming lawyers for several decades by

Such comments reveal how the first women lawyers embraced ideas about gender equality goals in different ways. For some, including Benjamin and Chauvin, the rhetoric of women's larger claims for legal and social equality proved useful in their claims for admission to the bar. By contrast, there were others for whom arguments about gender equality were focused on more pragmatic goals, including equality of access to paid work and to university education. It appears more than coincidental that women who did *not* succeed in gaining admission to the legal professions, including Sorabji, Langstaff and Orme, tended to focus on the need for narrower strategies, often adopting pragmatic arguments based on economic necessity. Yet, even for those who used equality rhetoric to gain admission to the bar, arguments about women's equality never challenged fundamental aspects of the culture of legal professions; women continued to be admitted to the bar 'on the same terms as men'.[55] Thus, it is important to examine the voices of women lawyers, not only in relation to admission to the bar, but also in relation to their experience of tensions between ideas of gender equality and professionalism in the practice of law.

Practising Law: 'Balancing' Gender Equality and Legal Professionalism

In response to Louis Frank's requests for information in the late 1890s concerning the experiences of women lawyers in different parts of the world, many women presented descriptions that confirmed their sense of full equality as members of the legal professions. For example, Clara Foltz's 1896 letter, without mentioning at all how she had been forced to initiate litigation to gain admission to law school, described her experiences as a member of the legal profession in completely glowing terms:

> With very few exceptions my relations with my clients have been most cordial and satisfactory. I have sometimes lost cases I thought I would win, but so have my opponents, and I have certainly won quite my share. Losing clients are not always amiable, but their wrath has never been directed toward me ... Between myself and the members of the bar the most friendly relations have always been maintained. Sometimes one of the rifraf of the profession made himself obnoxious, but the cases were few and I feel assured that I have received quite as much of a welcome at the bar and been shown quite as much courtesy by its members, as any other member of the profession.[56]

the end of the nineteenth century, some of them were still accepting work of all kinds. As Belva Lockwood, the first woman admitted to the US Supreme Court, explained in 1887, she accepted 'every case, no matter how difficult, occurring in civil, criminal, equitable and probate law': Drachman, above n 10, at 58.

[55] Above n 31.

[56] *Papiers Frank*, above n 44, #6031 (file 2): letter from Foltz to Frank, 23 Sep 1896.

Similarly, Belva Lockwood, ignoring her tireless efforts over several years to become the first woman admitted to the US Supreme Court in 1879, informed Frank that women and men experienced complete equality in their treatment in American courts:

> The admission of women to the bar in our country has not been the cause of any abuse, or of any inconvenience, either to themselves or others ... I do not think the court has ever shown any difference between male and female attorneys, but all are treated with respect and must respect each other.[57]

And Mary Greene, admitted to the bar of Massachusetts but not engaged in legal practice herself, confirmed that women lawyers were treated equally with respect to areas of legal practice: the

> special field of the woman lawyer is determined not by her sex but by her tastes, her talent, or her environment.[58]

These claims about women's full equality in the practice of law were, of course, written for the purpose of supporting Chauvin's application for admission to the bar in Paris in 1897. In such a context, it is perhaps understandable that American women lawyers wanted to emphasise the positive aspects of their relationships as members of the legal professions. Yet, their sense of equality must have been tempered, at least some of the time, by their exclusion from a number of local bar associations, and from the American Bar Association until 1918. In addition, women were not eligible for admission to several elite law schools in the United States, including Yale, Columbia and Harvard, until well into the twentieth century, and women's exclusion from these schools also ensured that they were not eligible for positions in elite law firms.[59] In this context, women lawyers' claims in their letters to Frank in 1896 may more accurately reflect their aspirations of equality rather than their experiences in practice. Significantly, Ethel Benjamin's experiences as a practitioner in New Zealand were similarly characterised by exclusion from bar dinners and other collegial events,[60] as well as from existing referral arrangements within the legal profession. As she explained in a letter to the Law Society in Wellington after there were complaints about her advertising practices:

---

[57] *Ibid*: letter from Lockwood to Frank, 9 Sep 1896. See also Norgren, J, *Belva Lockwood: The Woman Who Would be President* (New York, New York University Press, 2007).

[58] *Papiers Frank, ibid*: letter from Greene to Frank, 9 Sep 1896.

[59] Stevens, R, *Law School: Legal Education in America from the 1850s to the 1980s* (Chapel Hill, University of North Carolina Press, 1983) 84.

[60] Cullen, MJ, *Lawfully Occupied: The Centennial History of the Otago District Law Society* (Dunedin, Otago District Law Society, 1979) 68.

I know from experience that no business will be put my way by other Solicitors, and I must look to the Public for support.[61]

In addition, it is arguable that the letters from American women lawyers to Frank reveal, perhaps quite subtly, how they were increasingly adopting an identity as professionals, rather than as women. Indeed, Lelia Robinson had explicitly recommended, in a letter to the Equity Club in 1887, that women lawyers subdue their gender identities as members of the bar:

> Just go quietly on, getting a start in some established office if possible, and make practical lawyers of yourselves. If some little matters seem unpleasant, merely take them as matters of course, and pay no attention to them. *Do not take sex into the practice.* Don't be 'lady lawyers.' Simply be *lawyers*, and recognize no distinction – no existence of any distinction between yourselves and the other members of the bar. This will be your surest way to...achieve success. Let no one regard you as a curiosity or a *rara avis*. Compel recognition of your ability and respect for your industry from all. You can take this stand and yet in no wise cease to be ladies – true ladies in every sense of the word.[62]

Like the letters to Frank from Foltz, Lockwood and Greene, Robinson's advice suggests that, even if ideas about gender equality may have fostered women's admission to the bar, the rhetoric of gender equality was not useful in the practice of law. Indeed, women lawyers appear to have increasingly embraced ideas about professionalism, ideas which emphasised objectivity and rationality, and which did not, as Robinson had counselled, 'take sex into the practice'. As Nancy Cott argued, the ideal of 'dispassionate professionalism' was becoming increasingly magnetic in the late nineteenth and early twentieth centuries; in this context, women lawyers increasingly defined themselves as professionals, not as women:

> The professional ethos, with its own promise of freedom from sex-defined constraints, was released to flourish in aspiring women's minds. Women...did not deny the instrumentality of feminism in breaking down barriers to women's first entry to the professions, but they assumed that since women had been admitted to professional ground and no formal bar remained, the professions' supposedly neutral and meritocratic ideology was not only their best armor but their only hope. As the scientific areas...led the way, emphasizing that the professions' hallmarks were objectivity, empiricism, rationality, impersonality, and collegially determined standards, feminism seemed more openly to conflict with those hallmarks. The intensification of the perceived conflict between

---

[61] Brown, above n 32, at 34–5, citing correspondence from Benjamin to the Secretary of the Wellington District Law Society, 19 Sep 1907. See also Gatfield, above n 32.

[62] Drachman, above n 10, at 66: letter of Lelia J Robinson, 1887. See also Robinson, LJ, 'Women Lawyers in the United States' (1890) 2 *The Green Bag* 10.

feminism and professionalism was part and parcel of a larger process of purging politics, advocacy, or reform from within professional definition.[63]

Thus, women lawyers increasingly embraced ideals of (ungendered) equality embedded in ideals about professionalism, subduing the gender equality rhetoric which they had sometimes adopted to gain admission to the bar.[64] In this way, ideas about equality remained important for the first women lawyers, but their focus shifted from equality for women to (ungendered) egalitarian ideals within legal professionalism.

To some extent, this shift was reflected in women lawyers' ambivalence about the women's equality movement at the end of the nineteenth and the beginning of the twentieth centuries. For example, although Chauvin had been an active participant in *L'Avant-Courrière*, an organisation involved in lobbying for reforms to the *Code Civil* in France to permit women to retain their earnings and to allow them to give testimony in public,[65] it is less clear that she remained actively involved in this work after she was admitted to the *barreau* in 1900. Likewise, Benjamin had only a brief connection with the women's movement in New Zealand, parting company with its women reformers early on.[66] In Britain, Orme tried to distance herself from 'strong-minded women', an uncomplimentary term applied to outspoken women, including some of those campaigning for women's equal rights:

'Strong-minded' unfortunately suggests a host of weaknesses of which a very typical one is that peculiar taste which a few women have for trying to dress like men. The women who have been driven into notoriety by the refusal of just and moderate recognition, and those who try to enliven the dullness of a purposeless life by being uselessly eccentric, are generally called strong-minded. Society has adopted the word to describe the abnormal result of its own over-restrictions. How, then, can we speak of women who can take a journey by railway without an escort, who can stand by a friend through a surgical operation, and who yet wear ordinary bonnets and carry medium-sized umbrellas?[67]

Moreover, women lawyers' efforts to avoid being regarded as 'strong-minded' were also reflected in their perceptions of each other; for example,

---

[63] Cott, NF, *The Grounding of Modern Feminism* (New Haven, Yale University Press, 1987) 233–4.

[64] This process of primary identification as professionals, rather than as women, was well illustrated a few decades later in the comment of one of Canada's leading 'woman' lawyers: 'Only the fact that I am a lawyer matters. That I am a woman is of no consequence. I make a point of not knowing how many women lawyers there are in Canada.' See Hyndman, M, 'The Legal Lady', *Maclean's Magazine* (1949) 23.

[65] Mossman, above n 10, at 260–62.

[66] Nicholls, above n 5.

[67] Orme, E, 'Sound-Minded Women' (Aug 1874) *The Examiner* 820.

when Sorabji wished to be considered 'rational' in her claim for admission to the bar, she emphasised in a letter to friends that she was certainly not at all 'a Miss Orme'![68]

In addition, some women lawyers increasingly eschewed connections with suffrage campaigns. For example, Mary Greene explained to Frank that she was not at all involved with the suffrage movement in the United States:

> I do not know enough about the methods of the woman suffragists in this country to tell you much about them. My views on the subject differ in so many ways from those of the leaders that I cannot work with them. I do not believe that the ballot will cure all ills, nor do I believe that women are powerless without the ballot. I prefer to teach women how to use the power and the rights they already possess (which here in America are many) in order that they may know how to ask intelligently for changes in the laws. I do not like the way in which these leaders persistently misrepresent the present laws.[69]

Similarly, although Orme had been a leader of the Women's Liberal Federation in Britain, she promptly resigned when the Federation voted to put suffrage on its agenda before it had been adopted as policy by the Liberal Party.[70] And, although Mabel Penery French participated in the meeting of the International Council of Women in Toronto in 1909, there is no evidence of her further involvement in activities of the women's movement.[71]

Thus, while a rhetoric of *women's legal equality* had been successful in permitting some women to gain admission to the bar at the end of the nineteenth century, the rhetoric of ungendered *equality within professionalism* increasingly masked women lawyers' real inequality in professional and collegial relationships as members of the bar. Indeed, the metaphor of equality as 'masked' within women's professional identities is of interest in a context in which so many of these first women lawyers were described in nineteenth century news reports as 'Portias', a reference to Shakespeare's character in *The Merchant of Venice*.[72] Yet, while Portia represented an excellent model of effective advocacy in the trial scene in the Venetian court, it is clear that all her accomplishments occurred while she was

---

[68] Sorabji Papers, above n 40, F165/16: letter to Lady Hobhouse, 16 Oct 1898.

[69] *Papiers Frank*, above n 44, #7791–6 (envelope 1): letter from Greene to Frank, May 1895.

[70] See Orme, E, 'A Commonplace Correction' (1892) 1 *Welsh Review* 467.

[71] French, MP, 'The Legal Parental Rights of Women in New Brunswick' in *Report of the International Congress of Women, vol 1* (Toronto, Geo Parker & Sons, 1910) 203.

[72] See Corcos, CA, 'Portia and Her Partners in Popular Culture: A Bibliography' (1998) 22 *Legal Studies Forum* 269; Menkel-Meadow, C, 'Portia in a Different Voice: Speculations on a Women's Lawyering Process' (1985) 1 *Berkeley Women's Law Journal* 39; Menkel-Meadow, C, 'Portia *Redux*: Another Look at Gender, Feminism, and Legal Ethics' in S Parker and C Sampford (eds), *Legal Ethics and Legal Practice: Contemporary Issues* (Oxford, Clarendon Press, 1995).

'masked' as a man. Thus, references to the first women lawyers as 'Portias' appeared to recognise women's potential for effective work as legal professionals, while also confirming a male model of legal professionalism. Similarly, the norms of professionalism required women lawyers to 'mask' their gender within their professional identities in accordance with ideas of an objective, rational and ungendered equality. In this way, ideas about legal professionalism increasingly displaced ideas about gender equality for women lawyers.

CONCLUSION

> How are those who cross the threshold received? If they belong to a group different from the group already 'inside,' what are the terms of their incorporation? How do the new arrivals understand their relationship to the place they have entered? What are the terms of identity they establish?[73]

In posing these questions, Joan Wallach Scott argued that the first women who 'cross[ed] the threshold' in the professions necessarily confronted new kinds of challenges, not only in terms of their reception by 'insiders' but also in the formation of professional identities. Thus, the first women lawyers often used equality ideas in their legal arguments before courts and legislatures to gain access to the legal professions; and many of them publicly expressed satisfaction with their treatment as (equal) members of the bar. Yet, the historical record suggests that, even when they were successful in gaining access to the legal professions, women were not fully accepted: they were often excluded from the professions' collegial and social activities, and they sometimes experienced difficulty in obtaining referrals of legal work from colleagues. In addition, many of them increasingly eschewed contact with women's equality movements. In this context, it appears that the rhetoric of equality emphasised the opening up of opportunities for women, particularly in terms of higher education and paid work, but it did not encompass more fundamental changes in ideas about legal professionalism. As Michael Grossberg concluded, *women entered the legal profession without challenging its gender premises.*[74] Thus, by gaining access to the legal professions 'on the same terms as men', women used ideas about gender equality to overcome their exclusion from the bar. But by contrast, an ungendered equality rhetoric, which was fundamental to emerging ideals of professionalism, increasingly served to render invisible women's unequal treatment as members of the legal professions.

---

[73] Scott, JW, 'American Women Historians, 1884–1984' in JW Scott, *Gender and the Politics of History* (New York, Columbia University Press, 1999) 179.
[74] Grossberg, above n 9, at 148. See also Thornton, above n 8.

Moreover, it seems that women who adopted equality rhetoric limited their claims to ideas of formal equality; they did not address more fundamental issues concerning the structure or culture of the legal professions. As Jane Rendall explained, however, women's arguments had to be presented in the context of existing (male) political discourse; thus, their arguments often:

combine[d] both the demands that arose from the perceived needs of women, and the contemporary language of the male political world.[75]

In such a context, claims on the part of the first women lawyers necessarily were framed within the context of 'what society prescribed as desirable and plausible for a person of their gender'.[76] At the same time, the ways in which the first women lawyers used equality rhetoric, or designed other kinds of strategies to accomplish their goals, have profound implications for contemporary legal professions. As the work of a number of modern scholars demonstrates,[77] *substantive* equality in the legal professions has not yet been achieved: for example, issues of work-family balance, glass ceilings, and gendered behaviour and expectations remain highly contested in a number of different jurisdictions.[78] Moreover, although the stories of the first women lawyers sometimes reflect the optimism of Louis Frank in 1898, modern women lawyers know, as Carol Sanger pointed out, that:

the biographies of women who chose to locate their professional lives in the law are likely to be stories of *piecemeal progress and circumscribed success.*[79]

---

[75] Rendall, J, *The Origins of Modern Feminism: Women in Britain, France and the United States 1780–1860* (Chicago, Lyceum Books, 1985) 4.

[76] Cohen, ES, 'Court Testimony from the Past: Self and Culture in the Making of Text' in M Kadar (ed), *Essays on Life Writing: From Genre to Critical Practice* (Toronto, University of Toronto Press, 1992) 84, 89–90. See also Rendall, J, 'Uneven Developments: Women's History, Feminist History and Gender History in Great Britain' in K Offen, R Roach Pierson, and J Rendall (eds), *Writing Women's History: International Perspectives* (Bloomington, Indiana University Press, 1991) 45.

[77] See Schultz and Shaw, above n 13; Brockman, J, *Gender in the Legal Profession: Fitting in or Breaking the Mould* (Vancouver, UBC Press, 2001); Sommerlad, H and Sanderson, P, *Gender, Choice and Commitment: Women Solicitors in England and Wales and the Struggle for Equal Status* (Aldershot, Ashgate/Dartmouth, 1998); Thornton, above n 8; Hagan, J and Kay, F, *Gender in Practice: A Study of Lawyers' Lives* (Oxford, Oxford University Press, 1995); Harrington, M, *Women Lawyers: Rewriting the Rules* (New York, Plume Books, 1995); Rhode, DL, *The Unfinished Agenda: Women in the Legal Profession* (Chicago, American Bar Association Commission on Women in the Profession, 2001).

[78] Kay, F, 'Review Essay: The Social Significance of the World's First Women Lawyers' (2007) 45 *Osgoode Hall Law Journal* 397, 420–22.

[79] Sanger, above n 2.

8

That Obscure Object of Desire: Sex Equality and the Legal Profession

HILARY SOMMERLAD*

INTRODUCTION

EQUALITY PROJECTS ARE in disarray. After a near century of expansion resulting in, for instance, re-distributive socio-economic policies and anti-discrimination legislation, equality is now being assailed by critiques levelled against other 'modernist' concepts. Disowned by some who might be expected to seek its shelter, it is increasingly undermined by the neo-liberal project – an inherently hierarchical paradigm, in which social rights are residual and the discourse of social justice equality substituted for one of individual freedom, formal equality and diversity. This chapter will use current research into the encounter between the legal profession and a sample of trainee solicitors in the UK as a prism through which to examine the assaults on equality projects.

A significant characteristic of the sample is that the majority do not fit the professional template of the white, male, middle class subject.[1] However, whilst for several decades such 'outsider' trainees were overwhelmingly white middle class women, today their composition is far more heterogeneous, challenging the essentialism implicit in the concept of sex equality and bolstering the longstanding critique of studies which 'homogenise' women by taking gender as their primary focus. This paper therefore considers a range of intersecting forms of inequality. However, since there

---

* I would like to thank Sophie Goodeve for her research help, and Lisa Geary and Darren Shaw for their assistance.

[1] There is no established term to describe such students, precisely because their disadvantage frequently spans more than one axis. Many are first generation entrants to Higher Education (HE), but this is not always the case, so I have generally referred to them as 'outsider' students.

is extensive evidence that the profession continues to reify women in terms of their gender,[2] I also focus on women as 'women'.

The outsider status of many of the trainees is encapsulated in an initial unfamiliarity with the profession which in itself tends to represent a barrier to entry and progression: the paper will therefore examine whether they have come to comprehend the profession or whether it remains obscure to them. Are they able to gain entry, despite their lack of insider knowledge and poor cultural capital? The discussion of the data will also consider how women and other 'non-traditional' trainees self-conceptualise – do they see themselves as inhabiting particular collective categories? And if so, are they motivated by wishing to contribute to collective equality and social justice? Or are these now outdated values, trumped by the lure of material reward and status articulated in the discourse of meritocracy? Even if their primary identification is with their collective category, do the processes of professional identity formation which the 'outsider' trainee must undergo in order to become an 'equal' professional, preclude the progression of a subordinated category?

The chapter begins by discussing the current decline of interest in the sociology and politics of equality. It then reflects on the significance of liberal feminism and women's entry into the legal profession. The subsequent section describes the methodology of the research project which supplies the data, discussion of which forms the main body of the chapter.

EQUALITY OR MERITOCRACY: COLLECTIVITY OR IDENTITY

Equality's problems as a concept derive in part from internal tensions. A fundamental Enlightenment principle, it has, from its origin, been characterised by ambivalence, sustaining both liberalism and collectivist discourses. In its individualist, economistic guise it transmutes into meritocracy, framing the discourse of the autonomous, freely contracting legal subject. But it also generated a collectivist, substantive connotation which challenged the inequality implicit in formal equality and meritocracy, and which underpinned modern social justice struggles.

Whilst the idea of equality was a key stimulus of early feminist struggles, the dichotomy between equality's individualised and collectivist meanings has been particularly problematic for later feminism. On the one hand the construction of women as a collectivity primarily defined by their sexual and/or reproductive functions (including domestic duties) has required a

---

[2]   See, eg Duff, L and Webley, L, *Women Solicitors: Equality & Diversity: Report to the Law Society of England and Wales* (London, University of Westminster, 2003); McKenzie Leiper, J, *Bar Codes: Women in the Legal Profession* (Vancouver, UBC Press, 2007) for evidence of the persistence of women's professional disadvantage.

corresponding solidarity – yet equality struggles organised around a gender-collectivist strategy, that is as equality of opportunity and of outcome, reify the very difference which is the motif for the initial subordination. On the other hand women's intersectionality has meant that more privileged women have been able to use, for instance, their class and/or ethnic identity in the deployment of formal equality strategies to differentiate themselves from other women, thereby transcending – and emphasising – the negativity or at least asymmetry of female cultural capital.

The tensions within the concept have been compounded by the material and ideological changes which have transformed the West in recent decades: most notably, on the one hand, de-industrialisation, an increase in material inequality and decline in the social justice agenda, and, on the other hand, the rise of neo-liberalism and the discourse of meritocracy. These and other related changes, such as the reconstruction of the family and of gender norms, and the fragmentation of society, have necessarily challenged the monolithic and static character of collectivist understandings of equality. The weakening of social structural processes and the consequently fluid nature of social categories,[3] the boundaries of which are seen as more dependent on who is constructing them and in what context[4] than on material circumstances, has shifted attention towards identity, social agency and the symbolic. Identity formation is viewed as ongoing and relational, meaning created by individuals through processes of social interaction, involving the mobilisation or performance[5] of 'a complex of occasional identities in response to shifting contexts'.[6]

The complexity of this perspective on identity, and the difficulties it poses for collective equality projects, is increased if we jettison the teleological understanding of the social world as constituted by a linear evolutionary trajectory, where systems of culture and identity supplant their predecessors, and instead recognise that societal change is accumulative.[7] This postulates the articulation of different modes of production and

---

[3] Anthias, F, 'Rethinking Social Division: Some Notes Towards a Theoretical Framework' (1998) 46 *The Sociological Review* 505.

[4] Eg post-structuralist analysis posits identity as formed and informed through the discursive practices and interactions in which individuals engage: MacLure, M, 'Arguing For Your Self: Identity as an Organising Principle in Teachers' Jobs and Lives' (1993) 19 *British Educational Research Journal* 311.

[5] Butler, J, *Excitable Speech: a Politics of the Performative* (London, Routledge, 1999) in which she argues that the entwinement of the material with the discursive/symbolic, together with the generalised and hence indeterminate process of subjectification, allows for appropriation and subversion of the performative.

[6] Stronach, I, Corbin, B, McNamara, O, Stark, S and Warne, T, 'Towards an Uncertain Politics of Professionalism: Teacher and Nurse Identities in Flux' (2002) 17 *Journal of Educational Policy* 109.

[7] Mattausch, J, 'Chance and Societal Change' (2003) 54 *The Sociological Review* 506.

the coexistence of cultural forms with very different historical connotations: in the legal profession the vestiges of the gentlemanly profession reside alongside the rapacious 24/7 world of the globalised capitalist law firm – so, on the one hand, the last two decades have seen the neo-liberal sponsorship of highly individualised mobility projects, but, at the same time, the retention, despite neo-liberalism, of systems of social closure based on ascriptive characteristics. Thus, just as identities are constructed using 'building materials from history',[8] so too are social contexts marked by the coexistence of numerous temporalities which are then enacted in social practice; that is, as Bourdieu has argued, the historical is embodied and thus enacted within the social.[9]

For social theorists such as Beck a socially contingent view of identity[10] is fundamental to reflexive modernity. Whilst recognising the persistence, even accentuation, of material inequality, this view posits the social world as characterised by individualised differentiation, producing recognition of hierarchy, and positioning within it, rather than consciousness of category.[11] This devaluation of structure has, in a mimesis of the neo-liberal replacement of citizenship with consumerism,[12] generated a discourse of 'prescriptive individualism' which posits significant potential for individuals to reflect and strategise in order to succeed in their individual mobility projects:[13] the 'axes of (socially organised) difference, such as class, gender and sexuality...are (now) more a matter of individual decisions'.[14] Correspondingly, the responsibility for individual inequality can be re-assigned, either to individuals' wilful choice of subordinated difference, or to their failure to be appropriately reflexive[15] (or subversive).

[8]   Castells, M, *The Information Age: Economy, Society and Culture Vol II:The Power of Identity* (Oxford, Blackwell, 1997) 6–7.

[9]   Eg 'the habitus, the product of history, produces individual and collective practices and hence history, in accordance with the schemes engendered by history': Bourdieu, P, *Outline of a Theory of Practice* (Cambridge, Cambridge University Press, 1977) 82.

[10]   Nias, J, *Primary Teachers Talking* (London, Routledge & Kegan Paul, 1989); Goffman, E, *The Presentation of Self in Everyday Life* (New York, Doubleday, 1959).

[11]   Beck, U and Beck-Gernsheim, E, *Individualization: Institutionalized Individualization and its Social and Political Consequences* (London, Sage, 2001) 203; see also Giddens, A, *Modernity and Self Identity* (Cambridge, Polity, 1991).

[12]   Which entails the positioning of some as 'flawed consumers': Bauman, Z, *Postmodernity and its Discontents* (Cambridge, Polity, 1997).

[13]   Strathern, M, 'Qualified Value: The Perspective of Gift Exchange' in C Humphreys and S Hugh-Jones (eds), *Barter, Exchange and Value: An Anthropological Approach* (Cambridge, Cambridge University Press, 1992).

[14]   Beck, U and Beck-Gernsheim, E, *The Normal Chaos of Love* (Cambridge, Polity, 1996) 29.

[15]   Eg Skeggs, B, 'Change Value and Affect: Bourdieu and "The Self" in L Adkins and B Skeggs (eds), *Feminism After Bourdieu* (Oxford, Blackwell, 2004).

However, this 'reflexive modernisation' thesis is critiqued by other theorists[16] who, whilst agreeing that traditional sources of identity have weakened, nevertheless argue for the continuing salience of structure. Theorised in terms of difference or expressed in the unequal relationship in which groups stand to one another, social forms of determination are held to be implicit in social relations and expressed in cultural practices.[17] Class cultures are viewed as 'modes of differentiation rather than types of collectivity',[18] and whiteness[19] and gender as still deeply embedded in social practice, naturalising and hence perpetuating existing hierarchies.[20]

The structuralist framework offered by Pierre Bourdieu, grounded in the mechanisms within social systems which guarantee their reproduction, represents the most powerful critique of the voluntarism of 'rational action theory'.[21] Bourdieu's sociology is constructed around the open-ended conceptual tools of field, habitus and capital which offer a bridge between objectivism and subjectivism. Conceived as a social space with distinct, objective properties, a field is organised around behaviours and practices which are strongly patterned by traditions. These form part of a field's 'doxa', that is the tacit, taken for granted presuppositions which produce the field's habitus and determine its cultural practice. Identity formation and hence the capacity for 'equality' is thus constrained by the field's mechanisms for producing bodies disciplined by durable dispositions that recognise and comply with the field's specific demands.

In this view identity formation and equality projects (whether individual or collective) take place within a social world which, despite the discourse of equality and diversity, remains strongly hierarchical, and within which cultural forms and practices characteristic of different periods and fields

---

[16] Savage, M, *Class Analysis and Social Transformation* (Buckingham, Open University, 2000) 35.

[17] Eg Crook et al argue that 'action is divorced from underlying material constraints…and enters the voluntaristic realm of taste, choice and preference. As it does so the boundaries between determined social groups disappear': Crook, S, Pakulski, J and Waters, M, *Postmodernization* (London, Sage, 1992) 35.

[18] Savage, above n 16, at 102.

[19] See the work of David Wilkins for discussion of the continuing salience of race; eg 'The claim that lawyers and those with whom they interact can ignore race even if they wanted to requires believing that there is an "essential" core of rationality free from the pervasiveness of racial imagery, or that individuals can "construct" such a self out of existing cultural materials': Wilkins, D, 'Identities and Roles: Race, Recognition, and Professional Responsibility' (1998) 57 *Maryland Law Review* 1502, 1536.

[20] See Bottero, W and Irwin, S, 'Locating Difference: Class, "Race" and Gender, and the Shaping of Social Inequalities' (2003) 51 *The Sociological Review* 463, for a useful discussion of current theorisations of (in)equality, difference and identity.

[21] Bourdieu, P and Wacquant, L, *An Invitation to Reflexive Sociology* (Cambridge, Polity, 1992) 123.

intermingle.[22] Another way of expressing this is to return to the relationality not just of individual identity, discussed above, but also of the categories of gender and ethnicity. As Beck argues, identity *is* socially contingent, but it is structured by actors' understandings of merit and valuations of cultural and symbolic capital which are historical, and which are themselves the product of cultural lag: that is, derived from antique status understandings of, for instance, gender, ethnicity and class.[23] As a result, whilst the greater autonomy that 'women' now enjoy, together with our intersectional understandings of womanhood, may be producing a new and more nuanced politics of equality,[24] at the same time, within that conjuncture women can have the abjections of their embodiment re-imposed on them in certain interactions – and at the whim of the dominant actors in the field.

Nevertheless because habitus is generative as well as produced by a field, change *is* possible – in fact, of course, inevitable – and may be particularly sweeping in times of social crisis, though the extent, pace and direction of the change will be constrained by the social conditions set by the field.[25] The pressures of the wider social changes which have characterised recent decades have generated a lengthy (and ongoing) transformation of the legal profession from one based on traditional status categories to one rhetorically committed to economically rational practices, and to equality and diversity.[26] Arguably, this transformation has and does still represent a social crisis for the profession, and thus provides ideal terrain for outsiders' equality projects.

EQUALITY PROJECTS AND THE SOLICITORS' PROFESSION

As a major domain of the symbolic, the source of formal equality, the site of collectivist equality struggles, a primary goal in individual social

---

[22] As Parr has observed, 'social identities...are forged in particular spatial and temporal settings': cited in Mossman, MJ, *The First Women Lawyers* (Oxford, Hart Publishing, 2006) 15.

[23] It has therefore been argued that 'a reflexive orientation towards the contemporary environment may itself be regarded as a form of habitus, itself the outcome of an adaptation to...the changing nature of the social terrain': Sweetman, P, 'Twenty First Century Dis-ease? Habitual Reflexivity or the Reflexive Habitus' (2003) 51 *The Sociological Review* 528, 543. This historicisation of agency underscores the power of traditional ideologies to constrain, through the continuing reification of others on the basis of their ethnicity or gender.

[24] Walby, S, 'From Community to Coalition. The Politics of Recognition as the Handmaiden of the Politics of Equality in an Era of Globalization' (2001) 18 *Theory, Culture and Society* 113, 118.

[25] 'Times of crisis in which the routine adjustment of subjective and objective structures is brutally disrupted, constitute a class of circumstances when..."rational choice" may take over': Bourdieu and Wacquant, above n 21, at 123.

[26] Abel, R, *English Lawyers Between Market and State* (Oxford, Oxford University Press, 2003).

mobility projects, and an arena strongly marked by different temporalities, law and the legal profession exemplify important dimensions of the equality/identity problematic. As the first outsiders to seek entry to the profession, women deployed a collectivist equality rhetoric, but generally entered as individuals who had (uncharacteristically) acquired a masculine habitus (usually because they were drawn from the same social space as male lawyers) and were hence able to emulate those embodied (masculine) attributes deemed essential to lawyering, to 'pass' as almost male. Far from demonstrating gender consciousness, they tended to identify primarily as lawyers, exemplifying 'bleached out' professionalism.[27]

Nevertheless the history of women solicitors points to the durability of the traditional status groups of gender, ethnicity and class. The fact that until recently they tended to be of similar class background to that of the male lawyers meant that whilst their participation reinforced a 'fictitious universalism',[28] in practice it failed to produce synchronicity between doxic understandings of what it is to be 'woman', which are embedded in the general social field, and doxic understandings of what it is to be a lawyer. Nor, therefore, did it either disrupt the objective properties of the field or the law's nomination and reification of certain characteristics as female.[29]

Furthermore, to a great extent this continues to be the case, especially in the corporate sector where women lawyers tend to be middle class, white and committed to normative professionalism.[30] Their increased participation therefore exemplifies neo-liberal equality – that is, meritocracy: as *individual* access to privilege it contributes to the growing inequalities within a category, since it frequently involves highly gendered performances together with a denial of feminism,[31] and reliance on salaried female domestic labour.[32]

---

[27] Levinson, S, 'Identifying the Jewish Lawyer: Reflections on the Construction of Professional Identity' (1993) 14 *Cardozo Law Review* 1577; and see Wilkins, above n 19. See Mossman, above n 22, and in this volume, for discussion of early women lawyers' tendency to identify primarily as 'ungendered' lawyers.

[28] Bourdieu, P, *Masculine Domination* (Cambridge, Polity Press, 2001) 117.

[29] See Sommerlad, H and Sanderson, P, *Gender, Choice and Commitment* (Aldershot, Ashgate, 1998) 155.

[30] Skordaki, E, 'Glass Slippers and Glass Ceilings: Women in the Legal Profession' (1996) 3 *International Journal of the Legal Profession*, 16–17.

[31] Hunter, R, 'Talking Up Equality: Women Barristers and the Denial of Discrimination' (2002) 10 *Feminist Legal Studies* 113, 127, in which she describes how a significant group of her respondents deny both discrimination and their 'femininity (or at least its devalued aspects)' and 'present themselves simply as non-gendered barristers', whilst also conforming to 'standard gender stereotypes'.

[32] Anderson, B, *Doing the Dirty Work: the Global Politics of Domestic Labour* (London, Zed Books, 2000); and see Lovell, T, 'Rethinking Class and Gender' in Adkins and Skeggs (eds), above n 15, at 50–51.

Nevertheless, as we observed in the preceding section, identity is socially contingent and whilst its formation is shaped by structural forces, there is significant space for individual agency at times of great social change. On the one hand the profession continues to be a site where both masculinity and whiteness are simultaneously locations of structural advantage and also 'refer to a set of cultural practices that are usually unmarked and unnamed'.[33] On the other hand, social fragmentation and increasing material inequality has resulted in the legal profession's polarisation between the rich corporate sector and that which serves the private and legally aided client; its practices have undergone a process of de-traditionalisation; the last three decades have seen the large scale influx of women, and the profession now represents one of the most popular destinies for actors drawn from groups which are clearly differentiated from and stand in an unequal relationship to the group from which the professional elite is drawn.[34]

The research on which this chapter is based is therefore designed to explore the tensions between the objective structures of the professional field and subjective phenomena, that is between the career projects of outsiders and the persistence of gendered, classed and raced hierarchies. I have designated the cluster of choices and imaginary futures to which outsiders adhere as 'equality projects', though the data reveals this to be as deeply problematic a concept as the preceding discussion would lead us to believe. The projects formulated with the desire to achieve a place in the traditional hierarchy of law might apparently represent equality projects only in the liberal formal equality sense – that is, a desire to be treated comparably to any insider. As such, they could alternatively be designated 'mobility projects' or, following Witz, 'usurpationary strategies'.[35] However, this would be to ignore the extent to which, for many of these students, their planned trajectory is shaped by a network of real and perceived obligations to family and community,[36] and a consciousness of past exclusions, and is therefore very much informed by the concept of equality, even where this is represented by prospects of individual material gain. Similarly, although even the most idealistic venture into community-based lawyering reproduces the hierarchy of professional power, and may only weakly impact on substantive equality, that sense of obligation, most

[33] Frankenburg, R, 'White Women, Race Matters: The Social Construction of Whiteness' in L Back and J Solomos (eds), *Theories of Race & Racism* (London, Routledge, 2000).

[34] Shiner, M, 'Young, Gifted and Blocked! Entry to the Solicitors' Profession' in P Thomas (ed), *Discriminating Lawyers* (London, Cavendish, 2000) 93; see also Francis, A and McDonald, I, 'All Dressed Up and Nowhere to Go? Part-Time Law Students and the Legal Profession' in Thomas, *ibid.*

[35] Witz, A, *Professions and Patriarchy* (London, Routledge, 1992).

[36] Bagguley, P and Hussain, Y, *The Role of Higher Education in Providing Opportunities for South Asian Women* (Bristol, The Policy Press, 2007).

acutely felt by the children of economic migrants, imparts a collective element which mirrors the collective attempts of the dominant groups in the profession to marginalise 'outsider' lawyers in order to preserve their own position.

METHODOLOGY

The research project (which was piloted in 2003–04) was begun in September 2004 and is a longitudinal study of two cohorts of around 30 part-time and 60 full-time post-graduate students,[37] undergoing the academic stage of their vocational training (the Legal Practice Course (LPC))[38] at a new university in a large provincial city in the North of England.[39] The research is concerned with the processes of professional identity formation; specifically, it is designed to survey trainees' perceptions of the legal professional field and to track developments in career aspirations, levels of attainment and self conceptualisation, during and after the vocational training stage and into qualification.

The project's methodology comprises a mixture of methods, designed to combine the robust character of survey data with the insights available from in-depth qualitative techniques. Two questionnaires were administered to the student cohorts (both full and part-timers) at different stages in the LPC: the first during their first week and the second towards the end of their course (therefore the administration of questionnaire two to the part-time students in a cohort takes place a year after its administration to the full-timers). The questionnaires were designed to capture basic socio-demographic details; understandings of the profession; motivations and aspirations and their development; and success in obtaining training contracts. The data from the questionnaires was quality checked and,

---

[37] Cohort 1 comprised full-time students 2004–05 and part-time students 2004–06; cohort 2 2005–06 and 2005–07 respectively; the precise numbers varied slightly in each year of the study: 2004–05, 30 were part-time, 57 full-time; 2005–06, 33 part-time, 63 full-time.

[38] Currently becoming a solicitor in England and Wales is a lengthy and expensive process which generally comprises successful completion of either a qualifying law degree or a post-graduate diploma in law, followed by 3 or 4 years' vocational training comprising the LPC (either 1 year full-time or 2 years' part-time) and a 2 year training contract in practice. Contracts are increasingly difficult to obtain, especially for those from new universities and/or those without contacts in the profession.

[39] To explore the equality projects of students drawn from 'outsider groups' the research needed to be based in a 'new' university: the UK's highly stratified HE system comprises the 'Russell Group' of elite, traditional and 'redbrick' universities; the other 'pre-1992' universities, and the former polytechnics known as the 'post-1992' or 'new' universities; see Thomas, P and Rees, A, 'Law Students – Getting In and Getting On' in Thomas (ed), above n 34; Boon, A and Duncan, N, 'An Elite Profession and Elite Institutions Facing Demographic Change' (Spring 1990) *Journal of Access Studies* 47.

where appropriate, coded before being input into SPSS for analysis. Findings from the analysis in part determined the scope and nature of the in-depth qualitative follow up work.

The first questionnaire was followed by focus groups which were held about a third of the way through the full-time year (again these were held a year later for the part-timers in the cohort). Around one third of the student body participated in four groups of between four and nine students, who were selected to comprise various combinations: for instance, one group might be all female, one all male; one all non-white; one mixed both in terms of gender and ethnicity. Each group was led by a different member of the research team. The issues explored included law as a discipline, knowledge of the profession, the ideal job, and timelines charting the original desire to do law and the imagined career trajectory. In order to elicit internalised, and possibly tacit understandings of the profession, responses to questions were explored both in open discussion, and also by asking respondents to write descriptions and to draw what came into their minds when, for instance, they thought of solicitors. The focus group sessions lasted around two and a half hours. This focus group work was followed by semi-structured interviews with students, largely drawn from the full-time cohort but including some part-timers. In order to reduce bias, focus group participants were generally not selected for interview. Interviews are also being conducted with selected members of the cohorts at staged intervals during their training contract and through into their first two years post qualification, again at regular intervals.

The project is also undertaking research with representatives of the local legal labour market, deploying similar methods to those used with the student samples (this stage of the research is in progress at the time of writing). A questionnaire is being administered to all legal employers in the local county and in two nearby cities, which partly mirrors that administered to the students, with the addition of questions on how many trainees the employer takes and criteria for selection, methods of training together with questions about ideal qualities in a trainee. The questionnaire stage is to be followed by focus groups and interviews.

All the qualitative research is recorded and then transcribed.

THE DATA

Student Profile: Intersections of Class, Gender and Ethnicity

As discussed above, it is commonplace that de-industrialisation has problematised the concept of class. Nevertheless, research supports the view that all status categories and especially class continue to shape the potential for social agency in the legal profession.[40] It was therefore fundamental to the project to identify the sample's demographic profile.[41] The results discussed below are based on merging the two cohorts.

Because few 'old' universities run the (post-graduate) LPC,[42] the sample did contain some students who had been undergraduates in the pre-1992 sector; however the majority were 'outsiders'.[43] So, whilst the percentage of female students (55%) corresponded to the national average, the proportion of black or minority ethnic (BME) students exceeded it (41% as opposed to 23.9%).[44] Confounding Beck's description of class as a 'zombie category', around 45% categorised themselves as working class,[45] more of whom were Asian British than White British. The sample also included a higher than average percentage of mature students. No students identified themselves as gay and none as having a disability.

Students' self categorisation was triangulated with such indicators of socio-economic status as postcode, parental occupation, school attended and patterns of familial (non) attendance at university. The importance of educational institutions for encoding and then generating cultural and symbolic capital and hence reproducing class privilege[46] was demonstrated by firms' (especially the corporate firms') practice of basing their selection process in part on the school and category of university an applicant had

---

[40] Thus, one commentator observes that 'class appears to be the greatest obstacle to entry and progress within legal practice': Nicolson, D, 'Demography, Discrimination and Diversity: A New Dawn for the British Legal Profession?' (2005) *International Journal of the Legal Profession*, 201, 208.

[41] However, as discussed above, the erosion of occupation as a basis for social categorisation has problematised the conceptualisation of social categories. Yet social stratification not only persists but social mobility has actually decreased in the UK in recent years. We therefore used a combination of signifiers described above in the main text, some of which were socio-economic and some related to cultural practice, and based our percentages on the clusters of these signifiers and respondents' own self identification.

[42] When training in the craft of lawyering was deemed to require formal academic input rather than remain an apprenticeship process controlled by the profession, it became the province of polytechnics or HE colleges. These institutions, which in 1992 became the 'new' universities, continue to provide this technical part of a lawyer's formation whilst most 'old' universities continue to restrict themselves to law as a liberal art; this division is expressive of the status difference between new and old universities (see above n 39).

[43] As Shiner has noted 'students from less privileged social class backgrounds tend to be concentrated in new universities': Shiner, above n 34, at 115; and Francis and McDonald, above n 34.

[44] Cole, B, *Law Society Annual Statistical Report – Trends in the Solicitors' Profession* (London, Law Society, 2004).

[45] Beck and Beck-Gernsheim, above n 11, at 203; and likewise undermining the proposition that people are refusing 'the entire class discourse': Savage, above n 16, at 35.

[46] It was striking that the families of some students, especially those from a BME background, were central to individuals' conscious capital accumulating strategies. See Bourdieu, P and Passeron, JC, *Reproduction in Education, Society and Culture* (London, Sage, 1977); Dhavan, R, Kibble, N and Twining, W, *Access to Legal Education and the Legal Profession* (London, Butterworths, 1989) 275.

attended.[47] Relatedly, the lack of awareness by individuals whose family had had no experience of university of what would constitute a productive cultural accumulation strategy was revealed in students' 'choices' of institution, and their alienation from the pre-1992 institutions:

> The Russell Universities I visited, they seemed unapproachable, it was like 'yes we're selling you this and it's just a product and I'm a professor and you should know where you are'...very hierarchical...it made me think 'I don't want to be part of it because I won't fit in'.

However by the time of the research study, when the students had completed their first degree, all were very conscious of the class divide between HEIs; it was common to talk in terms of 'stigma' and the 'outsiders' readily nominated the provenance of their degree as a barrier they would need to overcome to realise their aspirations:

> There's elitism among the institutions...it borders on discrimination. If you've gone to a new university, not one of the red brick, top level institutions, then you're not fit to work for their firm – I've had that said to me.

One woman anticipated the intersections of different forms of marginalisation:

> You're at a disadvantage because you are female and also because you didn't go to a sort of proper university.

The implicit encoding of inferiority and superiority in different social and cultural practices is manifest in the following account by a white woman from a working class background who had first started a law degree at an old university but had given it up:

> I did a year there and loathed it...I just didn't seem to fit...I was terrified all the time...they made me feel inferior.

Her experience of the cultural mechanisms of closure extended to the way in which law was taught:

> It was very academic...they made it feel completely alien, the first sort of thing we had to do was...registered and unregistered land...but you didn't really feel you could ask for help if you were struggling...it was more a case of 'go and learn it for yourself and if you haven't understood then there is no point in your being here'.

---

[47] Whilst the twin policies of expansion and widening participation, sponsored by the state and the university sector in the UK since the 1990s, have produced a more diverse student base, this has been largely confined to the new university sector, and has tended not to produce equality of opportunity for their students; as Boon and Duncan observe, the concentration of resources in the 'old' universities has reinforced HE stratification and erected 'further career disadvantage to those who enter HE through non- traditional channels': above n 39, at 47; see also Shiner and Francis and McDonald, above n 34, and Thomas and Rees, above n 39.

Her second attempt to do law was at a new university, where she found a profound difference in 'the type of people – more like me'. There she also encountered a different approach to teaching: she explained that the university consciously aimed to deconstruct the mysteries of the law, to make transparent the opaque 'rules of the game': 'you were eased into it more gently from the start and...the tutors are definitely approachable'. However as Bourdieu has observed, the official language of a discourse community:

> reinforces the authority which is the source of its domination. It does this by ensuring among all members of the 'linguistic community'...the minimum communication which is the precondition for economic production and even for symbolic domination.[48]

And the shift in the meaning of class from a simple socio-economic category towards one signified by ignorance (that is, unmeritworthiness/ontological inequality) ensures that the more the new universities adapt to meet the needs of their students rather than transmitting the means by which students may in turn exercise symbolic domination, the more they may be viewed as producing besuited proletarians who have done 'dumbed down' or, in the words of an employer, 'mickey mouse degrees'. Further, as one student argued, the more accessible approach of the new universities may leave students 'ill equipped to deal with (the elitism) of the profession'.

In Bourdieu's theoretical model, power relations are most effective when they are 'somatised, that is inscribed as active ingredients in the bodies...as well as in the minds that perceive them'.[49] The inherent *lack* of authority in working class identities is also encoded in dress and speech.[50] The dress codes and bodily work of female outsider students tended to result in an aesthetic which could be coded as 'common', which clearly differentiated them from the subtle dress adopted by the middle class women, and from which ignorance could be read off.[51] And whilst students were conscious of the importance of dress in 'passing' as a professional in that all spoke of the need to wear a dark suit, they did not seem wholly conscious of what that involved:

> We had this woman come in from (*name of local firm*) and she said 'girls – black suits, trousers and white shirts and that's it' and I thought 'oh that's really

---

[48] Bourdieu, P, *Language and Symbolic Power* (Cambridge, Mass, Harvard University Press, 1991) 44.

[49] Bourdieu, above n 28, at 31.

[50] Over and above the indicators referred to above, students' class was manifest in everything about them – such as their hobbies, their dress and their accents: they embodied class; see Walkerdine, V, Lucey, H and Melody, J, *Growing Up Girl: Psychosexual Explorations of Gender and Class* (Basingstoke, Palgrave, 2001).

[51] Skeggs, B, *Formations of Class and Gender: Becoming Respectable* (London, Sage, 1997).

dull...[S]he said something like 'you're the face of the firm and you can't be seen to be different...you've got to follow in the footsteps of being smart and formal'.

Asked whether she would wear a low neckline, this student said 'yes, not too low but I wouldn't feel I had to wear a button up top'. Another student reported having been told on a placement that her skirt was too short.

On the other hand, Muslim students' use of religious dress produced an embodiment which was most alien to white professional normativity, and most revelatory of its structuration in terms of outsiders and insiders.[52] Thus one employer, when asked if her (large corporate) firm would be happy to take a British Asian woman who wore religious dress, said they would take one, as they had some public sector clients who 'would like that'.

Speech is of course a primary medium of communicating cultural capital and many students expressed concerns and even shame about their own accent as insufficiently 'neutral'. The following comments were representative:

> Things that might hinder me (in realising my aspirations): my educational history and the fact that I have quite a broad accent...I don't think it sounds as nice as some of the others...a BBC accent would help a lot.

The Nature of Students' Social Mobility/Equality Projects

How did such students, who were identifiably outsiders, conceive of the profession and what was the nature of their social mobility projects? One of the ways in which the woman who had started a law degree at an old university had recognised herself to be an outsider was in relation to the other students' clear understanding of normative professionalism, and their sense of future trajectory, a sense of becoming:

> Everybody else had wanted to do (law) since they were ten or something...a lot were from really privileged backgrounds, dads were lawyers, granddads lawyers, cousins lawyers...they sort of followed that path from being like at a good school to a good university.

The experience of another woman who had done her law degree at a Russell group university is an account of a lesson in symbolic domination and the receptiveness of her fellow students to this training for hierarchy:[53]

> My introductory lecture, the first thing they said was 'intelligence wise, you are in the top 1% of the country'. A lot of people carried that through with them,

---

[52] Amit, V and Rapport, N, *The Trouble with Community* (London, Pluto Press, 2002) 165. The research evidence for the persistence of racism within the profession is substantial; see, eg Vignaendra, S, Williams, M and Garvey, J, 'Hearing Black and Asian Voices – An Exploration of Identity' in Thomas (ed), above n 34.
[53] Kennedy, D, 'Legal Education as Training For Hierarchy' in I Grigg-Spall and P Ireland (eds) *The Critical Lawyers' Handbook* (London, Pluto Press, 1992).

they were confident, arrogant people...the lecturers didn't really talk to you about anything else apart from Magic Circle firms...it was all about money...no one said anything about job satisfaction or justice.

By contrast, those students from a working class background had few or no contacts with the profession and their understanding of it and aspirations had been formed by television programmes and films such as LA Law and Perry Mason. A member of the first cohort, in training with a firm when interviewed, said she had known nothing about the profession: 'no lawyers in the family...if I had known about it, it might have put me off'.[54]

When in the focus groups the students were asked to describe and draw what came into their minds when they thought of a solicitor, alien and, at times, negative images predominated; for instance 'aggressive, expensive because you know it just like exudes money'; 'male and middle aged, pedantic and probably abrasive'. Arrogant and elitist were words that surfaced repeatedly; furthermore, all the images bar two were male and white.

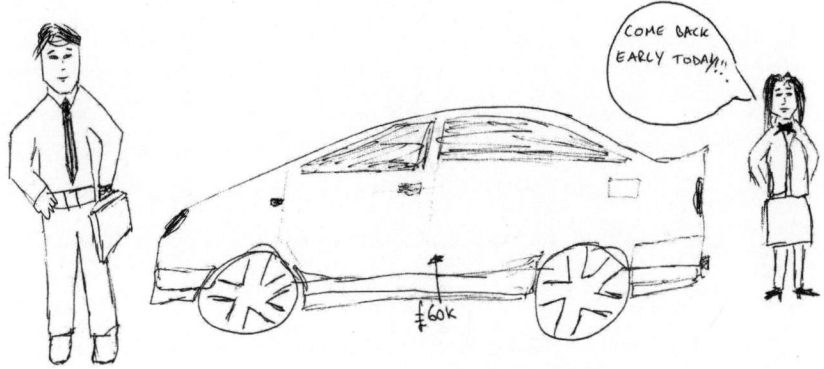

The resulting identity dissonance was particularly evident in an all women focus group. The caricatured narratives their images inspired drew on distinct modalities of normative professionalism:

He's about fifty, thick glasses, pinstripe suit, shiny shoes, chubby...'cause he earns lots of money; (no) time to get his hair done, so – bad hair...always in his office, working till like midnight; his wife doesn't do anything.

[54] This ignorance of the profession at the point of entering legal education has been found in other surveys; see, eg *Minority and Social Diversity in Legal Education* (2006), at www.Scotland.gov.uk/library5/justice/masd-02.asp, accessed 30 Mar 2006.

Pinstripe suit, short hair, glasses, between thirty and forty years old...married and his wife stays at home, looking after the house and children...he's quite straight-faced and serious...enjoys playing golf.

The images invoked by others drew on the new commercialised professionalism:[55]

I was thinking much younger, about thirty, sort of free and single...independent...more sort of out there, outgoing, works for a firm that gets involved in lots of things like sporting events, charity events...going to the gym...eating and drinking in expensive wine bars.

A City solicitor, white and male, only in his mid-twenties, middle-class, privately educated or very good state school...arrogant, well-dressed...work(s) late and long, not married – goes to the gym or drinking when not working.

Age 40 female. plain
Hair tied Back
No make-up!
Serious expression

pin-striped plain
Suit grey or
Blue.

Bulging with files!

The only depiction of a woman produced a description of someone evidently committed to embodying professionalism and signalling her differentiation from her gender:

---

[55] Hanlon, G, *Lawyers, the State and the Market* (Basingstoke, Macmillan, 1999).

She's about fortyish...very plain. She has her hair just tied back, no make-up...got a very serious expression on her face...plain pinstripe suit...flat shoes...she works for a big law firm, doesn't have children because she doesn't have time, she's not married and the free time that she does have, she probably stays in.

When asked why they wanted to join a group of people who they so clearly differentiated from themselves, 'profession', 'respected', 'status', 'empowerment' and 'money' were repeatedly cited.[56] However, the motivations expressed by some, especially women and working class BME students, tended to be ambivalent. Many (both in focus groups and interviews) nominated both the above reasons *and* 'serving the community' (and in particular members of their own community) as primary motivations. This articulation of a service ethic could be viewed as constituting a 'counternarrative...a representing race critique of bleached out professionalism',[57] and thus a collective equality project.

However, the prevalence of choice as the fundamental socio-political discourse and the marginalisation of value systems other than those centred round money combined to propel many students, especially the men, to aim at the corporate sector. On the other hand, other responses refuted the reality of choice and agency: for instance several outsiders said they would like to work in legal aid practice but could not afford to because of the large amount of debt they had amassed.[58] BME students in particular stressed familial obligation as a primary cause in their attempt to enter the corporate sector, both to repay debts and satisfy familial social mobility projects.

Other 'outsider' students, especially the women, said they wanted to work in 'ordinary' firms (some even specified legal aid practices), and some of those who had nominated corporate law as their first choice, in conversation subsequently shifted to High Street General Practices. Sometimes this was clearly prompted by a realistic assessment of their chances; for instance a mature female student explained that even though she had hoped that her wealth of experience and qualifications (including a degree in accountancy) would stand in her favour, she had been advised by corporate firms that she was too old.

---

[56] The Scottish survey referred to above, produced similar results. On the one hand, 'non-traditional' students saw the profession as 'white, male, middle aged and middle class', and yet at the same time they remained committed to entry and optimistic about their career opportunities: above n 54.

[57] Wilkins, above n 19, at 1518.

[58] See 'Twin Peeks at Career Expectations' (Summer 2005) 10 *Directions in Legal Aid* 13, which reports that 78% of students rejected a career in legal aid because of their level of indebtedness and poor career prospects in this sector; see also Norman, L, *Career Choices in Law: A Survey of Law Students* (London, Law Society, 2004).

Gender and Ethnicity

Recognition of the salience of gender varied both between respondents and within the accounts of individual respondents. For instance, the ambivalence that characterised all students' motivations and aspirations featured in women's views of potential barriers; some responses exemplified reflexive identity:

> I think you can be any sort of person really because whatever your strengths are there is going to be some aspect of law you can apply those to.

Another female student said:

> It *is* changing, even though that's still the stereotype, we're also recognising that there are a lot of women solicitors nowadays and they are becoming increasingly successful, and that it shouldn't stop you. And the more women you know who are good, who go into the law, the more they'll change the stereotype.

Nevertheless most students had come to recognise that entry to the profession would entail the formation of a new identity; for instance a male student from the first cohort who was interviewed at the training contract stage said:

> A lot of the pictures (representing the profession) we drew are the same and that's because there's some truth in it and ultimately you have to fit in with that a little bit.

The habitus endemic to capitalism is characterised by a narrative strategy in which actors perceive themselves as subjects in the process of constituting and transforming their future trajectory. It was striking that, asked to map out their future career on a time line, both outsider men and women produced narratives of seamless progression which for most men and a large proportion of women culminated in partnership and often extremely (unrealistically) high salaries,. Yet subsequently, sometimes only in response to questions, the women transmogrified from professionals into 'women', displaying an agency that did not simply unfold as part of the logic of habitus but was one which was characterised by breaks, a temporality which typifies women's engagement in the work of cultural production Their narratives of progression towards partnership would then be interrupted by predictions of breaks to have children, with most envisaging taking at least eight to 12 years off. This in turn provoked discussion and expressions of angst at the difficulty of reconciling the dual narratives of (goal directed) career and motherhood. Further evidence of cognitive dissonance was displayed by one of the women who had asserted that the profession was changing, who was already working (part-time) in a law firm; reflecting on the fact that there were no women with children there, she said:

> The female partner doesn't have a family...and the other lady who heads up departmental work doesn't have children either...grim future...they just leave...they end up feeling torn between children and work...One lady who's got two children had problems with her childcare...I suppose we sort of resented her really for not doing her share which is horrible really.

The BME students were similarly ambivalent about the extent to which their ethnicity might represent an obstacle to their ambitions. The majority came from working class backgrounds and had led highly segregated home lives in which it is inconceivable that racism had not featured. The difficulties for their equality projects posed by the taken for granted whiteness through to overt racism which characterises the profession, was rarely articulated as clearly as by this man:

> Pretty early on...there was a few people I knew that studied law before I did...and used to say how they were getting on with applications to get into a solicitors' firm and were getting declined...and all the rest of it.

His solution, however, was widely shared and represents the typical response of outsider groups: formation of an alternative network including the establishment of one's own practice:[59]

> You don't need to get into nobody's network if you can have your own thing I think...the old boy's network doesn't need to be cracked for me to get into a position.

However the inequalities *within* cultures are manifest in the gendering of these possibilities. This man's alternative network consisted of other, largely Asian, men. His brother's successful claims company had generated close links with both white and British Asian solicitors as a result of which he had obtained a training contract both for himself and his fiancé. His view of the future, however, embraced a family strategy in which his (future) wife's reproductive role trumped her professional and financial utility:

> We've discussed it a little. I think that having kids at the moment, no, not possible, for financial reasons ... there is time for that later on ... from what we've discussed she will get her training contract and then maybe a year or two – getting the financially stable position – so that I can say to her like 'you don't need to work any more, you can give it up and have kids'.

Given this, it is perhaps not surprising that on occasion British Asian women indicated that their gender trumped their ethnicity; for instance the

---

[59] This is, of course, the response of marginalised lawyers across jurisdictions; see, eg Wilkins, D, 'Straitjacketing Professionalism: A Comment on Russell' (1997) 95 *Michigan Law Review* 795.

sole woman in an all British Asian Focus group said: 'whilst we were talking about equality I think everybody was thinking about race; I was thinking about gender'.

Equality Projects in Practice

For Bourdieu one of the key ways in which the 'state nobility' demonstrates its cultural capital is through its embodied practices, notably bodily assurance and distinguished appearance. The following account by one male student of his impression of the legal profession and its source in his solicitor father, is illustrative:

> They seemed a rung above everyone else...the way they spoke, the way he reacted to other people...fairly draconian, almost judge like...they all seemed to act in the same manner, to speak in the same manner, it was almost as if they were a separate race...he was tall, imposing, always wore a pin-striped suit.

Interviewed nine months into his training contract (with his father's old firm) this man talked about how he had changed:

> I don't amble any more...I now have a busy important person's walk. It's a London walk – you know, it's a 'I have to rush walk because it's so important' and people have to know I'm busy and important. And sometimes maybe I'll talk with an air of importance.

This need to embody professionalism (and hence class and gender[60]) as status also featured in the reflections of a mature woman on the reasons some of her fellow students had got training contracts. Possession of a training contract was largely divided along socio-economic and ethnic lines. Those with contracts either had contacts in the profession (the latter group contained a significant proportion of British Asian students) and/or good degrees from pre-1992 or Russell group universities.[61] However, as this woman observed, these qualifications might not get you beyond an interview:

> To get a training contract you've got to have the qualifications, gone to the right school and so on – then you get the interview, but then it's the look. The correct look is a very important part of being a professional...some of the girls here are very dolly birdy...the girls who've got training contracts – certainly those with the big firms, they're all young, slim, blonde hair, attractive, well spoken. The men are generally attractive too...they do use their sexuality but subtly. They dress subtly, understated...confident in how they look and present themselves.

---

[60]   As Skeggs has convincingly argued, femininity is a classed sign: above n 51.
[61]   Shiner, above n 34.

The importance of being the right age also surfaced repeatedly in the accounts of older students and appeared related to a process of identity formation which involved as much compulsion as reflexivity.[62] The woman just cited explained that one firm had explicitly explained to her that she would be too old to undertake the menial tasks they would want to give her, in order to mould her into their ideal employee.

A part-time student, a legal executive with a medium sized General Practice who was re-training to become a solicitor in order to achieve recognition,[63] described a particularly brutal version of training for hierarchy:

It's always been very male orientated in the firm, although the majority of solicitors are now female...they are taking on females because they are the better ones...it's a worry because they're quite weak women and you always found them in the toilets crying because there is a lot of pressure on trainees...they're treated as the lowest of the low...like they would have to clean up sick from the steps and stuff like that...it's been said in the past that if we can break our trainees then we can build them up again then no client can do worse to them...they are made to feel like nothing...one partner...you can almost see it in his eyes...when she (a trainee) comes to him with something, you can see that he's thinking I can either help her along or I can really mess her up...and he goes down the messing her up sort of thing.

CONCLUDING REMARKS

The multiple tensions which beset the feminist equality project as a result of the contingency of equality, and the recognition of the fluidity and ambivalence of gender and its mediation by other, intersecting forms of disadvantage, have been compounded by social fragmentation and the 'cultural turn'. As a result it is argued that we now inhabit reflexive modernity, an age of shifting identities with wide scope for social agency: in the fields of both consumption and public policy this is epitomised by the talismanic status of 'choice'. Critics see this optimistic view as in part ideological: the complex interplay of identity and consumption renders opaque the underlying persistence of collective categories as determining instances in social trajectories.

This chapter has sought to contribute to this debate by exploring the cultural medium through which inequalities are perpetuated. Using the example of trainee lawyers, I have tried to trace the ways in which subjects apprehend equality in relation to the profession, and how they incorporate

---

[62]   Or as Sweetman argues, reflexivity is now compulsory: above n 23.

[63]   For discussion of the subordinate status of legal executives within the legal profession, see Francis, A, 'Legal Executives and the Phantom of Legal Professionalism: The Rise and Rise of the Third Branch of the Legal Profession' (2002) 9 *International Journal of the Legal Profession* 5.

this understanding into their social action and interaction. I have also explored the class dynamics which structure identities and cultural practices and determine the shape and outcome of equality projects, using a Bourdieusian approach which identifies the way in which cultural and symbolic practices represent objective structures constraining and disciplining subjects' acts.

The opening sections of this chapter posed a number of questions about the experience of 'minorities' attempting to enter the legal field. The first of these concerned the extent to which the ideology of meritocracy, the companion to the formal equality principle, was actually eroding the significance of social categories, and increasing the scope for genuine subjective choice in individual equality projects. The analysis of the data suggested the obduracy with which social categories persist in structural and cultural forms which bear the capacity to mark individuals. Class, for example, persists in the deeply embedded cultural hierarchies of the UK's binary HE system, to the extent that admission to the privileged 'Russell' group can enable an individual to slough off the integument of working class status by embracing those symbolic forms which mark its opposite. Middle class women with 'good' degrees from 'good' universities can apparently transcend their gender, as can middle class BME graduates who do not self-consciously mark their difference (for example through religious dress), and in some niche areas of the legal labour market an advantage may accrue to their gender and ethnicity. However, as Bourdieu would argue, this process involves the misrecognition of conformance to speech and dress codes as 'merit', and the foundations on which such transformations are based can be demonstrably shaky.

To understand the fragility of the equality projects of outsiders, one needs to appreciate both the complexity of the contemporary professional field, with its increasing pressures to rationalise and concentrate both financial and cultural capital, and the fact that, as a result, new forms and patterns of cultural hierarchy exist alongside the older, more explicitly raced and gendered modes of professional discourse. On the one hand this may appear to reconfigure the profession as a site of real diversity. On the other, such a complex patterning of desirable cultural capital also opens the way for a comprehensive set of strategies for blocking the entry and progress of outsiders. In this context, categories such as gender must be seen as relational, 'chameleon like, shifting in importance, value and effects from context to context or from field to field'[64] or from time to time. The nature of the field is such that powerful actors within it have the capacity to redefine the desired cultural capital for legal practice as that which

---

[64] Adkins, L, 'Introduction: Feminism, Bourdieu and After' in Adkins and Skeggs (eds), above n 15, at 6; see also Moi, T, *What is a Woman?* (Oxford, Oxford University Press, 1999) 288.

outsiders and women do not possess. This may be through obscure forms of cultural practice, or through quite overt forms of disciplining the body, through processes which, as reported by some respondents, resonate with Goffman's discussion of total institutions.[65] It may therefore be argued that the current reflexivity is not a freedom *from* gender (or other subordinated social categories) but an active reworking (of) them, 'especially in the economic field',[66] so that white masculinity as source of power re-creates itself. Correspondingly, the lack of inherent authority of working class or BME trainees obliges them to endure the symbolic violence entailed in internalising their essential difference and inferiority and working at passing as the other.[67]

Thus, should outsider trainees affirm what 'distinguishes them, that is, in the name of which they are dominated and constituted as (inferior)', or 'work at destroying what marks them out...and at appropriating that in relation to which they appear' as misplaced? '[I]s this submission? Resistance may be alienating and submission may be liberatory. Such is the paradox of the dominated'.[68]

This paradox appears to allow for two strategic approaches to the professional field: an individualised strategy which aims to maximise cultural and material returns on the investment in training, and alternatively a strategy which identifies the career as a means of validating collective status through involvement in justice struggles. Whilst there are indications that some outsiders, are, at least in part, motivated by a desire to contribute to social justice and equality, this motivation is sometimes subsumed by the need to pay off large debts or by the lure of the corporate world and the contrast it represents with the increasing impoverishment of legal aid practice. The elitist nature of the profession evoked similarly ambivalent responses. For many it appeared to form part of its appeal, whilst others appeared to accept the discourse of equality/meritocracy. And the significance of social contingency for equality projects was revealed by the fact that respondents would self identify in terms of their gender, class or ethnicity but at other times either explicitly or implicitly deny the significance of these categories, and acquiesce in the construction of feminism and other social struggles as reactionary and unnecessary.

The implications of the paradoxical nature of equality projects as outlined above are that the dominant discourse in thinking about equality and diversity points in the wrong direction. By endorsing individual

---

[65] Goffman describes the (male) entrant to a total institution as beginning 'a series of abasements, degradations and profanations of self. His self is systematically, if often unintentionally, mortified': Goffman, E, *Asylums* (London, Penguin, 1961) 24.

[66] Adkins, above n 64, at 9.

[67] See Vignaendra et al, above n 52.

[68] Bourdieu, P, *In Other Words: Essays Towards a Reflexive Sociology* (Cambridge, Polity, 1994) 155.

equality projects on the part of minority entrants as a means of overcoming collective subordination, the situation is created where in order to achieve equality, the cultural and linguistic attributes of collective identities must be abandoned. Diversity in this form becomes a merely somatic issue, the profession's absorption of different bodily forms, but not of their experience and biography. An alternative strategy is to shed light on those obscure cultural practices which seek to expel the vestiges of class, race and gender from the field, and thereby attempt to create a space for genuine difference in the legal field. However, the creation of this space demands alignment between the role of the profession and the collective struggles of those groups from whom the intending lawyers in my study have come: true access to a diverse profession is inextricably linked to the wider struggle for access to justice.

Index